Organizing E

Entrepreneurship, long neglected by economists and management scholars, has made a dramatic comeback in the last two decades, not only among academic economists and management scholars, but also among policymakers, educators, and practitioners. Likewise, the economic theory of the firm, building on Ronald Coase's (1937) seminal analysis, has become an increasingly important field in economics and management. Despite this resurgence, there is still little connection between the entrepreneurship literature and the literature on the firm, both in academia and in management practice. This book fills this gap by proposing and developing an entrepreneurial theory of the firm that focuses on the connections between entrepreneurship and management. Drawing on insights from Austrian economics, it describes entrepreneurship as judgmental decision made under uncertainty, showing how judgment is the driving force of the market economy and the key to understanding firm performance and organization.

NICOLAI J. FOSS is Professor of Strategy and Organization at the Copenhagen Business School and Professor of Knowledge-based Value Creation at the Norwegian School of Economics and Business Administration. He also holds a number of part-time and visiting professorships at other European universities.

PETER G. KLEIN is Associate Professor of Applied Social Sciences and Director of the McQuinn Center for Entrepreneurial Leadership at the University of Missouri. He also holds positions at the University of Missouri's Truman School of Public Affairs and the Norwegian School of Economics and Business Administration.

Organizing Entrepreneurial Judgment

A New Approach to the Firm

NICOLAI J. FOSS
Copenhagen Business School and Norwegian School
of Economics and Business Administration

PETER G. KLEIN
University of Missouri and Norwegian School
of Economics and Business Administration

CAMBRIDGE UNIVERSITY PRESS
Cambridge, New York, Melbourne, Madrid, Cape Town,
Singapore, São Paulo, Delhi, Mexico City

Cambridge University Press
The Edinburgh Building, Cambridge CB2 8RU, UK

Published in the United States of America by Cambridge University Press, New York

www.cambridge.org
Information on this title: www.cambridge.org/9780521697262

First published 2012

Printed in the United Kingdom at the University Press, Cambridge

A catalog record for this publication is available from the British Library

Library of Congress Cataloging in Publication data
Foss, Nicolai J., 1964–
Organizing entrepreneurial judgment : a new approach to the firm /
Nicolai J. Foss, Peter G. Klein.
p.   cm.
Includes bibliographical references and index.
ISBN 978-0-521-87442-7 – ISBN 978-0-521-69726-2 (pbk.)
1. Industrial organization (Economic theory)   2. Entrepreneurship.
I. Klein, Peter G.   II. Title.
HD2326.F667 2012
338′.0401–dc23
2011038183

ISBN 978-0-521-87442-7 Hardback
ISBN 978-0-521-69726-2 Paperback

Contents

Figures

Preface

Entrepreneurship, long neglected by economists and management scholars, has made a dramatic comeback in the last two decades. As the economic theory of the firm flourished following the rediscovery and reworking in the 1970s of Coase's path-breaking "The Nature of the Firm" (1937), the new field of "strategic entrepreneurship" has also begun to take off, along with a parallel rebirth of entrepreneurship studies in economic growth and development, sociology, and anthropology.

As management and organizations researchers with a particular and decade-long interest in entrepreneurship, we obviously welcome all these new developments, just as we have been heavily influenced by modern work on the theory of the firm. And yet, we think both sets of literature have missed important insights from the other. This book is written to fill the gap, proposing and developing an entrepreneurial theory of the firm that focuses on the links between entrepreneurship and management.

In particular, we develop Frank Knight's (1921) idea of entrepreneurship as *judgment*, a conceptualization also found in Richard Cantillon's (1755) pioneering treatment and in the works of the Austrian economist Ludwig von Mises (1949). "Judgment" gets some attention in the practitioner-oriented literature, in books with titles like *Judgment: How Winning Leaders Make Great Calls* (Tichy and Bennis, 2007), and in policy-oriented works like Amar Bhidè's *A Call for Judgment* (2010). But judgment plays very little role in conventional economic theories of the firm or the mainstream works in entrepreneurship and strategic management. More generally, we think judgment is undertheorized, particularly given its potential for an important role in theories of economic organization. Working out such a theory and its implications is the main rationale for this book.

ix

The book is aimed at social scientists with a similar interest in the intersection of entrepreneurship and organization, broadly conceived. More specifically, we have written the book for management researchers, particularly in entrepreneurship, strategic entrepreneurship, and strategic management, and economists who take an interest in the theory of the firm and entrepreneurship. Our aim is to influence existing research practice in management and economics research on entrepreneurship. However, we also offer observations and arguments of interest to historians of entrepreneurship and management and organization studies and to methodologists specializing in the development of social science theories. While many of our arguments deal specifically with the theory of the firm and the theory of entrepreneurship, it is not necessary to be interested in both fields to profit from this book. For example, an entrepreneurship scholar with little interest in the theory of the firm may still find the discussions in Chapters 2–5 valuable and interesting. Relatedly, while we have aimed at writing an integrated narrative, most of the chapters can be read usefully on their own.

Our analysis is rooted in economics, but we eschew formal modeling, decision theory, game theory, econometrics, and the like, and we avoid technical jargon as much as possible. We also deal extensively with recent developments in management theory, but our arguments presume little prior exposure to the management literature and its specialized language. In other words, the book should be accessible to researchers in a variety of fields and specialty areas, not just those who focus on economic and management theories of entrepreneurship.

We have been thinking, discussing, and writing on these issues for many years and it is impossible to thank adequately all those colleagues, students, manuscript reviewers, conference and workshop discussants, and other contemporaries who have influenced our work. But we do wish to single out some for special mention. In particular, we he have benefitted from conference and seminar discussant and audience feedback at the Copenhagen Business School, Ohio State University, Norwegian School of Economics and Business Administration, Stockholm School of Economics, University of Illinois, University of Missouri, Academy of Management, Austrian Scholars Conference, Strategic Management Society, and Wirth Institute Annual Meetings and Conferences. We thank (but do not implicate) Rajshree Agarwal, Jay Barney, Todd Chiles, Teppo Felin, Kirsten Foss, Sandra Klein,

Richard Langlois, Stefan Linder, Jacob Lyngsie, Henry Manne, Joe Mahoney, Joseph Salerno, Nils Stieglitz, Michael Sykuta, Randall Westgren, Sidney Winter, and Ulrich Witt for discussions and comments on the ideas in this book. We've benefitted from the research assistance of Per Bylund and Mario Mondelli.

Although much of the book represents fresh material, we have drawn from our previous work and are grateful to the following publishers for permission to incorporate some previously published material:

- Springer Publications for permission to use material from Nicolai J. Foss and Peter G. Klein, "Entrepreneurship and the Theory of the Firm: Any Gains From Trade?" in Rajshree Agarwal, Sharon A. Alvarez, and Olav Sorenson, eds., *Handbook of Entrepreneurship Research: Disciplinary Perspectives* (New York: Springer, 2005), pp. 55–80.
- Blackwell Publishing for permission to use material from Kirsten Foss, Nicolai J. Foss, Peter G. Klein, and Sandra K. Klein, "The Entrepreneurial Organization of Heterogeneous Capital," *Journal of Management Studies* 44(7) (2007): 1165–1186.
- Sage Publications for permission to use material from Kirsten Foss, Nicolai J. Foss, and Peter G. Klein, "Original and Derived Judgment: An Entrepreneurial Theory of Economic Organization," *Organization Studies* 28(12) (2007): 1893–1912.
- Sage Publications for permission to use material from Nicolai J. Foss and Ibuki Ishikawa, "Toward a Dynamic Resource-based View: Insights from Austrian Capital and Entrepreneurship Theory," *Organization Studies* 28(5) (2007): 749–772.
- Senate Hall Publications for permission to use material from Peter G. Klein and Nicolai J. Foss, "The Unit of Analysis in Entrepreneurship Research: Opportunities or Investments?" *International Journal of Entrepreneurship Education* 6(3) (2008): 145–170.
- Wiley for permission to use material from Peter G. Klein, "Opportunity Discovery, Entrepreneurial Action, and Economic Organization," *Strategic Entrepreneurship Journal* 2(3) (2008): 175–190.
- Sage Publications for permission to use material from Rajshree Agarwal, Jay B. Barney, Nicolai Foss, and Peter G. Klein, "Heterogeneous Resources and the Financial Crisis: Implications

of Strategic Management Theory," *Strategic Organization* 7(4) (2009): 467–484.

- The Mises Institute for permission to use material from Peter G. Klein, "Risk, Uncertainty, and Economic Organization," in Jörg Guido Hülsmann and Stephan Kinsella, eds., *Property, Freedom, and Society: Essays in Honor of Hans-Hermann Hoppe* (Auburn, AL: Ludwig von Mises Institute, 2009): 325–337.
- The Association of Private Enterprise Education for permission to use material from Nicolai J. Foss and Peter G. Klein, "Alertness, Action, and the Antecedents of Entrepreneurship," *Journal of Private Enterprise* 25(2) (2010): 145–164.
- Edward Elgar Publishing for permission to use material from Nicolai J. Foss and Peter G. Klein, "Entrepreneurial Alertness and Opportunity Discovery: Origins, Attributes, Critique," in Hans Landström and Franz Lohrke, eds., *The Historical Foundations of Entrepreneurship Research* (Cheltenham, UK: Edward Elgar, 2010): 91–120.

1 | *The need for an entrepreneurial theory of the firm*

The theory of entrepreneurship and the theory of the firm should be treated together. And yet, the important connections between these two bodies of literature have been largely overlooked. This is our book's basic motivation.

How, then, are entrepreneurs and firms connected? Do entrepreneurs need business firms to carry out their function? Or, do firms need entrepreneurs to survive in the competitive market process? And if there is a role for the entrepreneur in the firm, what is it, exactly? Where in the firm does entrepreneurial activity mainly take place? How does the organization of the firm influence entrepreneurial actions? Are business firms run by entrepreneurs, or rather by hired managers? How does firm organization (e.g., the allocation of residual income and control rights) affect the quantity and quality of entrepreneurial ideas? Can entrepreneurship be a property of a managerial team – or is it strictly an individual phenomenon?

To practitioners, policymakers, and other non-specialist readers, these questions seem to strike at the very core of our understanding of markets – price theory, industrial economics, strategic management, organization theory, even marketing and finance. Entrepreneurial behavior does not, after all, occur in a vacuum. Entrepreneurs, like other economic actors, employ scarce means to achieve their objectives, must economize on these means, must evaluate trade-offs at the margin, and so on.[1] Moreover, as both entrepreneurship and the theory of the firm deal with business ventures, new firm formation, new as well as sustained value creation, etc., one would expect substantial

---

[1] As we will see in Chapter 2 and elsewhere below, several important entrepreneurship theories abstract from scarcity, treating entrepreneurial ability as an extra-economic attribute or function that cannot, itself, be analyzed as a scarce resource. Even so, entrepreneurs need complementary factors of production – land, labor, capital – that are subject to the usual laws of supply and demand.

cross-fertilization to take place, simply because so many important, practical research questions appear at the intersection of these two fields. And yet, the study of entrepreneurship and the study of organizing in the economy lack contact. Indeed, the modern theory of the firm ignores entrepreneurship, while the literature on entrepreneurship in economics and management research has limited use for the economic theory of the firm.

As a result, there is no serious theory of the entrepreneurial firm to guide decision-making for the kind of problems that intimately involve both entrepreneurship and organizing. To be sure, there are theories of start-up firms in economics and in management and large literatures on product, process, and organizational innovation. But mature firms, as well as new firms, act entrepreneurially – witness the emphasis on "corporate renewal" and "entrepreneurialism" among practitioners – and entrepreneurship reveals itself in many activities besides innovation. Even non-market actors, including public officials, philanthropists, and university professors, are urged to be "entrepreneurial."

A good theory of entrepreneurship should explain the conditions under which entrepreneurship takes place, the manner in which entrepreneurship is manifested, and the interaction between entrepreneurial activity and firm, industry, and environmental characteristics. In the contemporary entrepreneurship literature, entrepreneurship is typically seen as a theory of firm creation; once created, however, the firm ceases to be "entrepreneurial" and becomes dominated by "managerial" motives – a partial legacy of Schumpeter's early and influential work on innovation (Schumpeter, 1911). However, processes of firm formation, growth, and ongoing operation are continuous, and things that matter at the early stages do not disappear overnight. A holistic view of entrepreneurship thus requires an understanding of the managerial and organizational aspects of the entrepreneurial function. In like manner, we think the economic theory of the firm can be improved substantially by taking seriously the entrepreneurial aspects of firm organization and strategy. In sum, the theory of entrepreneurship and the economic theory of the firm have much to learn from each other. However, they must first be brought into contact.

Prompted by what we see as a fundamental disconnect between these two strands of research literature, each of which has much to learn from the other, our basic aim in this book is to describe and exploit gains from trade by bringing entrepreneurship and the (theory of the) firm much closer together, to the benefit of both, as well as the fields and disciplines in which they are embedded. We see few substantial obstacles to doing so. The conventional separation between entrepreneurship and the theory of the firm is not due to any inherent incompatibility, but is largely an idiosyncratic consequence of the way the field of economics developed, particularly after WWII. Indeed, there is a certain historical irony in this separation because one of the key early contributions to the economic theory of entrepreneurship, Frank H. Knight's *Risk, Uncertainty and Profit* (1921), is also a pioneering analysis of basic issues about firms, markets, and competition that contemporary economists view as the foundational questions of the theory of the firm.

However, both the theory of the firm and the theory of entrepreneurship developed in a way that the original Knightian program of providing a unified treatment to the firm and the entrepreneur became stalled. Our overall aim is to revitalize this Knightian program. In the remaining part of this chapter, we further explain the need for such an integrated undertaking, describe some of the historical and disciplinary reasons why integration hasn't yet taken place, and provide a summary of our positive argument.

The theory of the firm in economics

The economic theory of the firm – also known as the economics of organization or organizational economics – is a well-established and influential area of economics. Thus, transaction-cost economics (Williamson, 1985), agency theory (Holmström, 1979), mechanism design, the nexus-of-contracts approach (Jensen and Meckling, 1976), and the property-rights theory of the firm (Hart and Moore, 1990) are now part of the standard discourse among academics, students, and practitioners studying firms and markets.[2]

In the management literature, resource and knowledge-based views of the firm have come to dominate the analysis of organizational performance (Wernerfelt, 1984; Barney, 1986, 1991; Peteraf,

---

[2] We here follow standard practice and include agency theory under the "theory of the firm," although strictly speaking this theory is not about the existence and the boundaries of firms (Hart, 1989).

1993; Peteraf and Barney, 2003), theories that in various ways build on earlier theories of the firm, be they behavioral (Cyert and March, 1963), evolutionary (Nelson and Winter, 1982), or neoclassical economic (Demsetz, 1973). Moreover, the economic theories of the firm mentioned above have also been hugely influential in management research for a long time (see Mahoney, 2005). Rumelt (1984) long ago argued that strategic management should rest on the "bedrock foundation" of the "economist's model of the firm." Many scholars in strategic management and neighboring fields followed his call (Foss, 1999; Becarra, 2009).

In short, the economic and managerial analysis of the firm is a vibrant area of research and application characterized by a diversity of competing theories and approaches and a robust empirical literature. Of course, the firm has long been central to economics, in the theory of production and exchange, the analysis of industry structure, labor economics, and a few other areas. Introductory textbooks all contain a section on the "theory of the firm" containing the familiar equations and diagrams describing the firm's production possibilities set, its cost and revenue curves, and the equilibrium pricing and production decisions. Firms are useful in basic economics because they are necessary parts of doing price theoretical analysis (Machlup, 1963). When economists address the industry- or economy-wide consequences of, say, a change in the price of an input, the analysis involves addressing how a representative firm will react to the change in terms of input substitution, product price, and so on.[3]

However, the theory of the firm as a contractual or organizational entity – the literature on the existence, boundaries, and internal organization of the enterprise spawned by Ronald Coase's "The Nature of the Firm" (1937) – is, in the history of economics, a relatively recent development. As discussed in Chapter 6 below, the economics of business organization emerged as a distinct field only in the 1970s with

---

[3] The idea of the "representative firm" comes from Marshall (1890), who imagined an entity that "has had a fairly long life, and fair success, which is managed with normal ability, and which has normal access to the economies, external and internal, which belong to that aggregate volume of production; account being taken of the class of goods produced, the conditions of marketing them and the economic environment generally." See Foss (1994a) on the role of this heuristic device in Marshallian and post-Marshallian thought more generally.

the path-breaking contributions of Williamson (1971, 1975, 1979), Alchian and Demsetz (1972), Hurwicz (1972), Marschak and Radner (1972), Ross (1973), Arrow (1974), Jensen and Meckling (1976), Klein, Crawford, and Alchian (1978), Holmström (1979), and others. Once economists realized they needed a theory of economic organization, the theory of the firm in this Coasean sense became part of the canon, and arguably one of the theoretical and empirical success stories of economics.[4] In important respects, as we argue below, the theory of the firm can further the entrepreneurship field, fundamentally because it addresses important issues regarding the locus of entrepreneurship that have not been addressed in entrepreneurship research.

Entrepreneurship

More recently, the analysis of entrepreneurship has seized the spotlight in economics. Other social sciences, including sociology (Thornton, 1999), anthropology (Oxfeld, 1992), political science (Klein, McGahan, Mahoney, and Pitelis, 2010), and economic and business history (Landes *et al.*, 2010), have begun to explore the entrepreneurial concept as well. In business schools, entrepreneurship is starting to be incorporated into management, marketing, finance, and accounting, rather than being a standalone program on new firm formation (business plan writing, venture funding, technology transfer, and the like). Indeed, the last decade has witnessed an explosion of university courses, faculty positions, research and educational centers, journals, publications, and grant funding dedicated to the study of entrepreneurship. Economists increasingly see entrepreneurship as a key to technological progress, and (therefore) an important part of the growth process (e.g., Blau, 1987; Aghion and Howitt, 1992; Baumol, 1994; Wennekers and Thurik, 1999; Blanchflower, 2000).

Recognition of the entrepreneur's importance predates even the *Wealth of Nations*, playing a central role in Richard Cantillon's (1755) pioneering treatise. One might thus expect the entrepreneur to be central to economic theorizing over the last two-and-a-half centuries. However, as we will explain later, this has not been the case; on the contrary, at least since WWII entrepreneurship has been left

---

[4] The term "success story" is Williamson's (2000: 605), describing the empirical work in transaction cost economics.

out of the economics mainstream, only be stressed by prolific and perhaps well-known, yet "heterodox" (and therefore rather uninfluential) economists, notably Austrian (e.g., Mises, 1949; Hayek, 1968; Kirzner, 1973) and Schumpeterian (Futia, 1980; Nelson and Winter, 1982). In fact, in spite of the appearance of two seminal papers about three decades ago that provided two fundamental "recipes" for modeling entrepreneurship in its self-employment sense (Lucas, 1978; Kihlstrom and Laffont, 1979), it is only over the last decade or so that mainstream economists have become seriously interested in the entrepreneur.

While it is widely recognized that formal modeling of the mainstream economics variety cannot do full justice to entrepreneurship,[5] at least some aspects of entrepreneurship can be captured using the standard tools of equilibrium and constrained maximization. An issue that has received much attention is the analysis of occupational choice (e.g., Holmes and Schmitz, 1990) and its implications for a host of policy issues (e.g., the incentives of minority groups to become entrepreneurs, access to credit as an entry barrier, the relative contribution to innovation of small and large firms, etc.). This research stream is virtually synonymous with contemporary economics research on entrepreneurship. Some work has also considered issues of direct relevance to management research, such as entrepreneurial learning (e.g., Parker, 1996). Overall, entrepreneurship is becoming a legitimate research subject in economics.[6]

The situation in management is similar in a number of respects. Entrepreneurship has long been an established field in management studies, but research in this area has been substantially transformed in the last decade. To some extent this is a result of a much closer liaison with strategic management (Baker and Pollock, 2007), giving rise to the field of strategic entrepreneurship.[7] But it is also, and

---

[5] Bianchi and Henrekson (2005: 354) survey many of the mainstream models of entrepreneurship and conclude that in these models "entrepreneurship is invariably narrowly defined and it cannot be said to capture the wide-ranging and complex functions suggested outside mainstream economics."

[6] Parker (2005) provides an excellent overview of recent entrepreneurship research in economics.

[7] Evidence for the spread of entrepreneurial ideas to strategic management research includes the 2008 launch of the *Strategic Entrepreneurship Journal*, a sister journal to the highly prestigious *Strategic Management Journal*. Representative strategic entrepreneurship papers include Hitt and Ireland

perhaps much more importantly, a matter of a drastic transformation of the field of entrepreneurship itself. While early research was mainly taken up with the management of small and family business, more recent research – drawing on insights from psychology, economics, and sociology – is directed toward a broader set of issues, theories, and phenomena, with more attention to defining constructs, formulating precise research questions, and establishing standard research procedures (see Shane [2003] for an overview).

This raises a more general issue: What, exactly, is entrepreneurship? An easy way of delineating different types of entrepreneurs and economic theories of entrepreneurship is to distinguish between those that define entrepreneurship as an *outcome* or a phenomenon (e.g., self-employment, start-ups) and those that see entrepreneurship as a *way of thinking or acting* (e.g., creativity, innovation, alertness, judgment, adaptation).

Much early work on entrepreneurship (e.g., Schumpeter, 1911; Knight, 1921) falls into the latter category, what Klein (2008b) calls "functional," in the sense that entrepreneurship was invoked as a necessary step to explaining other phenomena such as economic development (Schumpeter) or the existence of the firm and profit (Knight). Because the entrepreneur was merely a necessary analytical stepping stone to understanding other phenomena, typically at higher levels of analysis, they were treated in rather abstract, stylized terms. This is highly akin to the treatment of the firm in basic price theory (Machlup, 1967), where the firm receives a similarly abstract treatment. Some modern work in economics on the entrepreneur, specifically, Kirzner's (1973, 1985, 1992), has also treated the entrepreneur in highly abstract terms – and for similar reasons: In these approaches the interest is not in the entrepreneur per se, but in those phenomena that the presence of the entrepreneur help to explain. Moreover, these approaches do not pay much attention to the antecedents of entrepreneurial activity (Bjørnskov and Foss, 2008).

In contrast, the management research literature on entrepreneurship (and some work in labor economics) has given much more detail

(2000), Ahuja and Lampert (2001), and Ireland, Hitt, and Sirmon (2003). Foss and Lyngsie (2011) survey the strategic entrepreneurship field and discuss its relations to neighboring fields and theories such as the resource-based and dynamic capabilities views.

to the entrepreneur and entrepreneurial actions, describing the decision heuristics he makes use of (Sarasvathy, 2003), the biases he may suffer from (Busenitz and Barney, 1997), the experience base for his actions (Shane, 2000), the kind of uncertainty he confronts (Alvarez and Barney, 2010), the network structure that he is a part of (Sorenson and Stuart, 2005), his previous employment experience (Klepper, 2002; Braguinsky, Klepper, and Ohyama, 2009; Elfenbein, Hamilton, and Zenger, 2010), and so on. Much of this literature has been drawn to Kirzner's concept of entrepreneurship as "opportunity discovery" (Shane and Venkataraman, 2000), although, as we shall show (Chapter 2), this may be partially based on a misunderstanding of the nature of Kirzner's work.

Why entrepreneurship and the (theory of the) firm belong together

The firm as the locus of entrepreneurial activity

The research literatures on the theory of the firm and entrepreneurship can, we believe, be brought together to form a better theory of the firm and a fuller understanding of the nature and economic effects of entrepreneurship. From this perspective, the questions that arise in the intersection of entrepreneurship and the theory of the firm relate to the *locus* of entrepreneurship.[8] In an influential and programmatic statement, Shane and Venkataraman (2000: 218) argued that management scholars in strategy and organization are fundamentally concerned with three sets of research questions, namely why, when, and how (1) entrepreneurial opportunities arise, (2) certain individuals and firms and not others discover and exploit opportunities, and (3) different modes of action are used to exploit those opportunities. These issues include the issue of "how the exploitation of entrepreneurial opportunities are organized in the economy" (2000: 224). When they wrote their paper, Shane and Venkataraman could point to little work moving the field forward along these lines. Nearly a decade later the situation is not much better, though the need for integration is increasingly realized. We argue that economic theories of the firm are

---

[8] It is perhaps telling that one of the most influential entrepreneurship journals is (still) called *Small Business Economics*.

particularly well-equipped to understand not only the "exploitation," but also the discovery and even the evaluation of entrepreneurial opportunities. And these theories mesh even more closely with other approaches to entrepreneurship, as we shall see in later chapters.

One of our objectives is to explain, in this context, why entrepreneurs choose certain ways and not others for organizing their activities. These are questions that are becoming increasingly pertinent, as argued above, and, indeed, some of them are considered in the recent economics and management literature on entrepreneurship. However, they are only treated in a highly limited manner. Consider, for example, Lucas' (1978) general equilibrium model, the starting point for much modern economics work on entrepreneurship. The model examines the matching of firms and entrepreneurial talent, given that entrepreneurial talent is unequally distributed. "Entrepreneurial talent" is really a portmanteau variable that includes entrepreneurial, managerial, and ownership skills. Lucas describes a matching between firm size and entrepreneurial talent, the most able entrepreneurs running the largest firms. This suggests one association – albeit a highly stylized one – between firm organization and entrepreneurship.

One may question whether making entrepreneurship a factor of production and conceptualizing it solely as a coordinating function is really in the spirit of the classics of entrepreneurship (see Bianchi and Henrekson, 2005: 358). More to the point, however, it is unclear in Lucas' treatment why entrepreneurs would need firms at all. Why can't they perform their coordinating function simply by using contracts? Why are the governance mechanisms of the firm required? A similar critique may be directed at another important treatment, Kihlstrom and Laffont's (1979) model of self-employment. In this model, individuals differ in risk preferences but are otherwise identical. Picking up on a remark in Knight (1921) (on firm organization implying that the "venturesome" insure the "timid"), Kihlstrom and Laffont show the existence of an equilibrium with the population of agents divided into less-risk-averse entrepreneurs and more-risk-averse workers. Moreover, they link entrepreneurship to taking "responsibility for enterprise," and therefore bearing risk. It is clear from their discussion that they think this happens in the context of firms. However, it is not obvious why people need to form firms to share risks, when they could just as easily do it through contract. By implication, much of the subsequent research based on these two papers (and on Holmes and Schmitz, 1990) overlooks the issue of the locus of entrepreneurship in the proper comparative-institutional sense (Coase, 1964; Williamson, 1985): the relevant alternatives are not systematically identified and the net benefits compared.

Relatedly, most of the economics literature on entrepreneurship treats its *explanandum* as companies, implying that entrepreneurial activity ceases after the start-up phase. Much management research on entrepreneurship has simply *defined* entrepreneurship as the creation of new firms, or, more broadly: organizations. Either way, *established* firms are simply excluded from the set of entrepreneurial agents in the economy in very large parts of entrepreneurship research. However, as the recent strategic entrepreneurship literature argues, established firms may act in a highly entrepreneurial way, discovering and seizing new opportunities, exercising judgment over existing and potential resources, and introducing new products and processes (Hitt and Ireland, 2000). Seizing new opportunities through acquisition, divestiture, diversification, or refocusing constitutes a change in firm boundaries, one of the key issues in the Coasean theory of the firm. Or, established firms may wish to stimulate a kind of behavior inside the corporate hierarchy that seems fully "entrepreneurial" – what is often called "intrapreneurship" or "corporate venturing" in the management literature on entrepreneurship. Established firms can reorganize themselves by using incentive pay (Jensen and Meckling, 1992) or other devices such as "access" (Rajan and Zingales, 1998). This involves another key issue in the Coasean theory of the firm, namely that of internal organization.

As we have mentioned, management scholars in organization, strategic management, international business, etc. have often drawn eclectically on the theory of the firm. For example, many issues of strategic management (e.g., vertical integration or diversification decisions) are now routinely framed as problems of efficient governance. And among the most cited scholars in the top business administration journals is Oliver Williamson, perhaps the best-known representative of the modern theory of the firm (Williamson, 1975, 1985, 1996). However, if we turn our attention to recent management research literature on entrepreneurship, we see little on the *locus* of entrepreneurship, despite the earlier plea of Shane and Venkataraman (2000).

Advancing the theory of entrepreneurship

As noted above, over more than two centuries of social science work
on entrepreneurship, entrepreneurship scholars have sometimes
talked about entrepreneurship as an outcome (e.g., the creation of a
new firm), and other times as a behavior (e.g., discovery, judgment,
creativity). Empirical economics research on entrepreneurship typically adopts the outcome approach, mostly for pragmatic reasons (not
surprisingly, outcomes are usually easier to observe and measure than
behaviors). And yet, this approach may get it wrong, as when any new
Mom and Pop store is counted as an entrepreneurial venture, whereas
new innovative behaviors by established firms are not counted as
instances of entrepreneurship.[9]

Scholars who adopt the behavioral or functional understanding of
entrepreneurship have, since Cantillon, conceived it in various ways,
such as innovation, alertness, uncertainty-bearing, adaptation, creativity, and leadership. Chapter 2 surveys these various theories and
definitions and argues that one particular approach, the Knightian
conception of entrepreneurship as judgmental decision-making, provides an explanation of the entrepreneurial function that can be more
smoothly integrated with the economic literature on the firm than
other conceptions of entrepreneurship. In management research, the
dominant approach to entrepreneurship focuses on individuals' identification or discovery of profit opportunities, but pays less attention
to the means by which such opportunities are exploited. It tends to
focus on the cognitive and behavioral characteristics of individuals
who establish new enterprises (e.g., Baron, 1998). A parallel stream of
research, the "entrepreneurial orientation" literature (Lumpkin and
Dess, 1996; Wiklund and Shepherd, 2003), considers identification or
discovery of profit opportunities at the level of firms. Neither of these
two streams really focuses on the resources and capabilities necessary to transform opportunities or investments into realized profits.
However, analyzing the resources used by entrepreneurs, both for the

---

[9] This problem plagues the major databases on entrepreneurial activity such
as the Global Entrepreneurship Monitor. Some researchers and policymakers
try to avoid the problem by focusing on start-ups in particular industries,
such as information technology or pharmaceuticals. As an official at a major
foundation supporting entrepreneurship research told one of us, "We're not
looking for more restaurants and dry cleaners."

establishment of new ventures and the operation of existing ventures, sheds light on the manner in which perceived opportunities and real investments are transformed into value-creating activities.

More generally, entrepreneurship scholars in management are beginning to realize that entrepreneurship is closely linked to central issues of firm organization and strategy, not just to the particular management problems of small businesses (e.g., Shane and Venkataraman, 2000; Alvarez and Barney, 2005). Since Coase (1937) the fundamental issues in the economic theory of the firm have been taken as why firms *exist* (when non-firm, contractual means of allocating resources are available), what determines their *boundaries* (i.e., the allocation of productive activities across firms), and what determines their *internal organization* (i.e., organizational structure, reward systems, etc.). Thus, as we shall argue, entrepreneurial opportunities may be directly tied to why firms exist, because firms may be formed to exploit opportunities or facilitate entrepreneurial experimentation, and the allocation of ownership and property rights in firms may influence these activities within and across firms.

Advancing the theory of the firm

For several decades, William Baumol has criticized economists for neglecting the entrepreneur. His oft-cited quip that "[t]he theoretical firm is entrepreneurless – the Prince of Denmark has been expunged from the discussion of *Hamlet*" (Baumol, 1968: 68) still rings true, even if the meaning of the "theoretical firm" has changed in the meantime.

The theory of the firm (under which we included, as noted above, agency theory, transaction-cost economics, and the property-rights view) has often been criticized for its static nature (e.g., Boudreaux, 1989; Langlois, 1992; Furubotn, 2001).[10] While there are important, subtle differences between these theories (Foss, 1993a; Gibbons, 2005), for instance concerning the role of unanticipated contingencies

---

[10] Note that we do not consider resource-based, knowledge-based, and dynamic capabilities approaches to be theories of the firm per se, as they do not generally focus on the Coasean issues of existence, boundaries, and internal organization of the firm. However, a few attempts at this exist within this literature (e.g., Kogut and Zander, 1992), but these attempts have not, so far, been successful. For discussion of these issues, see Foss (1999).

and process features (e.g., the "fundamental transformation" in Williamson, 1985), they share a largely static and "closed" ontology. Specifically, they focus on solutions to given optimization problems, avoiding questions about the origin of these problems, or indeed of the firm itself. They build on the assumption of a given means-ends framework. Entrepreneurship scholars have traditionally argued, explicitly or implicitly, that breaking with this assumption is a necessary step towards building a theory of entrepreneurship (Schumpeter, 1911; Knight, 1921; Mises, 1949; Kirzner, 1973).

It is quite likely that such arguments have contributed to the disconnect between economics, including the theory of the firm, and entrepreneurship. As Coddington (1983: 61) comments in a different context (the "radical subjectivist" critique of mainstream economics),

a consistent or all-embracing subjectivism is, analytically a very self-denying thing ... One could, of course ... spend a good deal of time and energy in trying to convince those who engage in macroeconomics, econometric model-building, mathematical economics, general equilibrium theory and so on, of the folly of their ways. But, that task accomplished, there would be nothing left but for the whole profession to shut up shop.

Similarly, key themes often associated with entrepreneurship, such as process, uncertainty in its Knightian sense, ignorance, ambiguity, changing preferences, complexity, etc., are difficult to reconcile with the established economic theories of the firm. If these themes are taken to be the *sine qua non* of a theory of entrepreneurship, dialogue between entrepreneurship and these theories would indeed seem difficult.

However, one can offer more pragmatic critiques of the static approach of the contemporary theory of the firm that do not imply a fundamental rejection of the theory itself. Agency theory, for example, has generated important insights on the effects of incentives on effort and the relationship between incentive pay and risk that are highly relevant, for example, to understanding entrepreneurial activity within a firm (Jones and Butler, 1992). In explaining how a principal gets an agent to do something, however, the theory overlooks the more fundamental question of *what* the principal should want the agent to do, or indeed, how the principal got to be a principal in the first place. But it may be possible to tell a simple economics-based story about how and why the principal ended up as principal rather than agent. In fact, we shall tell such a story (Chapter 8). Likewise, one could accept the basic Coasean explanation for firm boundaries (based on minimization of transaction cost) while adding behavioral, experimental, or cognitive elements to broaden the scope and applicability of the theory. We seek to do this as well (Chapters 4 and 6).

While our arguments are offered in the form of verbal theorizing, rather than the mathematical model-building that has become the norm in cutting-edge work on the firm, we think these arguments advance the theory of the firm in various ways. For example, we link the existence of the firm to the cost of trading entrepreneurial judgment. We argue that the understanding of the boundaries of the firm need to be at least partly understood as involving commercial experimentation with resource combinations that grow from the entrepreneur's judgment. And we cast light on internal organization issues by examining how entrepreneur-managers can delegate entrepreneurial initiative to lower echelons in the firm. Of course, the value and scope of these contributions is left to the reader to decide.

The broader management context

Our approach also has implications for firm strategy, particularly in the context of the resource-based approach to the firm. In our perspective entrepreneurship is not simply another resource, like physical and financial capital, reputation, human capital, technical know-how, and the like, but a higher-level, coordinating factor – the source of what we shall later call "primary" or "original" judgment. Strategy research focuses on firm heterogeneity and on outliers, not representative firms. It also focuses on firm-specific coordinating capabilities (e.g., Kogut and Zander, 1992; Denrell, Fang, and Winter, 2003). Our approach suggests that the basic explanation for systematic differences in firm-level performance is that entrepreneurs differ in their abilities to exercise original judgment and to delegate "derived judgment" to subordinates. Here our approach complements the conventional resource-based literature, which focuses on the returns to individual factors but neglects the returns to the firm, that is, the idiosyncratic combinations of factors selected by particular entrepreneurs (see also Foss *et al.*, 2008). The ability to organize resources is itself a capability, an ability to create and recognize strategic opportunities in the language of Denrell *et al.* (2003).

For example, while firms may "empower" employees partly because employees increasingly demand a certain level of autonomy, and partly because leaving decision rights with better-informed employees may make much economic sense (Jensen and Meckling, 1992), empowerment, delegation, etc. also aim to stimulate initiative in a way that is best called "entrepreneurial." Such localized entrepreneurial efforts may contribute to the many process improvements that together add up to the "learning curve" phenomenon (Zangwill and Kantor, 1998), may lead to interaction with outside parties (customer, supplies, universities, etc.) who control potentially important knowledge (Foss, Laursen, and Pedersen, 2011), can assist in product improvements, and may in some cases lead to important breakthrough innovations. Thus, the exercise of entrepreneurship inside corporate hierarchies can have important implications for organizational performance.

An overview of our narrative

As we bring entrepreneurship and the theory of the firm together, we need to demonstrate to scholars in both fields the potential gains from trade. A main part of our narrative is to establish the potential for such gains and discuss whether they have not yet been recognized and seized. We hope to establish the existence of gains by example, that is, by showing concretely how both the field of entrepreneurship and the theory of the firm stand to gain from cross-fertilization.

Some unfortunate historical legacies

Why have these gains not already been recognized and seized? The most obvious reason is that economics, and with it the economic theory of the firm, developed throughout the twentieth century in a particular way, a way that effectively excluded a concern with the entrepreneur. The economic theory of the firm emerged and took shape as the entrepreneur was being banished from microeconomic analysis, first in the 1930s when the firm was subsumed into neoclassical price theory (O'Brien, 1984), and then in the 1980s as the theory of the firm was reformulated in the language of game theory and the economics of information (e.g., Holmström, 1979; Grossman and

Hart, 1986). The gradual "hardening" of the neoclassical approach in economics, including the mainstream approach to the theory of the firm, left little room for the entrepreneurship; Baumol (1994: 17) calls it "the specter which haunts economic models." Indeed, the terms "entrepreneur" and "entrepreneurship" do not even appear in the indexes of leading texts on the economics of organization and management such as Brickley, Smith, and Zimmerman (2008) or Besanko *et al.* (2010).[11] We discuss this in greater detail in Chapter 2.

Entrepreneurship research is also responsible for this state of affairs. Thus, many entrepreneurship scholars have implicitly or explicitly dissociated entrepreneurship and the firm. The entrepreneurial act is often conceived as an independent, free-floating cognitive act, divorced from subsequent processes of exploiting the entrepreneurial insight by assembling resources and producing goods and services. This comes through in the literature on the personal, psychological characteristics of individuals who start new businesses. It is common, particularly within the management literature, to associate entrepreneurship with boldness, daring, imagination, or creativity (Begley and Boyd, 1987; Chandler and Jansen, 1992; Aldrich and Wiedenmayer, 1993; Hood and Young, 1993; Lumpkin and Dess, 1996). Entrepreneurship, in this conception, is not a necessary component of all human decision-making, as argued by Knight (1921) and Mises (1949), but a specialized activity that some individuals are particularly well-equipped to perform. If these characteristics are the essence of entrepreneurship, then entrepreneurship has no obvious link to the theory of the firm; the relevant personal characteristics can presumably be acquired by contract on the market by purchasing consulting services, project management, and the like. In other words, the locus of entrepreneurship fundamentally doesn't matter.

Schumpeter's legacy has also played an unfortunate role in separating the theory of entrepreneurship from the theory of economic organization. Schumpeter is without any doubt the best-known economics contributor to the entrepreneurship field. He is certainly *the* entrepreneurship scholar that non-specialist economists or management

---

[11] Two British surveys of economics principles textbooks (Kent, 1989; Kent and Rushing, 1999) confirm a similar absence of the concept. A review of graduate textbooks used in Sweden (largely the same books used in the US and elsewhere [Johansson, 2004]) confirms the absence of the concept of the entrepreneur.

scholars are likely to associate with the field (e.g., Nordhaus, 2004). However, Schumpeter not only explicitly dissociated the firm and the entrepreneur; he also cast the latter in heroic terms as an almost genial *Gründer*, so that entrepreneurship tended to become an exceptional occurrence of massive importance; the entrepreneur is a person who by introducing "new combinations" – new products, production methods, markets, sources of supply, or industrial combinations – shakes the economy out of its previous equilibrium, starting a process Schumpeter termed "creative destruction."[12]

However, as we shall argue, entrepreneurship is very often something much more mundane, and, moreover, something that is closely tied to firm organization. In contrast, Schumpeter's entrepreneur need not own capital, or even work within the confines of a business firm at all. This suggests a rather tenuous relationship between the entrepreneur and the firm he owns, works for, or contracts with. Moreover, because Schumpeterian entrepreneurship is *sui generis*, independent of its environment, the nature and structure of the firm does not affect the level of entrepreneurship.

Concepts of entrepreneurship

The disconnect between entrepreneurship and the firm is also present in the notion of entrepreneurship as alertness to profit opportunities, a notion usually associated with the work of Israel Kirzner (1973, 1979a, 1992), which is probably only overshadowed by Schumpeter's in terms of its impact on social science research. In particular, Kirzner's work has become increasingly prominent in management work on entrepreneurship, directly inspiring the tendency in the field to move away from a conception of entrepreneurship as centered on small-business management to a conception of entrepreneurship as a general phenomenon, centering on opportunity discovery (Shane and Venkataraman, 2000; Shane, 2003).

As we discuss in greater detail below, there is something paradoxical about the fascination of management scholars with Kirzner's

---

[12] Schumpeter's thought evolved throughout his long career, however, and in later writings (e.g., Schumpeter, 1942), he adopted a more depersonalized, functional notion of entrepreneurial innovation. See, for discussion, Becker and Knudsen (2003).

work, for Kirzner's entrepreneurs do not own capital, they need only be alert to profit opportunities. Because they own no assets, they bear no uncertainty. For this reason, the link between Kirznerian entrepreneurship and the theory of the firm is weak. Owners, managers, employees, and independent contractors can all be alert to new profit opportunities; Kirzner's entrepreneur does not need a firm to exercise his function in the economy. Kirzner is not interested in the antecedents of entrepreneurship other than profit opportunities; in fact, Kirzner is not interested in entrepreneurship for its own sake, but only as an equilibrating force. His is a purely functional concept. In contrast, the entrepreneurship literature in management tends to paint a much less anonymous portrait of the entrepreneurship and to explicitly associate entrepreneurship with firms. We discuss Kirzner's views in detail in Chapter 3.

Other notions of entrepreneurship (e.g., charismatic leadership, Witt, 1998a, 1998b) are also largely disconnected from the issue of the locus of entrepreneurship. We provide a fuller discussion of these issues in Chapter 2. For now, we note only that the sole exception in the entrepreneurship literature is the notion of entrepreneurship as *judgment*, a notion put forward in the first economics contribution to entrepreneurship, Cantillon's *Essai sur la nature de commerce en général* (1755). While the view of entrepreneurship as judgment appears in many writers, it is most often associated with Frank Knight (1921), but can also be found in Mises (1949) (and, to a lesser extent, Mises' predecessors, such as Menger [1871]).[13] For Knight, firm organization, profit, and the entrepreneur are closely related. In his view, these arise as an embodiment, a result, and a cause, respectively, of commercial experimentation (Demsetz, 1988b).

As signaled already, much of what we are up to in this work may be seen as a reinterpretation, restatement, refinement, and updating of Knight's vision. Schumpeter's work has inspired a host of evolutionary economists, business historians, writers on technology strategy, and so on. Kirzner's work has been of great importance to management research on entrepreneurship. It is high time to restore Knight's fundamental work to the level where it belongs. In Chapters 3 and 4

---

[13] See Martin (1979) on the connection between Menger's and Knight's theories of entrepreneurship.

we discuss the specifically Knightian vision, adding more detail to, for example, his notion of judgment than Knight himself did.

The perhaps more subtle reason for the disconnect between the two fields lies in a conceptualization of entrepreneurship – dominant in the economics as well as in the management literature – in which the identification or imagination of profit opportunities is separated from the process of exploiting or realizing such opportunities. In fact, many contributors to the entrepreneurship literature put all the emphasis on the discovery of opportunities and suppress the exploitation aspects, neglecting the assembling of resources, learning about resource attributes, putting conjectures about resources to the test, etc. The process of resource deployment to seize opportunities is implicitly treated as the domain of established theories in strategy, organizational behavior, the economics of organization, etc. rather than something that belongs to the entrepreneurship field. Thus, Kirzner (1973, 1979a, 1985) thinks of entrepreneurial discovery as simultaneously discovering and seizing an opportunity. This may well fit Kirzner's paradigm example – the discovery of a dollar bill lying on the sidewalk – and it may be an innocuous assumption in the context of the purpose of Kirzner's theory of entrepreneurship: to explain the equilibrating market process. However, in general it misconstrues the nature of entrepreneurship, and disconnects entrepreneurship from the firm.

Likewise, management theories of economic organization and strategy, while paying substantial attention to the cognitive aspects of the discovery process (Lumpkin and Dess, 1996; Shane, 2003), tend to treat opportunities as *given* once the process of resource assembly begins.[14] In other words, established approaches both in entrepreneurship theory and in management treat opportunity discovery as a discrete event separating two distinct stages of the value creation process, giving rise to a separation into two sets of literatures, one on the processes by which plans are made, opportunities are perceived and evaluated, etc., and another in which plans, once formulated, are executed through the deployment of resources.

We argue that the separation of the value creation process into clearly delineated discovery, evaluation, and exploitation phases

---

[14] An important exception is Sarasvathy (2003).

without feedback loops is artificial and misleading.[15] In our perspective, opportunities for entrepreneurial gain do not exist, objectively, waiting to be discovered and exploited; rather, opportunities come into existence only as they are manifested in action. Of course, objective *indications* of an opportunity may exist, such as consumer research that reveals that consumers may demand certain not yet existing functionalities in certain products. However, such indicators do not automatically translate into opportunities, for two reasons. First, the objective indicators require *interpretation*; survey results may be objective data, but the knowledge embodied therein contains an essential subjective element (Foss *et al.*, 2008). Second, unmet market demands, once perceived, do not become opportunities without substantial commitment of resources on the part of the entrepreneur, including his own work. In other words, opportunities are largely created through forward-looking entrepreneurial action.

Organizing the entrepreneurial process

This is essentially the concept of entrepreneurship as judgmental decision-making under uncertainty, a concept we trace through Cantillon (1755), Say (1803), Knight (1921), and Mises (1949). In this approach entrepreneurs are modeled as decision-makers who invest resources based on their judgment of future market conditions, investments that may or may not yield positive return. Because markets for judgment are closed, the exercise of judgment requires starting a firm; moreover, judgment implies asset ownership. In Knight's formulation, entrepreneurship represents judgment that cannot be assessed in terms of its marginal product and which cannot, accordingly, be paid a wage (Knight 1921: 311). In other words, there is no market for the judgment that entrepreneurs rely on, and therefore exercising judgment requires the person with judgment to own productive assets. Of course, judgmental decision-makers can hire consultants, forecasters, technical experts, and so on. However, in doing so they are exercising their own entrepreneurial judgment. Judgment thus implies asset

---

[15] Note the parallel to Rosenberg's (1982) critique of the "linear" model in innovation studies.

ownership, for judgmental decision-making is ultimately decision-making about the employment of resources.[16]

We show how the notion of entrepreneurship as judgment illuminates these issues in novel ways. To develop a judgment-based approach to the firm, we also draw on ideas from Austrian economics (Mises, 1949; Rothbard, 1962; Kirzner, 1973) – the body of economics that is perhaps most intimately connected to ideas on entrepreneurship – and on property-rights economics (Hart, 1995; Barzel, 1997), an important part of modern organizational economics. In our approach, resource uses are not *data*, but are *created* as entrepreneurs envision new ways of using assets to produce goods. The entrepreneur's decision problem is aggravated by the fact that capital assets are *heterogeneous*, and it is not immediately obvious how they should be combined.

The entrepreneur's role, then, is to arrange or organize the capital goods he owns, as we explain in Chapter 5. In the words of Ludwig Lachmann (1956: 16), a key contributor to the Austrian theory of capital: "We are living in a world of unexpected change; hence capital combinations ... will be ever changing, will be dissolved and reformed. In this activity, we find the real function of the entrepreneur." Austrian capital theory provides a unique foundation for an entrepreneurial theory of economic organization. Neoclassical production theory, with its notion of capital as a permanent, homogeneous fund of value, rather than a discrete stock of heterogeneous capital goods, is of little help here.[17] Transaction-cost, resource-based, and property-rights approaches to the firm do incorporate notions of heterogeneous assets, but they tend to invoke the needed specificities in an ad hoc fashion to rationalize particular trading problems – for transaction-cost economics, asset specificity; for capabilities theories, tacit knowledge; and so on. The Austrian approach, starting with Menger's (1871) concepts of higher- and lower-order goods and extending through Böhm-Bawerk's (1884–1912) notion of roundaboutness, Lachmann's (1956) theory of multiple specificities, and Kirzner's (1966) formulation of capital structure in terms of subjective

---

[16] Note that we define the firm here in terms of resource ownership, not the employment relation. A firm, in this sense, can consist of an individual resource owner – a craftsman who owns his own tools is a firm, while an identical craftsman who works with someone else's tools is an employee.

[17] Ironically, the notion of capital as a homogeneous fund owes its popularity to Knight (1936).

entrepreneurial plans, offers a solid foundation for a judgment-based theory of entrepreneurial action.

One way to operationalize the Austrian notion of heterogeneity is to incorporate Barzel's (1997) idea that capital goods are distinguished by their *attributes*. Attributes are characteristics, functions, or possible uses of assets, as perceived by an entrepreneur. Assets are heterogeneous to the extent that they have different, and different levels of, valued attributes. Attributes may also vary over time, even for a particular asset. Given Knightian uncertainty, entrepreneurs are unlikely to know all relevant attributes of all assets when production decisions are made. Nor can the future attributes of an asset, as it is used in production, be forecast with certainty.

Ownership, the boundaries of the firm, and internal organization

Entrepreneurs who seek to create or discover new attributes of capital assets will want ownership titles to the relevant assets, both for speculative reasons and for reasons of economizing on transaction costs. These arguments provide room for entrepreneurship that goes beyond deploying a superior combination of capital assets with "given" attributes, acquiring the relevant assets, and deploying these to producing for a market. Entrepreneurship may also be a matter of *experimenting* with capital assets in an attempt to discover new valued attributes.

Such experimental activity may take place in the context of trying out new combinations through the acquisition of or merger with another firm, or in the form of trying out new combinations of assets already under the control of the entrepreneur. The entrepreneur's success in experimenting with assets in this manner depends not only on his ability to anticipate future prices and market conditions, but also on internal and external transaction costs, the entrepreneur's control over the relevant assets, how much of the expected return from experimental activity he can hope to appropriate, and so on. These aspects of our theory are covered in chapters 6, 7 and 8.

2 | *What is entrepreneurship?*

Entrepreneurship is one of the fastest-growing subfields in management research, and is increasingly appearing in economics, sociology, anthropology, finance, and even law. Entrepreneurship became a Division (specialized interest group) within the Academy of Management in 1987 and now has its own subject code (L26) in the *Journal of Economic Literature* classification scheme. Research and policy organizations such as the World Bank, the US Federal Reserve System, the European Commission, the United Nation's FAO, the OECD, agencies involved in agricultural and rural development, and others show a growing interest in studying and encouraging entrepreneurship. The Kauffman Foundation has substantially increased its funding for data collection, academic research, and education on entrepreneurship.

Entrepreneurship is also becoming one of the most popular subjects at colleges and universities (Gartner and Vesper, 1999; Solomon, Duffy, and Tarabishy, 2002). Entrepreneurship courses, programs, and activities are emerging not only in schools of business, but throughout the curriculum. In 2008 US colleges and universities offered over 2,200 entrepreneurship courses at over 2,000 schools (Cone, 2008), over 600 schools offered majors in entrepreneurship, and an additional 400 with concentrations in entrepreneurship (Kuratko, 2008). The number of Ph.D. programs conferring degrees in entrepreneurship has also increased in the last 20 years (Katz, 2007) and the number of refereed academic entrepreneurship journals have risen in impact factor ratings among peer-reviewed management journals (Gatewood and Shaver, 2009). While the field remains a minority specialization among business school faculties (Katz, 2003), during the 1990s the number of entrepreneurship positions increased by over 250 percent and the number of candidates nearly doubled (Finkle and Deeds, 2001). Besides the usual business school offerings, courses in Social Entrepreneurship, Family Business Management, Technical

Entrepreneurship, Performing Arts Entrepreneurship, and the like are popping up in colleges of arts and sciences, engineering, education, social work, and even fine arts.

The enigmatic entrepreneur of economic theory

Because the entrepreneur in many ways personifies market forces, one might expect entrepreneurs to be *the* central figures in economics. However, while the entrepreneur is fundamentally an *economic* agent – the "driving force of the market," in Mises' (1949: 249) phrase – modern economics maintains an ambivalent relationship with entrepreneurship. It is widely recognized that entrepreneurship is somehow important, but there is little consensus about how the entrepreneurial role should be modeled and incorporated into economic theory. Indeed, the historical "classics" in the economic literature on entrepreneurship – Schumpeter's account of innovation, Knight's theory of profit, and Kirzner's analysis of entrepreneurial discovery – are typically viewed as interesting but idiosyncratic insights that do not easily generalize to other contexts and problems and are difficult, and perhaps impossible, to formally model. Similarly, because most entrepreneurial ventures somehow involve a firm, entrepreneurship would seem to be a central subject in the economic theory of the firm. However, as noted in the previous chapter, one seeks in vain for references to the entrepreneur in the leading textbooks and research articles on the theory of the firm. Within modern economics, the entrepreneur remains an enigma.

Similarly, the strategic management literature has not traditionally given a strong role to the entrepreneur.[1] And yet, entrepreneurship is ultimately the main source of value creation at the firm level. Indeed, the firm's key strategic decisions – strategy formulation, market analysis, industry positioning, diversification, vertical integration and outsourcing, organizational design – are ultimately entrepreneurial decisions (Yu, 2005; Matthews, 2006). But it is only over the last decade that a close liaison has developed between the

---

[1] Within the Academy of Management, the Entrepreneurship interest group is separate from the Business Policy and Strategy and Organization Theory groups.

strategic management and entrepreneurship fields, resulting in the new "strategic entrepreneurship" literature.[2]

The absence of entrepreneurship – relative to its presumed importance – in economics and management is largely a product of the historical development of economics. (Sociologists appear to have had rather little interest in entrepreneurship.) While classical economists such as Adam Smith and, particularly, Jean-Baptiste Say gave the entrepreneur a central role in their accounts of the market process, this is hardly characteristic of modern economics.[3] The historian of economic thought Paul McNulty (1984: 240) notes that

The perfection of the concept of competition ... which was at the heart of the development of economics as a science during the nineteenth and early twentieth centuries, led on the one hand to an increasingly rigorous analytical treatment of market processes and on the other hand to an increasingly passive role for the firm.

The "increasingly rigorous analytical treatment" of markets, notably in the form of general equilibrium theory, not only made firms increasingly "passive," it also made the model of the firm increasingly stylized and anonymous, doing away with those dynamic aspects of markets that are most closely related to entrepreneurship (O'Brien, 1984).

In particular, the development of what came to be known as the "production function view" (Williamson, 1985; Langlois and Foss, 1999) – roughly, the firm as it is presented in intermediate microeconomics textbooks with its fully transparent production possibility sets – was a deathblow to the theory of entrepreneurship in the context of firm organization. If any firm can do what any other firm does (Demsetz, 1991), if all firms are always on their production possibility

---

[2] The *Strategic Entrepreneurship Journal* was established in 2008 as a companion to the established *Strategic Management Journal*. (A third journal, the *Global Strategy Journal*, was added in 2010.)

[3] As Machovec (1995: 109) observes, to the classical economists "specialization and commercial freedom spawned opportunities for alert individuals." Unlike later economists, the classical economists held what is essentially a process view in which competition was seen "as a tapestry of aggressive commercial behaviors which created pure profits by speculating on price futures, engineering new methods of production, and inspiring new product lines to better serve consumers" (Machovec, 1995: 136).

frontier, and if firms always make their equilibrium choices of input combinations and output levels, then there is no room for entrepreneurship. Even in more advanced models of asymmetric production functions, hidden characteristics, and strategic interaction, firms or agents are modeled as behaving according to fixed rules subject to formalization by the analyst. The entrepreneur makes an occasional appearance in business history and in Schumpeterian models of innovation and technical change, but is largely absent from contemporary economic theory.

Given this historical development, it is not surprising that much of the important work on the economics of entrepreneurship was done prior to World War II (i.e., Schumpeter, 1911; Knight, 1921), and that, until the recent surge of work on self-employment (Parker, 2005), most work by economists on entrepreneurship has been done largely outside of the confines of mainstream economics (e.g., Kirzner, 1973, 1979a, 1985; Casson, 1982; Littlechild and Owen, 1980). There have been some attempts to incorporate aspects of entrepreneurship into traditional models – via equilibrium models of the self-employment decision (Kihlstrom and Laffont, 1979; Lazear, 2004), the choice of new-venture creation (Holmes and Schmitz, 2001), or the R&D investment decision (Aghion and Howitt, 1992).[4] But these models treat entrepreneurship in a highly stylized and abstract fashion, not clearly distinguishing entrepreneurship from "management" or other economic functions.

Much of strategic management theory is based on economics. In particular, strategy's dominant perspective, the resource-based view (Lippman and Rumelt, 1982; Barney, 1991; Peteraf, 1993), is built upon the neoclassical model of perfect competition and the production-function view of the firm (Foss and Stieglitz, 2011). Penrose's (1959) approach to firm capabilities and firm growth, by contrast, shares more with Austrian and evolutionary concepts of the firm and market than with neoclassical economics (Foss *et al.*, 2008), though the "real" Penrosian model, rather than the resource-based interpretation of Penrose (Barney, 1991; Peteraf, 1993), remains in the minority within mainstream strategic management.[5] It is thus not surprising

---

[4] See Bianchi and Henrekson (2005) for an excellent review of attempts to incorporate entrepreneurship into neoclassical models.

[5] On the differences between Penrose and mainstream strategy thinking, see Foss (2000).

that it has been difficult to define a role for the entrepreneur in strategic management theory.

By contrast, the Austrian school of economics – discussed more fully in Chapter 5 below – has always given the entrepreneur a central role in the economy, going back at least to the proto-Austrian contribution of Richard Cantillon (1755).[6] For this reason, one would expect Austrian economics to figure prominently in the modern entrepreneurship literature. However, this is not the case. While Kirzner's concept of "alertness" is frequently invoked in particular strands of the entrepreneurship literature, particularly in management (e.g., Shane, 2003) this literature tends to misunderstand fundamentally the nature and purpose of Kirzner's metaphor of entrepreneurial discovery. Moreover, the overall causal-realist account of the market process that characterizes the Austrian approach has had little impact on contemporary entrepreneurship scholarship, which takes its underlying economic framework from the neoclassical account of production and exchange.

Austrian economics has much to offer to entrepreneurship research, not only through the well-known Austrian concepts of distributed, tacit knowledge and entrepreneurial discovery, but also, and even more fundamentally, we think, through the Austrian theory of capital. Careful attention to capital theory, and the heterogeneous, subjectively perceived characteristics of capital goods, is a hallmark of Austrian economics. It figures prominently in the Austrian theory of the business cycle, which reappeared in the public consciousness during the financial crisis of 2008–2009 and the subsequent economic downturn, as scholars, pundits, and policymakers began looking for alternatives to the dominant Keynesian perspective, which eschews capital theory altogether.[7]

Because capital is heterogeneous, the attributes of capital goods are not always known, *ex ante*. Production takes time, and the results are uncertain, so the economy's capital structure does not fall into place

---

[6] On Cantillon's place in the Austrian tradition see the Fall 1985 issue of the *Journal of Libertarian Studies* along with Hayek (1931b), Rothbard (1995, chapter 12), and Thornton (1998).
[7] We discuss Austrian capital theory in more detail in Chapter 5 below. For overviews of Austrian capital theory see Lachmann (1956) and Lewin (1999). On the recent revival of Austrian business-cycle theory, and the relationship between Austrian and Keynesian economics, see Garrison (2001).

automatically. Rather, capital goods must be deployed and redeployed in various combinations in attempts to produce particular consumer products, and someone has to do the deploying and redeploying. In the entrepreneurship theory developed by Cantillon, Knight, and Mises, that person is the entrepreneur, and the entrepreneur's primary role is to exercise *judgment* about the use of productive resources under uncertainty. While Cantillon and Knight did not share the Austrians' approach to capital – Knight, in fact, was a frequent sparring partner with Austrian F. A. Hayek on this very subject – we maintain that the judgment approach, combined with the Austrian subjectivist account of capital heterogeneity, provides a natural path between entrepreneurship theory and the economic theory of the firm and firm strategy.

We begin our discussion by reviewing classical and contemporary entrepreneurship theories, asking if, and how, within each theory, the entrepreneur needs a firm. The answers are not obvious. Some approaches to entrepreneurship – Schumpeter's concept of the entrepreneur as innovator, for instance – treat the entrepreneur as an uncaused cause, a pure genius who operates outside the usual constraints imposed by resource owners and other market participants and is thus unaffected by the firm. Other approaches treat entrepreneurs as skilled managers, exercising their entrepreneurial talents through skillful arrangements of productive factors, thus being an integral part of the firm's operation.[8]

Concepts of entrepreneurship and the firm

Entrepreneurship: occupational, structural, and functional perspectives

Entrepreneurship theories can be usefully divided into occupational, structural, and functional perspectives (see Klein, 2008a). *Occupational* theories define entrepreneurship as self-employment and treat the individual as the unit of analysis, describing the characteristics of individuals who start their own businesses and explaining the choice between employment and self-employment (Kihlstrom

---

[8] On the history of the entrepreneurship concept in economic theory, see Elkjær (1991), Van Praag (1999), and Ibrahim and Vyakarnam (2003).

and Laffont, 1979; Shaver and Scott, 1991; Parker, 2004). The labor economics literature on occupational choice, along with psychological literature on the personal characteristics of those who choose to become self-employed, fits in this category. For example, McGrath and MacMillan (2000) argue that particular individuals have an "entrepreneurial mindset" that enables and encourages them to find opportunities overlooked or ignored by others (and that this mindset is developed through experience, rather than formal instruction). In these approaches, being an entrepreneur means holding a particular job title. Of course, most countries collect data on employment status, and self-employment is a common measure of entrepreneurship in the empirical literature – because it is easy to measure.

Structural approaches treat the firm or industry as the unit of analysis, defining the "entrepreneurial firm" as a new or small firm. The literatures on industry dynamics, firm growth, clusters, and networks have in mind a structural concept of entrepreneurship (Acs and Audretsch, 1990; Aldrich, 1990; Audretsch, Keilbach, and Lehmann, 2005). Indeed, the idea that one firm, industry, or economy can be more "entrepreneurial" than another suggests that entrepreneurship is associated with a particular market structure (i.e., many small or young firms). As is the case with occupational concepts, the widespread use of structural concepts of entrepreneurship in the research literature may be driven by data availability; information on start-ups, venture funding, IPOs, and, to a lesser extent, firm size and age, are provided by the usual statistical agencies and services.

By contrast, the classic contributions to the economic theory of entrepreneurship from Schumpeter, Knight, Mises, Kirzner, and others model entrepreneurship as a *function*, activity, or behavior, not an employment category or market structure. They are typically oriented towards behaviors in the context of a process. In contrast, occupational and structural conceptions tend to focus on outcomes, while neglecting process. However, the outcomes most often used in the research literature on entrepreneurship – self-employment and start-ups – do not map easily into these broader functional concepts. Entrepreneurial thinking can be manifested in large and small firms, in old and new firms, by individuals or teams, across a variety of occupational categories, and so on. By focusing too narrowly on self-employment and start-up companies, the contemporary literature may be understating the role of entrepreneurship in the economy and in business organization.

What exactly is the entrepreneurial function? Various candidates have been proposed: small-business management; imagination or creativity; innovation; alertness to opportunities; the ability to adjust; charismatic leadership; and judgment. Let us consider each in turn.

Entrepreneurship as small-business management

In the entrepreneurship curricula of many business schools, the phenomenon under investigation is simply small-business management. Entrepreneurs are pictured as the managers of small, family-owned businesses or start-up companies. Entrepreneurship consists of routine management tasks, relationships with venture capitalists and other sources of external finance, product development, marketing, and so on. In this sense, entrepreneurship and the theory of the firm – the theory of *some* firms, at least – are inextricably linked. The theory of entrepreneurship in this approach is the theory of how small-business owners organize and manage their assets. Entrepreneurship courses and programs focus on writing business plans, making elevator pitches to potential resource providers, and leading small student teams, and the like. Groups like Students in Free Enterprise (SIFE) hold competitions at which students can test their skills.

While these are clearly important activities, limiting the domain of entrepreneurship to small-business management makes entrepreneurship at one level too narrow, and at another, too broad. It deems "entrepreneurial" virtually all aspects of small or new business management, while excluding the identical tasks when performed within a large or established business. Although the research literature moved away from this conception more than two decades ago, it still holds sway on university campuses. It is not difficult to understand the pragmatic reasons why: Entrepreneurship courses are designed for students who plan to start, or have already started, a company, and they need to understand the management problems that arise as a consequence of this. Entrepreneurial behavior in the context of established firms is addressed in other courses in the business curriculum that usually do not have "entrepreneurship" in their titles, such as "innovation management" or "corporate renewal." And yet, if entrepreneurship is simply a set of management activities, or any management activity that takes place within a particular type of firm, then it is unclear why we should bother to add this label "entrepreneurial" to those activities.

Entrepreneurship as imagination or creativity

The management research literature sometimes associates entrepreneurship with boldness, daring, imagination, or creativity (Begley and Boyd, 1987; Chandler and Jansen, 1992; Aldrich and Wiedenmayer, 1993; Hood and Young, 1993; Lumpkin and Dess, 1996). These accounts emphasize the personal, psychological characteristics of the entrepreneur. Entrepreneurship, in this conception, is not a necessary component of all human decision-making, but a specialized activity that some individuals are particularly well-equipped to perform.[9]

If these characteristics are the essence of entrepreneurship, then entrepreneurship has no obvious link to the theory of the firm (or, at least not without further arguments). The relevant personal characteristics can presumably be acquired by contract on the market by purchasing consulting services, project management, and the like. A "non-entrepreneurial" owner or manager, in other words, can manage the day-to-day operations of the firm, purchasing "entrepreneurship" on the market as needed. Moreover, the literature does not explain clearly whether imagination and creativity are necessary, sufficient, or incidental conditions for entrepreneurship. Clearly the founders of many firms are imaginative and creative. If not, are they not entrepreneurs?

Entrepreneurship as innovation

Probably the best-known concept of entrepreneurship among economists is Joseph Schumpeter's idea of the entrepreneur as innovator. Schumpeter's entrepreneur introduces "new combinations" – new products, production methods, markets, sources of supply, or industrial

---

[9] As Gartner (1988: 21) noted over two decades ago, this literature employs a host of different (and frequently) contradictory notions of entrepreneurship. A "startling number of traits and characteristics have been attributed to the entrepreneur, and a 'psychological profile' of the entrepreneur assembled from these studies would portray someone larger than life, full of contradictions, and, conversely, someone so full of traits that (s)he would have to be a sort of generic 'Everyman.' "

combinations – shaking the economy out of its previous equilibrium through a process Schumpeter termed "creative destruction." The entrepreneur-innovator is introduced in Schumpeter's groundbreaking *Theory of Economic Development* (1911) and developed further in his two-volume work *Business Cycles* (1939). Realizing that the entrepreneur has no place in the general-equilibrium system of Walras, whom Schumpeter greatly admired, Schumpeter gave the entrepreneur a role as the source of economic change (which could include, but is not limited to, the establishment of new ventures):

[I]n capitalist reality as distinguished from its textbook picture, it is not [price] competition which counts but the competition from the new commodity, the new technology, the new source of supply, the new type of organization ... competition which commands a decisive cost or quality advantage and which strikes not at the margins of profits and the outputs of existing firms but at their foundations and their very lives.

(Schumpeter, 1942: 84)

While there are substantial bodies of "Schumpeterian" and "Neo-Schumpeterian" literatures, especially in technology management and evolutionary economics,[10] these literatures are influenced by evolutionary economics, complexity theory, development economics, and other approaches as much as by the ideas of Schumpeter himself (Hanusch and Pyka, 2005). Much of the modern literature attempts to model small, continuous changes, while Schumpeter sought to explain radical, discontinuous shifts in technologies and markets. Schumpeter also paid little attention to natural selection, taking the successful innovation as the unit of analysis. As Rosenberg (1986: 197) remarks, "many of Schumpeter's contributions to economic and social thought remain neglected – even by people who would not shrink from the label 'Neo-Schumpeterians'."

Schumpeter carefully distinguished the entrepreneur from the capitalist (and strongly criticized the neoclassical economists for confusing the two).[11] His entrepreneur need not own capital, or even work within the confines of a business firm at all. While the

---

[10] And even an International Joseph A. Schumpeter Society, founded in 1986.

[11] We are oversimplifying a bit, as Schumpeter's views on the entrepreneur evolved throughout his career. For example, his initial formulation (Schumpeter, 1911) emphasized not only the depersonalized function of

entrepreneur could be a manager or owner of a firm, he is more likely to be an independent contractor or craftsman. In Schumpeter's conception, "people act as entrepreneurs only when they actually carry out new combinations, and lose the character of entrepreneurs as soon as they have built up their business, after which they settle down to running it as other people run their businesses" (Ekelund and Hébert, 1990: 569).

This suggests a rather tenuous relationship between the entrepreneur and the firm he owns, works for, or contracts with. Entrepreneurship is exercised within the firm when it introduces new products, processes, or strategies, but not otherwise. The day-to-day operations of the firm need not involve entrepreneurship at all. Moreover, because Schumpeterian entrepreneurship is *sui generis*, independent of its environment, the nature and structure of the firm does not affect the level of entrepreneurship. Corporate R&D budgets, along with organizational structures that encourage managerial commitment to innovation (Hoskisson and Hitt, 1994), have little to do with Schumpeterian entrepreneurship per se.[12]

Entrepreneurship as alertness to opportunities

Over the last decade, a different conception of the entrepreneurial function – alertness to profit opportunities – has come to dominate the management literature on entrepreneurship (Shane and Venkataraman, 2000; Shane, 2003). Critical to this perspective is the notion of "opportunities," defined as situations in which resources can be redeployed to create value through various forms of arbitrage.

establishing new combinations, but also the leadership qualities of the individual entrepreneur, held to possess "superhuman powers of energetic will" (Becker and Knudsen, 2003: 200). Here Schumpeter's entrepreneur is a causal agent "characterized by 'the disposition to act' in terms of 'the ability to subjugate others and to utilize them for his purposes, to order and to prevail, which leads to successful deeds – even without particularly brilliant intelligence' " (Becker and Knudsen, 2003: 207). By the time of *Business Cycles* (1937), Schumpeter had abandoned this emphasis on personal attributes.

[12] Other writers influenced by Schumpeter, however, such as Baumol (1994), do view public and private R&D, the scale and scope of patent protection, and basic science education as important determinants of the level of entrepreneurial activity.

While present in Cantillon's and J. B. Clark's notions of entrepreneurship, this concept has been elaborated most fully by Israel Kirzner
(1973, 1979a, 1985, 1992) (we provide a fuller characterization and
discussion of Kirzner's work in Chapter 3). The modern management
literature discusses opportunity recognition, evaluation, and exploitation, but for Kirzner, recognition is the primary entrepreneurial act;
the rest is management.

Kirzner's formulation emphasizes the nature of competition as what
Hayek (1968) called a "discovery process." The source of entrepreneurial profit is superior foresight – the discovery of something (new
products, cost-saving technology) unknown to other market participants. The simplest case is that of the financial-market or commodity
arbitrageur, who discovers a discrepancy in present prices that can be
exploited for financial gain. In a more typical case, the entrepreneur
is alert to a new product or a superior production process and steps
in to fill this market gap before others. Success, in this view, comes
not from following a well-specified maximization problem, but from
having some knowledge or insight that no one else has – that is, from
something beyond the given means-end framework.[13]

Kirzner's entrepreneurs do not own capital; they need only be alert
to profit opportunities. Because they own no assets, they bear no
uncertainty. Critics have seized on this point as a defect in Kirzner's
conception. According to this criticism, mere alertness to a profit
opportunity is not sufficient for earning profits. To reap financial
gain, the entrepreneur must invest resources to realize the discovered
profit opportunity. As Rothbard (1985: 283) argues, "[e]ntrepreneur-
ial ideas without money are mere parlor games until the money is
obtained and committed to the projects." Moreover, excepting the few
cases where buying low and selling high are nearly instantaneous (say,
electronic trading of currencies or commodity futures), even arbitrage
transactions require some time to complete. The selling price may fall

---

[13] It is important to distinguish Kirzner's view of superior foresight from
Stigler's (1961, 1962) search model in which the value of new knowledge is
known in advance, available to anyone willing to pay the relevant search
costs. "Stigler's searcher decides how much time it is worth spending
rummaging through dusty attics and untidy drawers looking for a sketch
which (the family recalls) Aunt Enid thought might be by Lautrec. Kirzner's
entrepreneur enters a house and glances lazily at the pictures which have
been hanging in the same place for years. 'Isn't that a Lautrec on the wall?' "
(Ricketts, 1987: 58).

before the arbitrageur has made his sale, and thus even the pure arbitrageur faces some probability of loss. In Kirzner's formulation, the worst that can happen to an entrepreneur is the failure to discover an existing profit opportunity. Entrepreneurs either earn profits or break even, but it is unclear how they suffer losses.

For these reasons, the connection between Kirznerian entrepreneurship and the theory of the firm seems weak. Owners, managers, employees, and independent contractors can all be alert to new profit opportunities. Kirzner's entrepreneurs do not need a firm to exercise their function in the economy. They do not require a particular institutional context. More generally, the link between Kirznerian entrepreneurship and other branches of economic analysis, such as industrial organization, innovation, and the theory of the firm, is weak. Hence Kirzner's concept has not generated a large body of direct applications.[14]

Klein (2008b) offers a more general critique of the opportunity-discovery perspective, arguing that under uncertainty, "opportunities" can only be defined *ex post*, and that actions, not opportunities, should be the unit of analysis in entrepreneurship studies. The notion of "opportunity" is metaphorical, not literal, and emphasis on opportunities can be misleading. Microeconomic theory, for example, deals with agents' subjective preferences, but preferences are not observed in action, only behavior in markets. Preferences are *inferred* from choices made, and there is little need to say what preferences "are," in some deeper, ontological sense. Opportunities, likewise, do not exist, but are inferred (*ex post*) from market behavior – if action generates net profit, we say that the actor seized an opportunity. As we note below (and in Chapter 4), viewing investments, not opportunities, as the entrepreneurial act may be a more parsimonious way to describe the phenomenon.[15]

---

[14] Exceptions include Ekelund and Saurman (1988), Holcombe (1992), Harper (1995), Sautet (2001), Pongracic (2009), and Huerta de Soto (2010). Harper (1995) tries to blend Kirzner's emphasis on the purely logical, analytical function of discovery with a more institutional, cognitive approach that incorporates individual psychology.

[15] As Huerta de Soto (2010: 15) notes, "both the Spanish word '*empresa*' and the French and Latin expression '*entrepreneur*' derive etymologically from the Latin verb *in prehendo-endi-ensum*, which means to discover, to see, to perceive, to realize, to attain; and the Latin term *in prehensa* clearly implies action and means to take, to catch, to seize. In short, *empresa* is synonymous with action."

Entrepreneurship as the ability to adjust

Nobel Prize-winning economist Theodore Schultz's (1975, 1979, 1980) approach to entrepreneurship, while less known today, is also worth considering (Klein and Cook, 2006). Schultz's view of the entrepreneurial function is akin to Kirzner's in certain key respects, notably the conceptualization of the entrepreneur's function as that of adjustment to equilibrium. Like Schumpeter, Schultz works in the Walrasian tradition, broadly defined. However, Schultz recognizes that markets do not automatically and instantaneously return to equilibrium following an exogenous shock. "[R]egaining equilibrium takes time, and how people proceed over time depends on their efficiency in responding to any given disequilibrium and on the costs and returns of the sequence of adjustments available to them" (Schultz, 1975: 829).

Surprisingly, economists have devoted little attention to this problem, perhaps because of the great difficulties of modeling disequilibrium adjustment processes where trades may take place at "false" (non-equilibrium) prices (Hicks, 1946; Fisher, 1983). Even Schumpeter, who saw economic progress as the result of disruptions to existing equilibrium states, assumed that equilibrium would be regained following such a disruption. Schultz, by contrast, took innovation as given, and focused on how economic agents adjust to exogenous shocks. An example is farmers in a developing economy. Such people must "deal with a sequence of changes in economic conditions, which are in general not of their own making because they originate mainly out of the activities of people other than farm people. For this reason Schumpeter's theory of economic development is far from sufficient to explain most of these changes" (Schultz, 1975: 832). Moreover, the atomistic nature of agriculture and the unique aspects of farm production generate problems of collective action and by-product behavior (Olson, 1965), making such adjustments lengthier.

In Schultz's formulation, entrepreneurship is the ability to adjust, or reallocate one's resources, in response to changing circumstances. As such, entrepreneurship is an aspect of all human behavior, not a unique function performed by a class of specialists. "No matter what part of the economy is being investigated, we observe that people are consciously reallocating their resources in response to changes in economic conditions" (Schultz 1979: 2). Businessmen, farmers, housewives, students, and even university presidents, deans, and research directors make Schultz's (1979) list of entrepreneurs.

Somewhat paradoxically, the degree to which entrepreneurship is manifested in a society is itself determined by supply and demand. The demand for entrepreneurial services is given by the expected gains from adjusting one's resources in the face of the disequilibrium, itself a function of some characteristics of that disequilibrium. The supply of entrepreneurial capacities is given by agents' abilities to perceive and exploit opportunities. Like any economic good, entrepreneurship is valuable and scarce (Schultz, 1979: 6). Knight and Kirzner treat entrepreneurship as "extra-economic," meaning that it is the driving force behind the pricing process, but is not itself traded and priced on the market. In contrast, Schultz (1979) insists that entrepreneurial ability, like other services available for hire, is a resource with a market price and quantity, though he did not develop this insight into a fully specified theory of the supply of and demand for entrepreneurship.

Schultz conceives entrepreneurial ability as a form of human capital. Like other forms of human capital, this ability can be increased through education, training, experience, health care, and so on. While education and other human-capital investments also lead to improvements in technical and allocative efficiency, Schultz argues that efficiency improvements cannot account for all of the effects of education on economic performance, particularly in agricultural communities during periods of modernization. At least part of the returns to education are the returns to improved abilities to adjust to change, for instance by adopting new technology and organizational practices. Moreover, an economy's aggregate stock of entrepreneurial ability can also be increased by the immigration of people with particular entrepreneurial experiences and skills (presumably in response to increased opportunities for entrepreneurial gain).

Entrepreneurship as charismatic leadership

Another strand of literature, incorporating insights from economics, psychology, and sociology and leaning heavily on Max Weber, associates entrepreneurship with charismatic leadership. Entrepreneurs, in this view, specialize in communication – the ability to articulate a plan, a set of rules, or a broader vision, and impose it on others.

Casson (2000) calls these plans "mental models" of reality. The successful entrepreneur excels at communicating these models to others, who come to share the entrepreneur's vision (and become his followers). Such entrepreneurs are also typically optimistic, self-confident, and enthusiastic (though it is not clear whether these are necessary conditions).

Witt (1998a, 1998b) describes entrepreneurship similarly as "cognitive leadership." He outlines an entrepreneurial theory of the firm that combines recent literature on cognitive psychology with Kirzner's concept of alertness. Entrepreneurs require complementary factors of production, he argues, which are coordinated within the firm. For the firm to be successful, the entrepreneur must establish a tacit, shared framework of goals, which governs the relationships among members of the entrepreneur's team. As Langlois (1998) points out, it is often easier (less costly) for individuals to commit to a specific individual, the leader, rather than an abstract set of complex rules governing the firm's operations. The appropriate exercise of charismatic authority, then, reduces coordination costs within organizations.

A possible weakness of this approach, in our view, is its emphasis on human assets, rather than the inalienable physical assets the entrepreneur controls. Must the charismatic leader necessarily own physical capital, or can he be an employee or independent contractor? Formulating a business plan, communicating a "corporate culture," and the like are clearly important dimensions of business leadership. But are they attributes of the successful manager or the successful entrepreneur? Even if top-level managerial skill were the same as entrepreneurship, it is unclear why charismatic leadership should be regarded as more "entrepreneurial" than other, comparatively mundane managerial tasks such as structuring incentives, limiting opportunism, administering rewards, and so on.

Entrepreneurship as judgment

An alternative to the foregoing accounts is that entrepreneurship consists of judgmental decision-making under conditions of uncertainty. We discuss judgment in detail in Chapter 4. For now, simply define judgment as decisive action about the deployment of economic resources when outcomes cannot be predicted according to known probabilities. In a judgment-based approach, bearing uncertainty – that is, making decisions without knowing the consequences for sure – is the entrepreneur's *raison d'être*. Of course, all human action (to use Mises' [1949] term) involves uncertainty, such that there is an element of entrepreneurship in all human behavior. To understand resource allocation in a market setting, however, we are mainly interested in a specific kind of uncertainty-bearing, namely the deliberate deployment of productive resources in anticipation of financial gain.

While alertness tends to be passive (perhaps even hard to distinguish from luck, Demsetz 1983), judgment is active. Alertness is the ability to react to *existing* opportunities while judgment refers to the creation of *new* opportunities.[16] Entrepreneurs "are those who seek to profit by actively promoting adjustment to change. They are not content to passively adjust their ... activities to readily foreseeable changes or changes that have already occurred in their circumstances; rather, they regard change itself as an opportunity to meliorate their own conditions and aggressively attempt to anticipate and exploit it" (Salerno, 1993: 123). Decision-making under uncertainty is entrepreneurial, whether it involves imagination, creativity, leadership, and related factors or not.

Knight introduces the notion of judgment to link profit and the firm to the existence of uncertainty. Judgment primarily refers to the process of businessmen forming estimates of future events in situations in which there is no agreement or idea at all on probabilities of occurrence. It may be defined as a service that enhances the quality of decisions in novel situations that require an urgent decision, a service that is learned and has a large tacit component. Entrepreneurship represents judgment that cannot be assessed in terms of its marginal product and which cannot, accordingly, be paid a wage.[17] This is

[16] In Kirzner's treatment, entrepreneurship is characterized as "a responding agency. I view the entrepreneur not as a source of innovative ideas *ex nihilo*, but as being alert to the opportunities that exist already and are waiting to be noticed" (Kirzner, 1973: 74).

[17] "The receipt of profit in a particular case may be argued to be the result of superior judgment. But it is judgment of judgment, especially one's own judgment, and in an individual case there is no way of telling good judgment from good luck, and a succession of cases sufficient to evaluate the judgment or determine its probable value transforms the profit into a wage ... If ... capacities were known, the compensation for exercising them can be competitively imputed and is a wage; only, in so far as they are unknown or known only to the possessor himself, do they give rise to a profit" (Knight, 1921: 311).

because entrepreneurship is judgment in relation to the most uncertain events, such as starting a new firm, defining a new market, and the like. As we explain in greater detail later (Chapter 7), there is no market for the judgment that entrepreneurs rely on, and utilizing judgment therefore requires the person with judgment to start a firm. Moreover, judgment implies asset ownership. Judgmental decision-making is ultimately decision-making *about the employment of resources*. An entrepreneur without capital goods is, in Knight's sense, no entrepreneur.[18]

This implies an obvious link with the theory of the firm, particularly those (transaction-cost and property-rights theories) that define asset ownership as a crucial ingredient of firm organization (Hart, 1995; Williamson, 1996). The firm, in this sense, is the entrepreneur and the assets he owns, and therefore ultimately controls. The theory of the firm is essentially a theory of how the entrepreneur exercises his judgmental decision-making – what combinations of assets will he seek to acquire, what (proximate) decisions will he delegate to subordinates, how will he provide incentives and employ monitoring to see that his assets are used consistently with his judgments, and so on.

Entrepreneurship as uncertainty-bearing is also important for Mises' theory of profit and loss, a cornerstone of his well-known critique of economic planning under socialism. Mises begins with the marginal productivity theory of distribution developed by his Austrian predecessors. In the marginal productivity theory, laborers earn wages, capitalists earn interest, and owners of specific factors earn rents. Any excess (deficit) of a firm's realized receipts over these factor payments constitutes profit (loss). Profit and loss, therefore, are returns to entrepreneurship. In a hypothetical equilibrium without uncertainty (what Mises calls the "evenly rotating economy"), capitalists would still earn interest, as a reward for lending, but there would be no profit or loss.

Entrepreneurs, in Mises' understanding of the market, make their production plans based on the current prices of factors of production and the anticipated future prices of consumer goods. What Mises calls

---

[18] Knight (1921: 267, 271) explains that "[w]ith uncertainty entirely absent, every individual being in possession of perfect knowledge, there would be no occasion for anything of the nature of responsible management or control of productive activities ... Its existence in the world is a direct result of the fact of uncertainty."

"economic calculation" is the comparison of these anticipated future receipts with present outlays, all expressed in common monetary units. Under socialism, the absence of factor markets, and the consequent lack of factor prices, renders economic calculation – and hence rational economic planning – impossible. Mises' point is that a socialist economy may employ workers, managers, technicians, inventors, and the like, but it cannot, by definition, employ entrepreneurs, because there are no money profits and losses. Entrepreneurship, and not labor or management or technological expertise, is the crucial element of the market economy. As Mises puts it: Managers of socialist enterprises may be allowed to "play market," to act as if they were managers of private firms with their own interests at stake, but entrepreneurs cannot be asked to "play speculation and investment" (Mises, 1949: 705). In the absence of entrepreneurship a complex, dynamic economy cannot allocate resources to their highest valued use.[19]

Conclusion: entrepreneurial judgment as a natural complement to the theory of the firm

All the foregoing accounts of the entrepreneurial function are interesting and important. But, we think, the judgment approach provides the most natural and useful links to the theory of the firm. In Chapter 6 we will review the dominant theories of the firm in organizational economics and strategic management, and approach the links with entrepreneurship theory from that direction. Again, we will conclude

[19] Mises and Kirzner are usually treated together as offering a unified Austrian account of the entrepreneur. Indeed, Kirzner, a leading member of the modern Austrian school, received his Ph.D. under Mises at New York University and has described his work as the working out of various parts of Mises' system. However, we see Mises in the Cantillon–Knight tradition of viewing entrepreneurship as judgment over the deployment of resources, not alertness per se. Kirzner (1973: 39–40) agrees that in a world of uncertainty, resource owners exercise entrepreneurial judgment in allocating their resources to particular uses. But he goes on (1973: 40–43) to introduce the analytical device of "pure entrepreneurship," the act of discovery or alertness to profit opportunities by those with no resources under their control, and claims that this function, rather than uncertainty-bearing, is the "driving force" behind the market economy. We do not find the concept of pure entrepreneurship or the "alertness" metaphor useful to understanding the nature of the market system. For more on this see Klein (1999a: 24–25), and the next chapter.

that the judgment approach fits most naturally with most of these theories. The reason is simple: firms are bundles of resources, and an entrepreneurial theory of the firm must be a theory about resources. Mental processes of recognition, perception, vision-setting, and social processes of leadership and culture-formation provide critical *contexts* for resource allocation – we may regard them as antecedents to decisions about resource use – but they do not constitute market action. Like Mises, we are ultimately interested in purposeful human action, and we want an entrepreneurship theory that focuses on deeds, not words or thoughts. The notion of judgment calls attention to decisions in the service of an entrepreneurial plan or at least intention about buying, selling, and using productive assets (while not being strictly identical to them). Such decisions have been remarkably underemphasized in much of the research literature on entrepreneurship, notably in the "opportunity discovery" research stream. We discuss this stream in the following chapter.

3 | *Entrepreneurship: from opportunity discovery to judgment*

In this chapter we discuss and confront two of the conceptions of entrepreneurship that were discussed in the preceding chapter, namely Israel Kirzner's concept of entrepreneurship as alertness to profit opportunities and the concept of entrepreneurship as judgment associated with Cantillon, Say, Knight, and Mises. As both concepts have a pedigree in Austrian economics, we also discuss some of the key tenets of the Austrian approach.

Kirzner's notion of alertness to previously undiscovered profit opportunities is a dominant strand of the contemporary entrepreneurship literature, along with Schumpeter's notion of entrepreneurship as innovation and Knight's idea of entrepreneurship as judgment. The distinction between "Schumpeterian" and "Kirznerian" entrepreneurs has become standard in the literature (although Kirzner [2009] himself contests the distinction). Among Austrian economists, Kirzner's understanding of the market as "an entrepreneurially driven process" (Kirzner, 1997: 67) of "mutual discovery" (Kirzner, 1997: 71) is one of the leading perspectives on production, exchange, and market efficiency.[1]

More recently, Kirzner's concept of entrepreneurship has also become highly influential in the management literature on entrepreneurship (e.g., Shane and Venkataraman, 2000; Shane, 2003). The "opportunity identification" or "opportunity recognition" strand of this literature seeks to build a positive research program by operationalizing Kirzner's idea of alertness or discovery and pinpointing its cognitive, motivational, and environmental antecedents. The goal is to understand how and why particular individuals are alert and, in

---

[1] Kirzner's work has given rise to much critical discussion since its original statement in Kirzner's *Competition and Entrepreneurship* (1973), mainly (but not exclusively, e.g., Demsetz, 1983) among Austrian economists (Rothbard, 1974; High, 1982; Salerno, 1993, 2008).

some cases, how to increase the degree of alertness in an organization or in society (Cooper, Folta, and Woo, 1995; Gaglio and Katz, 2001). While Kirzner himself doubts the connection between his alertness construct and the study of actual decision-making – "my own work has nothing to say about the secrets of successful entrepreneurship" (Kirzner, 2009: 145) – the management research literature in entrepreneurship sees "discovery entrepreneurship" as a fundamentally Kirznerian concept (Klein, 2008b).

Shane and Venkataraman's (2000: 218) influential assessment defines entrepreneurship research as "the scholarly examination of how, by whom, and with what effects opportunities to create future goods and services are discovered, evaluated, and exploited." As such, "the field involves the study of sources of opportunities; the processes of discovery, evaluation, and exploitation of opportunities; and the set of individuals who discover, evaluate, and exploit them." Shane's *General Theory of Entrepreneurship* (2003) cites Kirzner more than any writer except Schumpeter. More generally, the entrepreneurial opportunity, rather than the individual entrepreneur, the start-up company, or the new product, has become the unit of analysis in much of the academic literature on entrepreneurship (Shane and Venkataraman, 2000; Gaglio and Katz, 2001; Shane, 2003).

Kirzner's framework builds on one particular strand of Austrian economics, what is sometimes called the "market process" approach. Kirzner himself sees his contribution as primarily an extension of the work of Mises and F. A. Hayek, in effect bridging Mises' (1949) emphasis on the entrepreneur with Hayek's (1946, 1968) concept of market competition as an unfolding process of discovery and learning.[2] Among mainstream economists, Kirzner has been cited in the literature on occupational choice, and there have been a few attempts

---

[2] More specifically: "The key to understanding the market process is to understand the dynamic character of market competition. But the neoclassical focus on perfect competition as an equilibrium *state of affairs* prevented appreciation of this insight. It was not until Hayek's pioneering, but insufficiently-appreciated work on the dynamically competitive market as a process of mutual discovery, that Austrian economics was able explicitly to grapple with this embarrassing hiatus. It was particularly in the work of Ludwig von Mises that this writer discovered, in the Misesian entrepreneur and in the Misesian dynamically competitive process, what he believed (and believes) to be the true solution. My 1973 work was written in order to spell out this solution" (Kirzner, 2009: 147).

to formalize his model of the market process (Littlechild and Owen, 1980; Yates, 2000), in the context of a more general interest in equilibration processes (Fisher, 1983). Kirzner has explained the Austrian model of the entrepreneurial market process to readers of the prestigious *Journal of Economic Literature* (Kirzner, 1997). Still, his work has been more influential among management scholars than among economists, who tend to view equilibration as a second-order phenomenon; the main focus of theoretical work in economics today (both microeconomic and macroeconomic) remains identifying and characterizing market equilibria in terms of existence, uniqueness, and stability.

This chapter traces the origin and development of the concept of entrepreneurial alertness and its place as the centerpiece of the opportunity-discovery approach to entrepreneurship. In particular, we place Kirzner's contribution within the broader context of the Austrian school of economics. We argue that while Kirzner's contribution is often thought of as *the* Austrian conception of the entrepreneur (e.g., Van Praag, 1999; Casson, 2005; Landa, 2006), there is in fact an alternative Austrian tradition that emphasizes the entrepreneur as an uncertainty-bearing, asset-owning individual and that this tradition offers advantages over the discovery approach (whether in the Kirznerian or modern-management incarnations). We also critically discuss the way Kirzner's work has been interpreted and used in the theoretical, empirical, and experimental literatures looking into the antecedents and consequences of such opportunity discovery. As we argue, this literature goes much beyond Kirzner's work, making opportunity discovery and its determinants the key feature of the theory, whereas Kirzner's real interest lies in explaining market equilibration, a higher-level phenomenon.

The Austrian school of economics

The Austrian school (Menger, 1871; Böhm-Bawerk, 1884–1912; Hayek, 1933, 1948, 1968; Mises, 1949; Lachmann, 1956; Rothbard, 1962; Kirzner, 1973), one of the three revolutionary schools in the "marginalist revolution" of the 1870s, has made fundamental contributions to the theory of markets, capital and interest theory, comparative systems theory, business cycle theory, the economics of information – and entrepreneurship. However, like all "heterodox" approaches, the Austrian school currently occupies a marginal position among contemporary, mainstream economists, though Hayek's theory of the business cycle has attracted renewed interest since the turn of the century (e.g., Oppers, 2002), not the least under the impact of the current slump (Tempelman, 2010).

Besides the Austrian critique of socialism and the Mises–Hayek business cycle theory, the Austrian theory that is perhaps best generally known (i.e., outside the Austrian school) is Kirzner's theory of entrepreneurship. Thus, Kirzner is increasingly well-known in management studies for his contributions to the theory of entrepreneurship and the complementary "market process" account of economic activity (Jacobson, 1992; Hill and Deeds, 1996; Langlois, 2001; Chiles and Choi, 2000; Chiles, 2003; Roberts and Eisenhardt, 2003). Other characteristically Austrian ideas such as the time structure of capital (Hayek, 1941) and the heterogeneity of capital goods (Lachmann, 1956) have received less attention (but see Chiles, Bluedorn, and Gupta, 2007).

Here we offer a brief sketch of the history and development of the Austrian school, with particular reference to its approach to the entrepreneur. As we discuss in more detail below, the Austrian tradition is more diverse than is conventionally recognized. For example, we see important differences between Kirzner's approach to entrepreneurship and that of Menger, the early twentieth-century American representatives of the Austrian school, and Mises, Kirzner's teacher and the most important and influential of the modern Austrian economists.

Menger and the early Austrian school

The Austrian tradition begins with Carl Menger (1871), who sought to develop a causal, realistic account of price formation (and other economic phenomena) in contrast to the inductive, historicist approach that dominated late-nineteenth-century German economics. Menger's approach emphasized the subjectivity of economic value, marginal analysis, resource heterogeneity, distributed knowledge, and the time structure of production. The entrepreneur figures prominently in Menger's account of production (Martin, 1979), though not in the sense emphasized by Kirzner. The entrepreneur is described by Menger (1871: 68) as a coordinating agent who is both capitalist and a manager:

Entrepreneurial activity includes: (a) obtaining information about the economic situation; (b) economic calculation – all the various computations that must be made if a production process is to be efficient (provided that it is economic in other respects); (c) the act of will by which goods of higher order (or goods in general – under conditions of developed commerce, where any economic good can be exchanged for any other) are assigned to a particular production process; and finally (d) supervision of the execution of the production plan so that it may be carried through as economically as possible.

This formulation emphasizes the importance of uncertainty and knowledge, and the deliberate, decisive action of the entrepreneur in arranging the productive resources at his disposal. Menger also makes the entrepreneur a resource owner, as does Knight (1921).

In his emphasis on uncertainty-bearing Menger picks up a theme introduced by Richard Cantillon, often considered a forerunner of the Austrian tradition (Rothbard, 1995; Thornton, 1999). Cantillon was the first economist to analyze the entrepreneur systematically. In *Essai sur la nature du commerce en général* (1755), he described three classes of economic agents: landowners, wage workers, and entrepreneurs whose main purpose is to engage in arbitrage, motivated by the profit that may stem from "buying at a certain price and selling at an uncertain price" (Cantillon, 1755: 54):

Entrepreneurs work for uncertain wages, so to speak, and all others for certain wages until they have them, although their functions and their rank are very disproportionate. The General who has a salary, the Courtier who has a pension, and the Domestic who has wages, are in the latter class. All the others are Entrepreneurs, whether they establish themselves with a capital to carry on their enterprise, or are Entrepreneurs of their own work without any capital, and they may be considered as living subject to uncertainty; even Beggars and Robbers are Entrepreneurs of this class.

Thus Cantillon saw uncertainty as an integral part of understanding profits and emphasized that entrepreneurs, rather than a distinct group of individuals, are all those who bear commercial risk. He also emphasized the importance of foresight and argued that entrepreneurs do not need to own capital, a characteristic of Kirzner's approach that we discuss in more detail below.

In the 1880s and 1890s an Austrian school coalesced around
Menger and his disciples, most notably Eugen von Böhm-Bawerk and
Friedrich Wieser. Important British and American economists such as
Philip Wicksteed, John Bates Clark, Herbert J. Davenport, and Frank
A. Fetter also adopted and developed Menger's principles of pricing
and his causal-realistic approach to economic theorizing. Clark, for
example, developed a theory of the entrepreneur based on the distinction between the "static state" and "dynamic societies" (Salerno,
2008: 197). Under static conditions, the entrepreneur's function is
"purely passive ... the *entrepreneur* in his capacity of buyer and seller
does not even do the work which purchases and sales involve ... Sales
and purchases are made in his name, but he does none of the work
that leads up to them" (Clark, 1918: 122). There is essentially nothing for the entrepreneur to do under static conditions because under
such conditions all factors of production are already allocated to their
optimal uses, so that profits and losses will be zero. However, in the
"dynamic society" profits and losses are unavoidably present, because
under such conditions and the uncertainty that accompanies them,
the entrepreneur "makes the supreme decisions which now and again
lead to changes in the business" (Clark, 1918: 124). The entrepreneur,
in Clark's view, is the ultimate decision-maker, and that "part of the
management of a business which consists in making the most far-
reaching decisions cannot safely be entrusted to a salaried superin-
tendent or other paid official, and must get its returns, if at all, in the
form of profits" (Clark, 1918: 157). This means that the entrepreneur
must also be the owner of the business.

Clark's contemporary Frank A. Fetter, known primarily for his
contributions to the theory of capital and interest, also gave the entrepreneur a central role in the process of resource allocation (Fetter,
1905, 1915, 1977). Fetter's explanation of the differences between
short-run and long-run profits anticipates both Knight's (1921) distinction between "risk" and "uncertainty" and Kirzner's concept of
market equilibration. In the long run, Fetter argued, the net returns
to production are determined by interest rates, themselves determined
by the market's rate of "time preference," or the relative valuation of
present and future consumption. In the short run, business incomes
fluctuate around these "normal" returns because some entrepreneurs are better able than others to anticipate future prices and can
thus acquire resources at prices below the present discounted values

of their eventual contributions to output, leaving profit in addition to interest. In doing so, these entrepreneurs bid up the prices of the "underpriced" factors and help bring about the long-run equilibrium in which such profits are eliminated.[3]

Fetter's (1905: 286–287) description of the entrepreneur (Fetter uses the term "enterpriser") identifies uncertainty-bearing as the key entre-preneurial function. The entrepreneur (1) "guarantees to the capitalist-lender a fixed return," (2) "gives up the certain income to be got by lending his own capital, and, becoming a borrower, offers his cap-ital as insurance to the lender," (3) "gives to other workers a definite amount for services applied to distant ends," and (4) "risks his own services and accepts an indefinite chance instead of a definite amount for them." He also serves as an "organizer" and "director," possessing "unusual foresight" and the "ability to judge men and tact in relations with them" (Fetter, 1905: 268). In short, the entrepreneur "is the eco-nomic buffer; economic forces are transmitted through him."

As the specialized risk-taker, he is the spring or buffer, which takes up and distributes the strain of industry. He feels first the influence of changing conditions. If the prices of his products fall, the first loss comes upon him, and he avoids further loss as best he can by paying less for materials and labor. At such times the wage-earners look upon him as their evil genius, and usually blame him for lowering their wages, not the public for refusing to buy the product at the former high prices. Again, if prices rise, he gains from the increased value of the stock in his hand that has been produced at low cost. If the employer often appears to be a hard man, his disposition is the result of "natural selection." He is placed between the powerful, selfish forces of competition, and his economic survival is conditioned on vigi-lance, strength, and self-assertion. Weak generosity cannot endure.

(Fetter, 1905: 287–288)

---

[3] As Rothbard (1977: 16) puts it: "Why does an entrepreneur borrow at all if in so doing he will bid up the loan rate of interest to the rate of time preference as reflected in his long-run normal rate of profit (or his 'natural rate of interest,' to use Austrian terminology)? The reason is that superior forecasters envision making short-run profits whenever the general loan rate is lower than the return they expect to obtain. This is precisely the competitive process, which tends, in the long run, to equalize all natural and loan rates in the time market. Those entrepreneurs 'with superior knowledge and superior foresight,' wrote Fetter, 'are merchants, buying when they can in a cheaper and selling in a dearer capitalization market, acting as the equalizers of rates and prices.' "

As in Knight and Kirzner, the entrepreneurial role is not limited to new-venture creation or the introduction of new products, services, production methods, and the like, but lies at the heart of the everyday affairs of production and exchange.

Mises, a student of Böhm-Bawerk, and Mises' younger colleague Hayek, more a student of Wieser than of Böhm-Bawerk, would develop and extend the Austrian tradition in the early twentieth century, with Kirzner, Murray Rothbard, both Mises students, and Ludwig Lachmann, a Hayek student, making critical contributions in the 1950s, 1960s, and 1970s. Recent scholars have noted considerable variety within the Austrian school, particularly in its modern interpretations. Salerno (1993), in particular, argues that there are two distinct strands of Austrian economics, both tracing the origins to Menger. One strand, manifest in the works of Wieser, Hayek, and Kirzner, emphasizes disequilibrium, the informational role of prices, discovery of already existing opportunities, and profit-seeking behavior as an equilibrating force. Another strand, developed by Böhm-Bawerk, Mises, and Rothbard, focuses on monetary calculation and forward-looking, uncertainty-bearing, entrepreneurial appraisal and investment, rather than discovery.[4] The concept of entrepreneurship as alertness to profit opportunities created by disequilibrium comes out of the Wieser–Hayek–Kirzner strand. There are, however, important precursors to both strands.

Wieser and Hayek: the beginnings of the discovery view

In his treatise *Social Economics* (1914) Wieser presented an eclectic definition of the entrepreneur as owner, manager, leader, innovator, organizer, and speculator. He noted that the entrepreneur "must possess the quick perception that seizes new terms in current transactions as his affairs develop" (Wieser, 1914: 324), the first hint of alertness as an entrepreneurial attribute.

Wieser's student Hayek did not contribute to the theory of entrepreneurship per se, but his discovery view of competition, developed

---

[4] Schumpeter is often classified with the Austrian economists but, despite being trained by Böhm-Bawerk, was most heavily influenced by Walras and is better classified as a neoclassical equilibrium theorist. See also Klein (2008b) on these two strands within the Austrian tradition.

in a series of essays from the mid-1940s (notably Hayek, 1945, 1946) as a critical reaction to the perfect-competition model, is a crucial input into the opportunity-discovery approach. Competition, Hayek argued, should not be understood as a static state of affairs, but as a rivalrous process that is essentially a procedure for discovering "*who* will serve us well: which grocer or travel agency, which department store or hotel, which doctor or solicitor, we can expect to provide the most satisfactory solution for whatever personal problem we may have to face" (Hayek, 1946: 97). The basis for this conceptualization is the characteristically Austrian emphasis on dispersed knowledge, present already in Menger, but fully articulated by Hayek. Competition, Hayek maintains, is the mechanism that makes best use of dispersed knowledge – it is an effective way to discover knowledge we do not yet know is available or indeed needed at all (Hayek, 1968).

However, Hayek is not entirely forthcoming on how exactly the market performs this discovery function. Entrepreneurs are mentioned only in passing.[5] Indeed, different mechanisms underlying the market's discovery process can be imagined, depending on how much intention, rationality, and learning ability are ascribed to market participants. At one extreme lies a selection mechanism that selects effectively among various entrepreneurial ventures formed essentially in ignorance of consumer preferences (Alchian, 1950; Becker, 1962). Such a process is heavily error-prone, and, more importantly, no one learns from past errors. While Hayek's writings may sometimes describe such processes in which the system, and not individual agents, are "rational" (Langlois, 1985), most other Austrians have strongly emphasized the intentions of entrepreneurs in coping with uncertainty and ignorance, allowing for various degrees of error. Indeed, Kirzner has often conceptualized the market process as one of a *systematic* elimination of errors. Interestingly, one of Kirzner's earliest papers is

[5] Hayek (1968: 18) mentions that competition "is important primarily as a discovery procedure whereby entrepreneurs constantly search for unexploited opportunities that can also be taken advantage of by others." He adds that this "ability to detect certain conditions ... can [be used] effectively only when the market tells them what kinds of goods and services are demanded, and how urgently," (Hayek, 1968: 13) that is, how effectively the price system works. Hayek also uses the term "entrepreneur" in his earlier writings on socialist calculation and capital theory, but he seems to mean simply "businessman," and does not distinguish sharply among entrepreneurs, managers, capitalists, and other business professionals.

a strong critique of Becker's (1962) evolutionary argument that one can dispense entirely with the rationality of market participants in doing basic price theory (Kirzner, 1962). Kirzner's entrepreneur is highly rational, or, perhaps more precisely, extra-rational, in going beyond the given means-ends frameworks and noticing previously undiscovered opportunities for pure profit. Kirzner, then, supplies a crucial mechanism (or micro foundation) for the Wieser–Hayek discovery view: A competitive market is a superior setting because it generates entrepreneurial discoveries through the exercise of alertness. As Kirzner (1973: 14) argues, "our confidence in the market's ability to learn and to harness the continuous flow of information to generate the market process depends crucially on our belief in the benign presence of the entrepreneurial element." Although the entrepreneur may not search for any profit opportunity in particular, the lure of pure profit may nevertheless lead him to continually scan the horizon, as it were (Kirzner, 1997: 72).

Böhm-Bawerk, Mises, and Rothbard

Böhm-Bawerk was one of Austria's most prominent economists, not only as a theorist but as a three-time Austrian minister of finance (whose picture still graces Austria's 100 schilling note). His work was mainly on the theory of capital and interest (Böhm-Bawerk, 1884–1912), and his approach has largely been abandoned within mainstream macroeconomic theory. (He also authored a penetrating and original critique of Marx; Böhm-Bawerk, 1898.) Perhaps for this reason, his work is little known to contemporary management scholars.

Böhm-Bawerk's two most important students were Joseph Schumpeter and Ludwig von Mises. Mises is often considered the most important twentieth-century representative of the Austrian school, and his work, along with that of Hayek, provided a main impetus to the "Austrian revival" of the 1970s (Vaughn, 1994; Salerno, 1999). Mises became an internationally known monetary theorist with the publication of his *Theory of Money and Credit* in 1912, followed by an important 1920 article and 1922 book on the economic theory of socialism (Mises, 1920, 1922). Mises' best known book is his 1949 treatise, *Human Action*, which continues to be a foundational text for Austrians.

Kirzner has always described his work as an extension of Mises' theory of the market process.[6] Mises, Kirzner's mentor and teacher at New York University, and Kirzner are usually lumped together as offering a unified Austrian account of the entrepreneur. However, as we clarify later, we see Mises as closer to the Cantillon–Knight position that entrepreneurship is judgment over the deployment of resources, not alertness per se. Kirzner (1973: 39–40) agrees that in a world of uncertainty, resource owners exercise entrepreneurial judgment in allocating their resources to particular uses. But he goes on (1973: 40–43) to introduce the analytical device of the pure entrepreneur, the agent who discovers profit opportunities without putting any resources at stake, and claims that this function, rather than investment under uncertainty, is the "driving force" of the market economy. This view, we maintain, and the Wieser–Hayek–Kirzner account in general, is very different from the view found in Cantillon, Knight, and Mises.

Mises' own position is somewhat ambiguous (Salerno, 2008). The economist, Mises writes, "shows how the activities of enterprising men, the promoters and speculators, eager to profit from discrepancies in the price structure, tend toward eradicating such discrepancies and thereby also toward blotting out the sources of entrepreneurial profit and loss." Describing this equilibrating process "is the task of economic theory" (Mises, 1949: 352–353). Elsewhere, however, Mises describes the entrepreneur as an investor, an economic actor who bears uncertainty, rather than discovering (certain) opportunities for gain. "[T]he outcome of action is always uncertain. Action is always speculation" (Mises, 1949: 253). Consequently, "the real entrepreneur is a speculator, a man eager to utilize his opinion about the future structure of the market for business operations promising profits. This specific anticipative understanding of the conditions of the uncertain future defies any rules and systematization" (Mises, 1949: 582).

This emphasis on action under conditions of uncertainty calls to mind Cantillon's (1755) brief account of the entrepreneurial function

---

[6] "I have always emphasized that my own contribution is simply an expansion and deepening of insights articulated by my teacher, Ludwig von Mises" (Kirzner, 2009: 146). See also Kirzner (1982b) for Kirzner's most extensive reflections on the relations between his and Mises' work.

and Knight's (1921) concept of entrepreneurial judgment. Judgment is business decision-making when the range of possible future outcomes, let alone the likelihood of individual outcomes, is generally unknown (what Knight terms uncertainty, rather than mere probabilistic risk). Exercising judgment thus requires the investment of resources (primarily, the purchase of factors of production in the present, in anticipation of future receipts from the sale of finished goods).[7] Alertness, or awareness of particular conditions, does not itself involve judgment, and does not, in this understanding, have a direct effect on the allocation of resources.

Kirzner's contemporary Murray Rothbard, another influential modern Austrian economist, was among the first to question Kirzner's strict separation between the "discovery" and "ownership" functions of the entrepreneur (Rothbard, 1995). Rothbard argued that unless buying and selling are instantaneous, even arbitrageurs bear uncertainty, in that selling prices may change after goods and services are acquired for arbitrage. More generally, the driving force of the market economy is not Kirzner's "pure entrepreneur," but the capitalist-entrepreneurs who invest resources in anticipation of uncertain rewards:

Kirzner's entrepreneur is a curious formulation. He need not, apparently, risk anything. He is a free-floating wraith, disembodied from real objects.

---

[7] Knight (1921) introduces the concept of judgment to decompose business income into two elements, interest and profit. Interest is a reward for forgoing present consumption, is determined by the relative time preferences of borrowers and lenders, and would exist even in a world of certainty. Profit, by contrast, is a reward for anticipating the uncertain future more accurately than others and exists only in a world of "true" uncertainty. In such a world, given that production takes time, entrepreneurs will earn either profits or losses based on the differences between factor prices paid and product prices received. This understanding of entrepreneurship is central to Mises' argument that rational economic planning is "impossible" under socialism (Mises, 1920). Entrepreneurs make production plans based on the current prices of factors of production and the anticipated future prices of consumer goods. What Mises calls "economic calculation" is the comparison of these anticipated future receipts with present outlays, all expressed in common monetary units. Under socialism, the absence of factor markets, and the consequent lack of factor prices, renders economic calculation – and hence rational economic planning – impossible. Mises' point is that a socialist economy may assign individuals to be workers, managers, technicians, inventors, and the like, but it cannot, by definition, have entrepreneurs, because there are no money profits and losses.

He does not, and need not, possess any assets. All he need have to earn profits is a faculty of alertness to profit opportunities. Since he need not risk any capital assets to meet the chancy fate of uncertainty, he cannot suffer any losses. But if the Kirznerian entrepreneur owns no assets, then how in the world does he earn profits? Profits, after all, are simply the other side of the coin of an increase in the value of one's capital; losses are the reflection of a loss in capital assets. The speculator who expects a stock to rise uses money to purchase that stock; a rise or fall in the price of stock will raise or lower the value of the stock assets. If the price rises, the profits are one and the same thing as the increase in capital assets. The process is more complex but similar in the purchase or hiring of factors of production, the creating of a product and then its sale on the market. In what sense can an entrepreneur ever make profits if he owns no capital to make profits on?

(Rothbard, 1985: 282–283)

Summary

In short, the Austrian tradition comprises a variety of diverse elements, some complementary but others distinct. In particular, we distinguish a Wieser–Hayek–Kirzner strand, emphasizing knowledge, discovery, and process, and a Böhm-Bawerk–Mises–Rothbard strand, emphasizing monetary calculation and decision-making under uncertainty. Management scholars, particularly those working on entrepreneurial discovery and opportunity identification, may wish to study these strands more carefully, and to consider Austrian insights that have not made appearances in contemporary management theory.

Kirzner and entrepreneurial alertness

Kirzner's *Competition and Entrepreneurship* (1973) is conventionally seen as *the* seminal modern Austrian statement on entrepreneurship. Kirzner's later work on entrepreneurship has mainly consisted in clarifying the positions in that book (Kirzner, 1979a, 1992, 1997, 2009), as well as relating them to other theories of entrepreneurship, and applying them to, for example, regulation (e.g., Kirzner, 1984, 1985) and ethics (Kirzner, 1989).

Kirzner's contribution

In Kirzner's framework, profit opportunities result from prices, quantities, and qualities that diverge from their equilibrium values. Some individuals tend to notice, or be alert to, these opportunities, and their actions bring about changes in prices, quantities, and qualities. The simplest case of alertness is that of the arbitrageur, who discovers a discrepancy in present prices that can be exploited for financial gain. In a more typical case, the entrepreneur is alert to a new product or a superior production process and steps in to fill this market gap before others. Success, in this view, comes not from following a well-specified maximization problem, such as a search algorithm (High, 1980), but from having some insight that no one else has, a process that cannot be modeled as an optimization problem (which is not to say that it escapes formal treatment; see Littlechild and Owen, 1980, and Yates, 2000).[8] Entrepreneurship, in other words, is the act of grasping and responding to profit opportunities that exist in an imperfect world. Unlike other approaches in modern economics, the imperfections in question are not seen as temporary "frictions" resulting from ill-defined property rights, transaction costs, or asymmetric information. While those imperfections can be cast in an equilibrium mold – as in the modern economics of information – Kirzner has in mind a market in permanent and ineradicable disequilibrium.[9]

As explained in Chapter 2, Kirzner's approach, like that of Knight, Schumpeter, and other key contributors to the economic theory of entrepreneurship, sees entrepreneurship as an economic function, not an employment category (i.e., self-employment) or type of firm (i.e., a start-up company). The main effect of the entrepreneurial function is market equilibration: by closing pockets of ignorance in the market, entrepreneurship always stimulates a tendency towards equilibrium (Selgin, 1988). While Kirzner's "pure entrepreneur," an ideal type, performs *only* this function, and does not supply labor or own capital, real-world business people may be partly entrepreneurs in this sense, partly laborers, partly capitalists, and so on. As we suggested in the previous section, the relationship between entrepreneurial discovery and capital investment distinguishes Kirzner's approach sharply from Knight's (and, arguably, from Kirzner's mentor Ludwig von

---

[8] As discussed above, Kirzner is careful to distinguish alertness from systematic search, as in Stigler (1961, 1962). See also Kirzner (1997) for his most extensive discussion of the distinction between "sheer ignorance" and asymmetric information, and the role of alertness in overcoming the former.

[9] For details on Kirzner's treatment of equilibrium see Klein (2008b).

Mises'). Because Kirzner's (pure) entrepreneurs perform only a discovery function, rather than an investment function, they do not own capital; they need only be alert to profit opportunities. Kirznerian entrepreneurs need not be charismatic leaders, do not innovate, and are not necessarily creative or in possession of sound business judgment. They do not necessarily start firms, raise capital, or manage an enterprise. They perform the discovery function, and nothing else.

Key in Kirzner's work is his distinction between "Robbinsian maximizing" and "entrepreneurial alertness." The first conforms to the standard picture of economic man as applying given means to best satisfy given but conflicting ends in a fundamentally mechanical way (Robbins, 1932). Because everything is given, action becomes purely a matter of calculation. Kirzner argues that this conceptualization of behavior cannot accommodate the discovery of new means, new ends, and the setting up of new means-ends structures. As a result, the dynamic market process cannot be captured by the model of Robbinsian maximizing; another behavioral quality is needed, namely the quality of entrepreneurial alertness to previously unexploited profit opportunities.[10]

Alertness ranges from the discovery of a ten dollar bill on the street to the discovery of a new, highly profitable drug. Thus, entrepreneurs are discoverers; they discover new resource uses, new products, new markets, new possibilities for arbitrage – in short, new possibilities for profitable trade. Alertness is not the same as search (Stigler, 1961), the deliberate search for new information. Rather, entrepreneurship is the act of discovering, or being alert to, information and opportunities that others fail to perceive. It is not only that entrepreneurial activity

---

[10] See Salerno (2009b) for a defense of Robbins against Kirzner, arguing that Robbins also appreciated the importance of novelty, learning, and discovery, but thought that once agents have settled on particular ends, it is the analyst's job to take them as given. "[E]nds and means are assumed as data given to the economic theorist and not to the economizing agent whose choices are the subject of analysis" (Salerno, 2009b: 99). Moreover, "for the Robbinsian economizer, it is entrepreneurial anticipations of future market conditions that are part of the 'given data' that constitute his framework of choice at any moment. But these given data are not known with certainty by him because of the continual emergence of unexpected exogenous changes. The result is a dynamic market process in which endogenous changes are induced by adjustment to the irrevocable errors of the past, at the same time that economizers are struggling to anticipate and adapt to exogenous changes" (Salerno, 2009b: 106).

reduces our lack of knowledge about which products, processes, new organizational forms, etc. are needed; it is more fundamentally that entrepreneurial activity alleviates our ignorance about what we don't know. What Kirzner calls "sheer ignorance" is "necessarily accompanied by the element of surprise – one had not hitherto realized one's ignorance" (Kirzner, 1997: 62).

Combining his notion of entrepreneurial behavior with Hayek's notion of the market as a dynamic process, Kirzner develops a view of the market process as a continual process of entrepreneurial discovery of previously unnoticed opportunities for pure profit. The profits earned in this process reflect the discovery and exploitation of profit opportunities that would not have been grasped in the absence of entrepreneurial activity. Thus, the entrepreneurial function is beneficial because it alleviates the problems of coordination introduced by the division of knowledge (Hayek, 1945). Here Kirzner invokes the welfare concept, borrowed from Hayek, of "plan coordination," a concept that has generated considerable controversy within the Austrian school.[11]

Kirzner's fiction of the pure entrepreneur is introduced to elucidate the coordinating function of entrepreneurship. While Clark and Mises introduced similar devices to emphasize selected aspects of entrepreneurship, Kirzner sees his construct as capturing its very essence. Kirzner has been insistent that the pure entrepreneur is a non-owner (Kirzner, 1975). "An important point," Kirzner argues (1973: 47), "is that ownership and entrepreneurship are to be viewed as completely separate functions. Once we have adopted the convention of concentrating all elements of entrepreneurship into the hands of pure entrepreneurs, we have automatically excluded the asset owner from an entrepreneurial role. Purely entrepreneurial decisions are by definition reserved to decision-makers who own nothing at all." Thus, the entrepreneur is a pure decision-maker, and nothing else. As such, anyone can be a pure entrepreneur.

[11] O'Driscoll and Rizzo (1985: 80–85) argue that plan coordination – they call it "Hayekian equilibrium" – is not consistently defined in the Austrian literature. On plan coordination see also Salerno (1991), Lewin (1997), Klein (2008b), and Klein and Briggeman (2009).

The notions of decision-making in the context of entrepreneurship raise several pertinent questions. For example, the notions of "alertness" and "discovery" suggest that there are separate phases in the act of entrepreneurship. Similarly, Kirzner often talks about the exploitation of opportunities, which adds another possible phase (following discovery). These phases could conceivably be separated by long stretches of time. Relatedly, they could have widely different antecedents or determinants. However, Kirzner seems to treat alertness, discovery, and exploitation as parts of one *Gestalt* – inseparable parts of a whole – and does not seem interested in exploring their relationship. As we argue below, this is presumably because his explanatory concern is equilibration, not the entrepreneur as such.

However, even if entrepreneurship is ultimately a means to understanding a higher-level phenomenon, equilibration, the antecedents of entrepreneurship can still be important and worthy of academic study. The modern entrepreneurship literature in economics and management research has suggested several possible antecedents such as the personal skills (Lazear, 2005), cognitive biases (Busenitz and Barney, 1997), and prior experience (Shane, 2000), as well the characteristics of the parent company (Gompers, Lerner, and Scharfstein, 2005), the institutional environment (Bjørnskov and Foss, 2008), and other background characteristics (Xue and Klein, 2010). However, like other contributors to the economic theory of entrepreneurship (notably Schumpeter and Knight), Kirzner is not interested in such antecedents, presumably because his aim is to construct a general theory of the equilibrating function of entrepreneurship. He does, however, argue that government interference with the price mechanism inhibits the entrepreneurial discovery process (e.g., Kirzner, 1979b).

[D]irect controls by government on prices, quantities, or qualities of output production or input employment may unintentionally block activities which have, as yet, not been specifically envisaged by anyone. Where these blocked activities turn out to be entrepreneurially profitable activities (perhaps as a result of unforeseen changes in data), the likelihood of their being discovered is then sharply diminished. Without necessarily intending it, the spontaneous discovery process of the free market has thus been, to some extent, stifled or distorted. (Kirzner, 1982a)

Debates on the Kirznerian discovery approach

Kirzner's approach has stimulated considerable controversy, both within and outside the Austrian school of economics. Among Austrians, debate has focused on the inherently equilibrating aspect of entrepreneurial discovery. Kirzner wants to maintain equilibrium (as understood by mainstream economists) as a meaningful and useful analytical category. The Austrian quarrel with equilibrium economics is that we are "entitled to demand a theoretical basis for the claim that equilibrating processes systematically mold market variables in a direction consistent with the conditions postulated in the equilibrium models" (Kirzner, 1997: 65). However, this "theoretical basis" has not been offered by mainstream economists. This criticism of equilibrium economics echoes Hayek (1937), who argued that economists should devote analytical attention to understanding those learning processes that establish congruence between "subjective data" (i.e., agents' perceptions) and "objective data" (i.e., real scarcities and preferences). However, unlike Hayek, who argued that the "pure logic of choice" was not helpful in this regard, Kirzner claims that entrepreneurship is a logical category that supplies the "'story' which might account for the economists' confidence in the special relevance of the intersection point in [the] demand and supply diagram" (Kirzner, 1997: 66). This may be interpreted as implying that entrepreneurship is always and inherently equilibrating (Selgin, 1988).

However, by explicitly raising the need to theorize equilibrating processes, Kirzner may also be seen as linking up with work in mainstream economics that has dealt with the issue of how markets can converge to equilibria (see Selgin, 1988: 44), notably the so-called "stability theory" (Scarf, 1960), which studies perturbations and the processes by which equilibria is re-established. Also, some mainstream economists have argued that it is only meaningful to make use of the equilibrium construct if it can be theoretically demonstrated that there may exist a tendency to equilibrium (Fisher, 1983). Thus, Kirzner may be seen as forging linkages to important contributions from mainstream economics. However, overall this work demonstrates that strong assumptions must be made for convergence to take place – and no such assumptions are explicitly made in Kirzner's work (but see Yates, 2000).

There are several ways in which entrepreneurship may fail to equilibrate markets within Kirzner's own analytical system. First, if opportunities can be posited as existing objectively, then if entrepreneurs fail to discover all opportunities, equilibration does not take place (a possibility allowed for by Kirzner himself). Second, if by equilibrium Kirzner has in mind Hayek's sense of multi-period plan coordination, then Kirzner has introduced an intertemporal dimension that may wreak havoc with the whole notion of entrepreneurship as equilibrating. In parts of Kirzner's early work (e.g., Kirzner, 1973), the exercise of entrepreneurship does not seem to presuppose uncertainty. If entrepreneurship means overcoming sheer ignorance by the exercise of alertness, this is a logically correct inference. However, uncertainty is clearly a fundamental aspect of action (Mises, 1949) and it is difficult to see the usefulness of a theory of entrepreneurship that abstracts from it. However, introducing uncertainty may destroy the basis for the claim that entrepreneurship is equilibrating.

In particular, Ludwig Lachmann, drawing on English economist George Shackle's work on the radically uncertain, "kaleidic" economy, raised strong doubts in the 1970s concerning equilibration.[12] If the future is unknowable and emerges from creative acts in a kaleidic manner, current profits and losses – which are based on past actions – do not provide reliable guides to future-oriented current actions (Lachmann, 1976). Only a small subset (e.g., futures markets) of the full set of intertemporal prices exists. In other words, there is very little rational basis for entrepreneurs to form expectations of future consumer demands and resource scarcities, and such expectations are therefore more likely to be divergent than convergent.[13]

Selgin (1988) argues that these debates misunderstand the nature of the equilibration process. Correctly understood, "equilibration" does not refer to coordination of plans as in Hayek (1937), mainstream stability theory, convergence to rational expectations equilibrium, and the like; it refers to entrepreneurial profits and losses. These are strictly subjective categories and have no objective basis outside the minds of entrepreneurs:

---

[12] Lachmann's perspective has generated relatively little attention among management scholars. An exception is Chiles *et al.* (2007).

[13] Note that Lachmann (1986) allows for temporary market clearing, that is, Marshallian short-run equilibria or what Mises (1949) calls "plain states of rest."

It is necessary ... to treat entrepreneurial profit opportunities as the unique products of the valuations and understanding (*Verstehen*) of actors who will seek their exploitation. Upon the fact of action, these "imagined" or "understood" (rather than "perceived") profits are, logically and temporally, destroyed. Thus, action leads to the systematic elimination of entrepreneurial profit and loss; it is *equilibrating*.   (Selgin, 1988: 39)

Thus, equilibration in this (Misesian) meaning makes no reference to the state of knowledge of market participants and whether their plans are consistent or not. In fact, Selgin (1988) dismisses the very notion of coordination in a world in which profit opportunities cannot be thought of as "objectively existing," in which preferences have no existence apart from actions, etc. Klein (2008b: 182) argues, following Salerno (1991), that Mises has in mind a concept of coordination that refers only to real-world exchanges, not the movements of prices and quantities toward some hypothetical long-run equilibrium values:

In this sense, the existence or nonexistence of equilibrating tendencies in the unhampered market – the issue that divided "Kirznerians" and "Lachmannians," and dominated much of the Austrian discussion in the 1980s – is relatively unimportant. For Mises, the critical "market process" is not the convergence to equilibrium, but the selection mechanism in which unsuccessful entrepreneurs – those who systematically overbid for factors, relative to eventual consumer demands – are eliminated from the market.
(Klein, 2008b: 182)

Other economists have emphasized the contrast between the Kirznerian and Schumpeterian entrepreneurs, asking if Kirzner's entrepreneur can also innovate, be creative, take risks, and so on. Kirzner emphasizes that his "pure entrepreneur" performs only a discovery function and need not be an innovator in the Schumpeterian sense of disrupting an existing equilibrium allocation of resources by introducing new products, services, sources of supply, production methods, etc. Kirzner does not deny that businesspeople, resource owners, financiers, traders, and the like exercise boldness, creativity, and imagination, only that he *need* not exercise these functions to perform the role of alertness to previously unknown profit opportunities. "My entrepreneurs were engaged in *arbitrage*, acting entrepreneurially even when they might *not* be seen as Schumpeterian 'creators'," Kirzner explains. "In

so emphasizing the difference between Schumpeter's theory of entrepreneurship and my own, I was motivated by my primary scientific
objective. This was to understand the nature of the market process –
even in its *simplest* conceivable contexts" (Kirzner, 2009: 147).

The market versus the "market process"

Kirzner's understanding of the market process may be contrasted
with the price-theoretic tradition of the Austrian school that Klein
(2008a) terms "mundane Austrian economics." This tradition, sometimes called "causal-realist" analysis following Menger's emphasis
on causal explanation and a focus on real-world, day-to-day prices,
emerged in the early twentieth century, but was largely supplanted
by the Marshallian-Walrasian synthesis that dominated the economics profession after World War II (Salerno, 1993, 2002). Beginning
with Hayek's work on tacit knowledge (Hayek, 1937, 1945) and the
competitive process (Hayek, 1948, 1968), Austrians began challenging the neoclassical assumption that prices can be assumed to equal
their "equilibrium" values (Machovec, 1995). One interpretation of
Kirzner's theory of entrepreneurship is that it provides an equilibration process that justifies the welfare conclusions of "standard" economics (namely, that markets are efficient means of allocating scarce
resources).[14] However, as Klein (2008a) argues, causal-realist analysis
is not concerned with long-run Marshallian or Walrasian equilibrium
prices, but with actual, empirical, market prices, those occurring in
what Mises calls the "plain state of rest." In this understanding of
the market, the existence or non-existence of equilibrating tendencies – the issue that divided "Kirznerians" and "Lachmannians," and
dominated much of the Austrian discussion in the 1980s – is relatively

---

[14] Kirzner's approach, as Boettke and Prychitko (1994: 3) describe it,
"provided the disequilibrium foundations of equilibrium economics that
were required to complete the neoclassical project of explicating the
operating principles of the price system." Adds Boettke (2005): "Why is all
this important? Well as Franklin Fisher pointed out in his very important
book *The Disequilibrium Foundations of Equilibrium Economics* (1983)
that unless we have good reasons to believe in the systemic tendency
toward equilibrium we have no justification at all in upholding the welfare
properties of equilibrium economics. In other words, without the sort
of explanation that Kirzner provides the entire enterprise of neoclassical
equilibrium is little more than a leap of faith."

unimportant. For Mises, the critical "market process" is not the convergence to equilibrium, but rather the selection mechanism in which unsuccessful entrepreneurs – those who systematically overbid for factors, relative to eventual consumer demands – are eliminated from the market (Mises, 1951). It is this process that ensures that real-world, day-to-day prices are as "efficient" as they can be – in other words, that consumer sovereignty obtains at all times on the market.

In Mises' system, neither consumer goods nor factor prices "converge," in real time, to efficient, long-run equilibrium values, because the adjustment processes set in motion by profit-seeking entrepreneurs are frustrated, moment by moment, by exogenous changes in consumer preferences, technological knowledge, resource availabilities, and so on.[15] The efficiency of the market, for Mises, results simply from the fact that prices are determined by the voluntary interactions of buyers and sellers according to their preferences over marginal units of goods and services.[16]

As we interpret Mises, then, his entrepreneur plays a different role in the market system than that played by Kirzner's entrepreneur. Rather

---

[15] Nor do prices obtaining on real markets achieve a "coordination of plans," as final-goods prices may exceed or fall short of entrepreneurs' expectations (leading to profits and losses).

[16] In his "Mises and His Understanding of the Capitalist System," Kirzner (1999) simultaneously accepts and dismisses Mises' welfare analysis of plain-state-of-rest prices. "Once we have understood the central position of the doctrine of consumer sovereignty in Mises' overall system, we can surely sense and appreciate the deep respect Mises felt for the actual market prices of productive resources. Certainly these prices are likely to be 'false' prices, in that they necessarily imperfectly anticipate the true future valuations of consumers for the various possible potential products (at the times when these products might conceivably be made available to consumers). Nonetheless, these prices, and the transactions in which they emerge, are wholly governed ... by the preferences of consumers" (Kirzner, 1999: 225). And yet, Kirzner (1999: 216) writes, "Mises is clearly entirely aware that the market prices at any given date are almost certainly not the 'correct' prices" (i.e., they are not long-run equilibrium prices). For Mises, in Kirzner's interpretation, "[i]t is the market process, driven by the competition of profit-seeking entrepreneurs, that modifies those false prices and tends to ensure that they are replaced by prices more closely and 'truthfully' reflecting the underlying preferences of the consumers. What stimulates that process is the realization by entrepreneurs that the existing market-generated pattern of resource allocation is not the ideal one" (Kirzner, 1999: 216). If plain-state-of-rest prices are "wholly governed" by the preferences of consumers, then they are efficient, whether the market-process modifies them or not.

than an *equilibrator*, Mises' entrepreneur is a *resource allocator*. Mises begins with the marginal productivity theory of distribution developed by his Austrian predecessors. In the marginal productivity theory, laborers earn wages, landowners earn rents, and capitalists earn interest.[17] Any excess (deficit) of a firm's realized receipts over these factor payments constitutes profit (loss). Profit and loss, therefore, are returns to entrepreneurship. In a hypothetical equilibrium without uncertainty (what Mises calls the evenly rotating economy), capitalists would still earn interest as a reward for lending, but there would be no profit or loss. Outside the evenly rotating economy, however, factors may be priced above or below these equilibrium values, and shrewd entrepreneurs can acquire factors for less than their discounted marginal revenue products, leading to profit. Less capable entrepreneurs will overpay for factors, or choose inefficient factor combinations, or produce the wrong products, among other errors, and earn losses. This understanding of the market is central to Mises' argument about the impossibility of economic calculation under socialism (i.e., a world without factor markets).[18]

For Kirzner, the main effect of entrepreneurship is to push real-world, disequilibrium prices toward their long-run, equilibrium values.

---

[17] Following Fetter (1905), Rothbard (1962, 1977) characterizes all factor payments as rents, and emphasizes that in long-run equilibrium, only the "originary" factors land and labor earn net rents, while the gross rents accruing to capital goods are imputed back to the originary factors used to produce them.

[18] Entrepreneurs, in Mises' explanation, make their production plans based on the current prices of factors of production and the anticipated future prices of consumer goods. What Mises calls economic calculation is the comparison of these anticipated future receipts with present outlays, all expressed in common monetary units. Under socialism, the absence of factor markets and the consequent lack of factor prices render economic calculation – and hence rational economic planning – impossible. Mises' point is that a socialist economy may assign individuals to be workers, managers, technicians, inventors, and the like, but it cannot, by definition, have entrepreneurs, because there are no money profits and losses. Entrepreneurship, and not labor, management or technological expertise, is the crucial element of the market economy. As Mises puts it, directors of socialist enterprises may be allowed to "play market" – to make capital investment decisions as if they were allocating scarce capital across activities in an economizing way. But entrepreneurs cannot be asked to "play speculation and investment" (Mises, 1949: 705). Without entrepreneurship, a complex, dynamic economy cannot allocate resources to their highest-valued use.

He is not particularly interested in the determinants or welfare properties of day-to-day, plain-state-of-rest prices, but rather the presence or
absence of equilibrating tendencies. But is entrepreneurship necessarily
equilibrating markets within Kirzner's own analytical system? As mentioned earlier, several arguments have been advanced against Kirzner
in the Austrian literature (Lachmann, 1986; Buchanan and Vanberg,
1991; Vaughn, 1992). First, if opportunities can be described as existing, objectively, then if entrepreneurs fail to discover all opportunities,
equilibration does not take place (a possibility allowed for by Kirzner
himself).[19] Second, if by equilibrium Kirzner has in mind Hayek's sense
of multi-period plan coordination, then Kirzner has introduced an
intertemporal dimension that may wreak havoc with the whole notion
of entrepreneurship as equilibrating. In parts of Kirzner's early work
(e.g., Kirzner, 1978), the exercise of entrepreneurship does not seem to
presuppose uncertainty. If entrepreneurship means overcoming sheer
ignorance by the exercise of alertness, this is a logically correct inference. However, uncertainty is clearly a fundamental aspect of action
(Mises, 1949), and it seems difficult to argue that a theory of entrepreneurship can meaningfully abstract from it. However, introducing
uncertainty may destroy the basis for the claim that entrepreneurship is equilibrating in the sense of achieving Hayekian plan coordination. This formed the core of Lachmann's "equilibration skepticism"
(Lachmann, 1986): Because of pervasive uncertainty, there is very
little rational basis for entrepreneurs to form expectations of future
consumer demands and resource scarcities, and such expectations are
therefore more likely to be divergent than convergent.

The entrepreneur as capital owner

Kirzner's ideal type of the "pure entrepreneur" is used to explain the
coordinating function of entrepreneurship. While Clark and Mises
introduced similar devices to emphasize selected aspects of entrepreneurship (Salerno, 2008; see Chapter 2), Kirzner sees his construct
as capturing its very *essence*. Kirzner does not deny that business
people, resource owners, financiers, traders, and the like exercise
judgment, or that they possess boldness, creativity, and imagination,

[19] See Alvarez and Barney (2007, 2010) and Klein (2008a) on the objectivity or
subjectivity of entrepreneurial opportunities.

only that they need not exercise these functions to be alert to previously unknown profit opportunities. "My entrepreneurs were engaged in *arbitrage*, acting entrepreneurially even when they might *not* be seen as Schumpeterian 'creators' ... In so emphasizing the difference between Schumpeter's theory of entrepreneurship and my own, I was motivated by my primary scientific objective. This was to understand the nature of the market process – even in its *simplest* conceivable contexts" (Kirzner, 2009: 147).

In elucidating his conception of the entrepreneurial market process, Kirzner has consistently emphasized the highly abstract nature of his "metaphor" of the entrepreneur (Kirzner, 2009).[20] In contrast, most contributors to the entrepreneurship literatures in management and economics have given more detail to the entrepreneurial function. The amount of detail differs, however, depending on the explanatory purpose. For example, the opportunity-discovery literature in management research is taken up with the antecedents of specific, individual entrepreneurs and as such takes a rather detailed view of the entrepreneur (e.g., Shane, 2003).

The judgment approach as found in Mises is concerned with the more "functional" (Klein, 2008b) issue of understanding the market selection process in the context of the profit-and-loss mechanism, and of understanding profit as a reward to entrepreneurship. In elucidating these functions, the judgment approach provides a somewhat richer view of the entrepreneur than the ghost-like Kirznerian pure entrepreneurs. Kirzner has consistently emphasized that his "contribution is simply an extension and deepening of insights articulated by my teacher, Ludwig von Mises" (Kirzner, 2009: 146). Specifically, the key insight in Mises that Kirzner's work purportedly has sought to "expound and develop" (Kirzner, 2009: 148) is the following one: "What makes profit emerge is the fact that the entrepreneur who judges the future prices of the products more correctly than other people do buy some or all of the factors of production at prices which, seen from the point of view of the future state of the market, are

---

[20] Kirzner's use of the notion of "metaphor" to characterize his entrepreneur construct seems puzzling: At least in usual parlance, a "metaphor" is a figure of speech in which a term or concept is used as a reference to something that it does not literally denote so that a potentially illuminating similarity is revealed. Isn't Kirzner talking about real-world entrepreneurs? We return to this issue later.

too low" (Mises, 1951: 190). Kirzner argues that his notion of alertness (to price discrepancies) captures the essence of the Misesian view of entrepreneurship as described in this quotation, and therefore the simple model of the pure entrepreneur undertaking nearly instantaneous arbitrage applies even to situations where discrepancies between "future prices of the products" and imputed prices of the "factors of production" involve very long periods of time.

While Mises certainly sounds Kirznerian in this passage, we think Mises is more consistently read as a Knightian, emphasizing not the simple differences between current and future prices, but the uncertainty surrounding those future prices. "The term entrepreneur as used by [economic] theory means: acting man exclusively seen from the aspect of the uncertainty inherent in every action" (Mises, 1949: 254). At the same time, Mises also describes a class of economic agents who are "alert," in Kirzner's sense. As Mises notes, economists have not always used the term "entrepreneur" in his sense of uncertainty-bearing. Economics "also calls entrepreneurs those who are especially eager to profit from adjusting production to the expected changes in conditions, those who have more initiative, more venturesomeness, and a quicker eye than the crowd, the pushing and promoting pioneers of economic improvement" (Mises, 1949: 255). Mises notes that this concept of the entrepreneur is narrower than the precise, functional concept of uncertainty-bearing, and regrets that the same word has been used in such different senses, suggesting the term *promoter* for particularly alert individuals.[21]

The promoter, for Mises, is a loosely defined, historically contingent idea, not a purely formal, logical one. But clearly some individuals are more alert than others:

[E]conomics cannot do without the promoter concept. For it refers to a datum that is a general characteristic of human nature, that is present in all market transactions and marks them profoundly. This is the fact that various individuals do not react to a change in conditions with the same quickness and in the same way. The inequality of men, which is due to differences both in their inborn qualities and in the vicissitudes of their lives, manifests itself in this way too.   (Mises, 1949: 256)

---

[21] Huerta de Soto (2010: 19) suggests the Spanish adjective *perspicaz* (perceptive, shrewd) for Mises' promoter concept.

But this is hardly the abstract concept of Kirznerian alertness. Indeed, Mises describes creativity and leadership as similar attributes in the two sentences immediately following the previous quote: "There are in the market pacemakers and others who only imitate the procedures of their more agile fellow citizens. The phenomenon of leadership is no less real on the market than in any other branch of human activities" (Mises, 1949: 256). It is the real-world, flesh-and-blood entrepreneur, who not only bears uncertainty in his judgments about deploying the resources he owns and controls but is also alert, creative, and a leader – and not some abstract, hypothetical discoverer – who is the "driving force of the market."

Antecedents of opportunity discovery

Alertness to opportunities, the discovery of specific opportunities, and action based on those discovered opportunities are typically portrayed as discrete phases of market behavior. These phases could conceivably be separated by long stretches of time, and could have widely different antecedents or determinants. The management research literature on entrepreneurship typically distinguishes between opportunity recognition (discovery) and opportunity exploitation (investment, firm formation, etc.), and has devoted considerable attention to cognitive and learning processes that might lead to discovery (Short *et al.*, 2010: 55–56).

Mises, by contrast, does not distinguish between "discovery" and "exploitation" phases of entrepreneurship. Rather, as noted above, he makes action the unit of analysis, with discovery and its antecedents implied by action. In our own approach, investment under uncertainty is both necessary and sufficient for entrepreneurship to take place. Investment, as human action, already implies purpose or objective, so that invoking opportunities and discovery is simply a relabeling.[22]

---

[22] Salerno (1993: 119) describes Mises' position this way: "[F]or Mises, the moment of choice coincides with the emergence of a value scale that is the *raison d'être* and consummation of the actor's previous 'discovery' activities and that provides the framework for purposive behavior. Choice and action can only be conceived as occurring within such a 'given situation.' Contrary to Kirzner's later interpretation of Mises, discovery cannot serve as the core of the central axiom in a praxeological system, precisely because there is no possibility of inferring from it the 'given situation' prerequisite to the moment of choice. A being who is ever seeking to 'discover changes that have

While Kirzner separates "discovery" and "investment" or exploitation stages of the entrepreneurial process, he explicitly denies that the study of antecedents to discovery is part of the economic analysis of entrepreneurship. He maintains that his work "does not even aim to explore the roots and the determinants of individual entrepreneurial alertness" (Kirzner, 2009: 148).

Of course, arbitrage opportunities cannot exist in a perfectly competitive general-equilibrium model, so Kirzner's framework assumes the presence of competitive imperfections. Beyond specifying general disequilibrium conditions, however, Kirzner offers no theory of how opportunities come to be identified, who identifies them, and so on; identification itself is a black box. The claim is simply that outside the Arrow–Debreu world in which all knowledge is effectively parameterized, opportunities for disequilibrium profit exist and tend to be discovered and exploited. In short, what Kirzner calls "entrepreneurial discovery" is simply that which causes markets to equilibrate. The focus is solely on the market process as being driven by alertness. Opportunity discovery is an analytical primitive, meaning that Kirzner does not address its antecedents/determinants.

In terms of levels of analysis, then, Kirzner's focus is entirely on abstract, aggregate effects of individual acts of alertness (i.e., a micro → macro relationship). It is conceivable that richer models of opportunity discovery, however – including those incorporating the cognitive and motivational antecedents that characterize the opportunity-discovery literature in management research – may yield additional insights in aggregate outcomes, relating for example to the speed of adjustment, possible path-dependencies and informational cascades in the adjustment process, the nature of coordinated states,

occurred' in his situation can never act on those discoveries because he is incapable of creating the framework for choosing. In the newer Kirznerian interpretation, therefore, the Misesian *homo agens* has been transformed into *homo quaerens*, a perpetual and aimless seeker of new knowledge who is forever unable to turn it to account in improving his welfare; a shade who has become unstuck in (praxeological) time ... [A]ccording to Mises, 'discovery' is logically implied in the very concept of choice and need not be posited as an independent facet of human purposiveness ... Or, in other words, from the perspective of Misesian praxeology, entrepreneurial information gathering and forecasting are never autonomous and free-flowing activities directly expressing purposefulness, but are always rigidly governed by the exigencies of choosing under uncertainty."

etc. While such inquiries could be seen as natural extensions of some contributions to Austrian economics (particularly Hayek, 1937), they clearly go beyond the scope of Kirzner's interest and, perhaps, beyond his conception of what constitutes "pure theory."

However, Kirzner is ambiguous on these issues. First, he allows for error-correcting feedback effects from market interaction (i.e., a macro → micro relationship), not only from entrepreneurs who discover the profit opportunity introduced by other entrepreneurs' errors, but also from entrepreneurs recognizing their own earlier mistakes. It is not entirely clear whether such a learning capability is logically implied by the discovery notion. Moreover, Kirzner sometimes treats disequilibrium opportunities for profit as exogenous determinants of entrepreneurial activity. For example, he invokes an imagery of traffic lights (opportunities) that prompt behaviors (discovery) (Kirzner, 1992: 151). On the other hand, he also treats opportunities metaphorically, noting that opportunities are "metaphorically waiting to be discovered," not literally waiting to be discovered (Kirzner, 1997).

Kirzner's continued emphasis on the metaphorical nature of his constructs is somewhat puzzling. Arguing that a construct is a metaphor drives a wedge between the reality that the construct is supposed to throw light over and the construct itself. The construct and the reality it mirrors remain very different things (although illuminating the difference using the metaphor may be enlightening). In particular, use of metaphorical reasoning is different from using models, constructs, or ideal types meant to capture essential qualities of real phenomena (which a metaphor need not do). Perhaps Kirzner really means the latter, in which case the metaphor terminology appears misleading. Kirzner also insists that "the way in which policymakers understand the market economy is likely to carry enormously significant implications for encouragement or discouragement of entrepreneurial creativity" (Kirzner, 2009: 151), suggesting that the models or ideal-typical notions of entrepreneurship held by policymakers affect entrepreneurial activity.

More generally, Kirzner clearly argues that government interference with the price mechanism, such as regulation, antitrust, and other government policies that affect business decision-making, inhibits the entrepreneurial discovery process (e.g., Kirzner, 1979b, 1982) through their impact on the "presence" of profit opportunities:

[D]irect controls by government on prices, quantities, or qualities of output production or input employment may unintentionally block activities which have, as yet, not been specifically envisaged by anyone. Where these blocked activities turn out to be entrepreneurially profitable activities (perhaps as a result of unforeseen changes in data), the likelihood of their being discovered is then sharply diminished. Without necessarily intending it, the spontaneous discovery process of the free market has thus been, to some extent, stifled or distorted.   (Kirzner, 1982: 10)

Thus, government intervention seems to be capable of influencing the sheer amount of entrepreneurial activity through its impact on "discoverable" opportunities (in this case blocking certain opportunities). It is of course also possible that government intervention may create new opportunities à la the opportunities for destructive rent-seeking discussed by Baumol (1994). Moreover, various indications of a direct effect from government intervention to discovery can also be found in Kirzner's work. For example, he argues that while "[w]e know very little that is systematic about what 'switches on' alertness ... it does seem intuitively obvious that alertness can be 'switched off' by the conviction that external intervention will confiscate (wholly or in part) whatever one might notice" (Kirzner, 2009: 151). Taxation hampers discovery by converting "open-ended" situations into "closed-ended" ones (Kirzner, 1985: 111), while regulatory constraints "are likely *to bar the discovery* of pure profit opportunities" (Kirzner, 1985: 142, emphasis in original). The suggestion is that government intervention, while not eliminating discovery entirely, reduces its quantity and quality. The argument strikes us as ad hoc, and inconsistent with the purely exogenous character of Kirznerian profit opportunities. Moreover, even if true, the welfare implications are ambiguous. When it comes to discovery, is "more" necessarily better?

Kirzner and the management research literature on entrepreneurship

The contemporary opportunity identification literature seeks to build a positive research program by operationalizing the concept of alertness (Kaish and Gilad, 1991; Cooper *et al.*, 1995; Busenitz and Barney, 1997; Gaglio and Katz, 2001; Demmert and Klein, 2003; Kitzmann and Schiereck, 2005). How is alertness manifested in action? How do we recognize it, empirically? Can we distinguish "discovery" from systematic search? What are the psychological characteristics of particularly "alert" individuals? However, as discussed by Klein (2008a), this positive research program may miss the point of Kirzner's metaphor of entrepreneurial alertness: namely, that it is only a metaphor. Kirzner's aim is not to characterize entrepreneurship per se, but to explain the tendency for markets to clear. In the Kirznerian system opportunities are (exogenous) arbitrage opportunities *and nothing more*. Entrepreneurship itself serves a purely instrumental function; it is the means by which Kirzner explains market clearing. As Kirzner (2009: 145–146, original emphasis) explains, reviewing his main contributions and critiquing his own critics:

[M]y own work has *nothing* to say about the secrets of successful entrepreneurship. My work has explored, not the nature of the talents needed for entrepreneurial success, not any guidelines to be followed by would-be successful entrepreneurs, but, instead, the *nature of the market process set in motion* by the entrepreneurial decisions (both successful and unsuccessful ones!) ... This paper seeks (a) to identify more carefully the sense in which my work on entrepreneurial theory does *not* throw light on the substantive sources of successful entrepreneurship, (b) to argue that a number of (sympathetic) reviewers of my work have somehow failed to recognize this limitation in the scope of my work (and that these scholars have therefore misunderstood certain aspects of my theoretical system), (c) to show that, despite all of the above, my understanding of the market process (as set in motion by entrepreneurial decisions) *can*, in a significant sense, provide a theoretical underpinning for public policy in regard to entrepreneurship.

Contemporary entrepreneurship scholars, perhaps uneasy with the idea that Kirznerian opportunities are "out there," waiting to be found, have suggested that opportunities may be treated as subjective, rather than objective (McMullen and Shepherd, 2006; Companys and McMullen, 2007). Kirzner does tend to treat opportunities as objective, but this misses the point. Kirzner is not making an ontological claim about the nature of profit opportunities per se – not claiming, in other words, that opportunities *are*, in some fundamental sense, objective – but merely using the concept of objective, exogenously given, but not-yet-discovered opportunities as a device for explaining the tendency of markets to clear. To a certain extent this confusion is caused by the different levels of analysis, Kirzner moving on the level of markets, modern entrepreneurship scholars being concerned with entrepreneurs per se.

However, this may be a case of a fruitful misunderstanding, for the basic notion that opportunity discovery may be taken as the unit of analysis, and that analytical and empirical attention may center on the antecedents to such discovery, has generated some interesting research results about "occupational" and "functional" entrepreneurs. Studies have emphasized, for instance, the means by which individuals identify and react to opportunities, relying largely on survey data (Kaish and Gilad, 1991; Cooper *et al.*, 1995; Busenitz, 1996). These studies suggest that founders of new ventures (the operational definition of entrepreneurs) spend more time gathering information, and rely more heavily on unconventional sources of information, than managers of existing enterprises. The opportunity-discovery view has also served as a useful foil for critics.

Critiques of the opportunity discovery view

The alertness or discovery perspective faces several challenges, however. First, a precise definition of opportunities has remained elusive. Typically, opportunities are defined very broadly; Shane and Venkataraman's (2000: 220) influential paper defines entrepreneurial opportunities as "those situations in which new goods, services, raw materials, and organizing methods can be introduced and sold at greater than their cost of production." This involves not only technical skills like financial analysis and market research, but also less tangible forms of creativity, team-building, problem-solving, and leadership (Long and McMullan, 1984; Hills, Lumpkin, and Singh, 1997; Hindle, 2004). This may be too broad a concept to be operationally useful.[23]

---

[23] While value can of course be created not only by starting new activities, but also by improving the operation of existing activities, research in opportunity identification tends to emphasize the launching of new ventures (firms, products, or services). As summarized by Shane (2003: 4–5), "the academic field of entrepreneurship incorporates, in its domain, explanations for why, when and how entrepreneurial opportunities exist; the sources of those opportunities and the forms that they take; the processes of opportunity discovery and evaluation; the acquisition of resources for the exploitation of these opportunities; the act of opportunity exploitation; why, when, and how some individuals and not others discover, evaluate, gather resources for and exploit opportunities; the strategies used to pursue opportunities; and the organizing efforts to exploit them."

A debate since the start of the twenty-first century asks whether opportunities are "discovered" or "created." Alvarez and Barney (2007) distinguish, within the applied entrepreneurship literature, a "discovery approach," in which entrepreneurial actions are seen as responses to exogenous shocks, and a "creation approach," in which such actions are taken as endogenous. "Discovery entrepreneurs" focus on predicting systematic risks, formulating complete and stable strategies, and procuring capital from external sources. "Creation entrepreneurs," by contrast, appreciate iterative, inductive, incremental decision-making, are comfortable with emergent and flexible strategies, and tend to rely on internal finance. More generally, as noted by McMullen, Plummer, and Acs (2007: 273), "some researchers argue that the subjective or socially constructed nature of opportunity makes it impossible to separate opportunity from the individual, [while] others contend that opportunity is as an objective construct visible to or created by the knowledgeable or attuned entrepreneur."

However, we argue that opportunities are not best characterized either as discovered or created, but rather as *imagined*. The logic is simple: The creation metaphor implies that profit opportunities, once the entrepreneur has conceived or established them, come into being, objectively, like a work of art. Creation implies that something is created. There is no uncertainty about its existence or characteristics (though of course its market value may not be known until later). By contrast, the concept of opportunity imagination emphasizes that gains (and losses) do not come into being, objectively, until entrepreneurial action is complete (i.e., until final goods and services have been produced and sold).

Another issue relates to entrepreneurial opportunities and profit opportunities more generally. Shane and Venkataraman (2000) define profit opportunities as opportunities to create value by enhancing the efficiency of producing existing goods, services, and processes, reserving the term entrepreneurial opportunities for value creation through "the discovery of new means–ends frameworks," appealing to the Kirznerian distinction between Robbinsian maximizing and entrepreneurial alertness described above. They may misunderstand Kirzner (and the Austrians more generally) on this point, however. In a world of Knightian uncertainty, *all* profit opportunities involve decisions for which no well-specified maximization problem is available. Kirzner does not mean that some economic decisions really *are* the result of Robbinsian maximizing while others reflect discovery. Instead, Kirzner is simply contrasting two methodological constructions for the analysis of human action.

An alternative approach is to focus not on what opportunities "are," but what opportunities "do." Opportunities, in this sense, are treated as a latent construct that is manifested in entrepreneurial *action* – investment, creating new organizations, bringing products to market, and so on. Empirically, this approach can be operationalized by treating entrepreneurship as a latent variable or residual (Carnahan *et al.*, 2010; Xue and Klein, 2010). Moreover, by treating opportunities as a latent construct, this approach sidesteps the problem of defining opportunities as objective or subjective, real or imagined, and so on. If opportunities are inherently subjective, and we treat them as a black box, then the unit of analysis should not be opportunities, but rather the assembly of resources in the present in anticipation of (uncertain) receipts in the future. More generally, this perspective suggests that entrepreneurship research should focus on the execution of business plans. We return to this important point in the following chapter.

Finally, some critics have urged a move away from the opportunity concept in its entirety, arguing that real-world entrepreneurs do not think in terms of opportunities, but marginal changes to existing activities, as in Sarasvathy's (2008) notion of "effectuation," a model of entrepreneurial thinking that emphasizes control of resources at hand, under Knightian uncertainty, with ambiguous goals and an unpredictable future. The increasingly popular concept of "bricolage" (Garud and Karnøe, 2003) – engaging in entrepreneurial activities, incrementally, using whatever resources are at hand, rather than acquiring resources to achieve a particular vision – also stands in contrast to the opportunity-discovery framework.

Conclusions

The concept of entrepreneurial alertness continues to be one of the most heavily used, and potentially valuable, constructs in entrepreneurship research. It dovetails nicely with ideas from microeconomic theory about equilibration and arbitrage, and it appears to have recognizable empirical analogs in processes of decision-making, evaluation, assessment, environmental recognition, and the like. It is easy to see why the concept of alertness has become foundational in entrepreneurship studies.

However, as Kirzner's recent essay (2009) makes clear, the relationship between the theoretical construct of alertness and the applied study of opportunity recognition is subtle and complex. Kirzner (2009) sees his concept of the entrepreneurial market process as relevant to applied work not primarily to management research, but in public policy. After arguing that Schumpeterian creativity can, in an important sense, be subsumed as a category of alertness – even Schumpeter's innovations can, *ex post*, be seen as improvements that were waiting to be discovered – Kirzner (2009: 151) notes that "the way in which policymakers understand the market economy is likely to carry enormously significant implications for encouragement or discouragement of entrepreneurial creativity." Specifically, while "[w]e know very little that is systematic about what 'switches on' alertness ... it does seem intuitively obvious that alertness can be 'switched off' by the conviction that external intervention will confiscate (wholly or in part) whatever one might notice."

More generally, it suggests that we can analyze specifically the effects of the competitive, regulatory, and technological environment on entrepreneurial behavior, an approach that is not easily squared with the pure concept of alertness, as Kirzner conceives it. In essence, Kirzner wants to treat alertness as an analytical primitive, and there is indeed very little mention of antecedents to alertness in his work. However, as indicated by the above quotation Kirzner – like contemporary management scholars studying entrepreneurship – does allow antecedents to slip into the analysis. Kirzner has in mind regulation, antitrust, and other government policies that affect business decision-making. However, similar arguments could possibly also be applied to alertness within organizations: the belief that senior managers will appropriate the rent streams created by discovery or creation of new activities or uses of assets by lower-level employees will likely stifle "entrepreneurial" activity within the firm.

4 | *What is judgment?*

As we argued in the previous chapter, the key construct that links entrepreneurship and the theory of the firm is *entrepreneurial judgment*. But what is judgment, exactly? So far we have treated judgment in a highly formal and abstract way, as *that which generates profit and loss*. Here we are consistent with other approaches to the entrepreneurial function: Schumpeter takes entrepreneurship to be *that which generates economic growth*, while Kirzner treats it as *that which causes markets to equilibrate*. In all of these cases, entrepreneurship itself is largely a black box; it is invoked, instrumentally, to explain a particular set of phenomena.

Judgment, to be more specific, is residual, controlling decision-making about resources deployed to achieve some objectives; it is manifest in the actions of individual entrepreneurs; and it cannot be bought and sold on the market, such that its exercise requires the entrepreneur to own and control a firm. To simplify, we have collapsed into this notion the acts of creating and evaluating opportunities, and deciding on which resources need to be assembled, how they need to be combined, etc. to realize the opportunity.[1] We have made the point that judgment is a meaningful notion of decision-making that is intermediate between decision-making via formalizable rules and pure luck or random behaviour (see Casson, 1982). It is the kind of decision-making that concerns unique business investments for which it is difficult, or even impossible, to assign meaningful probabilities to outcomes, or even to specify the set of possible outcomes itself (Shackle, 1972; Zeckhauser, 2006). When confronted with such a situation, individuals will reach different decisions, even

---

[1] Langlois (2007a) argues that one can consider Kirzner's work about the discovery of opportunities, Schumpeter's (1911) about the exploitation of opportunities, and Knight's (1921) about the evaluation of opportunities. However, Knight's use of the notion of judgment would seem to also involve discovery (or creation) and exploitation.

if they share the same objectives and the data are presented to them in exactly the same manner, because they have access to different information, interpret the data in different ways, and so on (Lachmann, 1977; Casson and Wadeson, 2007). In Bayesian terms, priors are diffuse, and updating rules may differ.

For explaining the existence of the firm, such a highly abstract treatment may be perfectly fine. However, in later chapters we apply the notion of judgment more broadly, examining teams as *loci* of judgment, and arguing that judgment can, in an important sense, be delegated. We also explore how judgment helps explain the boundaries and internal organization of firms. Examining these issues requires us to be more explicit about the nature of entrepreneurial judgment. Similarly, to tease out policy and management implications of the judgment theory of the firm, we need to begin opening up the black box of judgment. Finally, it may also be useful to break down the act of entrepreneurial judgment into distinct imagination or discovery, evaluation, and exploitation phases of entrepreneurial action. Not only may these activities be temporally separated, they may also reside with different actors. Thus, since Schumpeter (1942) much work in innovation studies and corporate strategy has proceeded from the assumption that the large industrial firm is characterized by an "entrepreneurial division of labor," different entrepreneurial activities residing in different parts of the firm. The different activities that underlie this division of labor are underpinned by different skills and may represent different aspects of judgment.

Economists have usually discussed judgment in a specific epistemic context, namely that of "uncertainty," sometimes called "Knightian uncertainty" as homage to the first economist to discuss it systematically (Knight, 1921). Uncertainty is one of the most fascinating and perplexing concepts in economics, one that has also recently been picked up by management scholars in the entrepreneurship field (e.g., McMullen and Shepherd, 2006). We provide a brief account of its history as well as of its modern treatments. Following Knight we then link judgment to uncertainty, treating judgment as the exercise of a particular skill, namely that of dealing successfully with resource allocation decisions under uncertainty.

Certain entrepreneurs and investors – Warren Buffet comes to mind (Buffett and Clark, 1997) – seem to have a persistent, successful track record in making such decisions. One explanation for repeated entrepreneurial success, suggested by Alchian (1950) and Taleb (2007) (drawing on a famous thought experiment about coin-flipping by Emile Borél), is that this reflects persistent luck. This hypothesis is rooted in the idea that Knightian uncertainty is fundamentally debilitating, epistemologically, and hence might as well be randomness. Many economists hold this view. Schultz (1980: 437–438), for example, insists that "it is not sufficient to treat entrepreneurs solely as economic agents who only collect windfalls and bear losses that are unanticipated. If this is all they do, the much vaunted free enterprise system merely distributes in some unspecified manner the windfalls and losses that come as surprises." In other words, the future is either "anticipated," by which Schultz means "describable using expected utility theory," or pure surprise – that is, luck.

   Knight (1921: 298), however, clearly thought that some people systematically deal with uncertainty better than others: "Like a large portion of the practical problems of business life, as of all life, this one of selecting human capacities for dealing with unforeseeable situations involves paradox and apparent theoretical impossibility of solution. But like a host of impossible things in life, it is constantly being done." Mises (1949: 585) likewise attributes to the entrepreneur a

specific anticipative understanding of the conditions of the uncertain future [that] defies any rules and systematization. It can be neither taught nor learned. If it were different, everybody could embark upon entrepreneurship with the same prospect of success. What distinguishes the successful entrepreneur and promoter from other people is precisely the fact that he does not let himself be guided by what was and is, but arranges his affairs on the ground of his opinion about the future. He sees the past and the present as other people do; but he judges the future in a different way.

How, exactly, does the entrepreneur "judge the future in a different way"? Is this something that can be analyzed systematically, by decision-makers themselves or by analysts? Or do we conclude, like Lucas (1986), that economics cannot handle Knightian uncertainty?

   While traditional decision theory offers little on dealing with Knightian uncertainty, this does not leave decision-makers in epistemological bedlam. We argue that entrepreneurs can deal with uncertainty, and hypothesize that judgment is rooted in *skills* for handling uncertainty, an idea that was key to Knight's thought. Thus, while the exercise of judgment is a function (or, rather, a set of complementary functions), it is based on perceptions, skills, and heuristics. The link between those perceptions, skills, and heuristics, and the judgment they inform is not deterministic, of course; if it were, we would not be talking about judgment, but decision-making according to formal rules. As Phelps (2006: 5) puts it, citing Hayek, "actors in the world have to make judgments that are not fully implied by their formal models." And yet, as we shall see, we can peek somewhat into the black box of judgment.

Note that in suggesting a possible "operationalization" of judgment, we do not deny that the purely formal, logical notion of uncertainty-bearing, as the economic function uniquely responsible for economic profit and loss, is valid and useful. Indeed, the emergence of a correct theory of profit – not a standardized, automatic rate of return on invested capital (as in Ricardo), a "surplus" extracted from labor value (as in Marx), or a monopoly rent (as in Marshall), but a reward from successful bearing of uninsurable risks – was one of the most important developments in twentieth-century economics. From a managerial point of view, however, this strictly formal notion does not offer much insight or guidance. Here we suggest ways the formal idea of judgment can be extended, augmented, and applied, to build a theory of entrepreneurial organization with richer implications and applications.

Knightian uncertainty

[T]he truth is, there are things we know, and we know we know them – the known knowns. There are things we know that we don't know – the known unknowns. And there are unknown unknowns; the things we do not yet know that we do not know. Donald Rumsfeld

Former Defense Secretary Rumsfeld may not exactly be a bona fide epistemologist, but in the above quotation – ridiculed by commentators at the time it was uttered – he encapsulated some basic insights that go right to the heart of the fundamental issues in the nexus of entrepreneurship: risk/uncertainty/ignorance, and decision-making, and the social organization of these. Thus, when Kirzner (1979a: 181) points out that "entrepreneurship reveals to the market what the market did

not realize was available, or indeed, needed at all," he is pointing to
the importance of handling the third Rumsfeldian unknown. Hayek's
(1945, 1973) social thought, on which Kirzner builds, is all about
how evolved institutions deal with the unknown unknowns. Actually,
Rumsfeld's three unknowns correspond nicely to the way Knight constructs his key argument on probability in *Risk, Uncertainty, and Profit*
(1921), as we shall see. (Like Hayek, Knight also consistently related his
social thought to these epistemic problems.)

Knight on uncertainty

As indicated earlier the judgment theory of entrepreneurship ultimately derives from Cantillon who, in Hébert and Link's (1988: 21)
description, defined the entrepreneur as "someone who engages in
exchanges for profit; specifically, he or she is someone who exercises
business judgment in the face of uncertainty." Others, notably, Mises
(1949), have cultivated similar views. However, the *locus classicus* of
the judgment view of entrepreneurship remains Frank Knight's *Risk,
Uncertainty, and Profit* (Knight, 1921).

Interpretations of Knight's work. For several decades Knight's book
has generated a growing interpretive literature (e.g., Barzel, 1987;
LeRoy and Singell, 1987; Boudreaux and Holcombe, 1989; Langlois
and Cosgel, 1993; Foss, 1993b; Demsetz, 1988b; Runde, 1998;
Emmett, 1999, 2009, 2010; Brooke, 2010). This literature is akin to
the literature on "what Keynes really meant" (e.g., Coddington, 1983)
in striking ways. Thus, some scholars interpret Knight as making a
break with existing economics based on a radical epistemology stressing the unknowability of the future (e.g., Boudreaux and Holcombe,
1989; Langlois and Csontos, 1993) while others, armed with subjective probability theory and the economics of information, argue that
Knight's theory of profit and the firm is entirely consistent with mainstream economics. For example, there is an argument that Knight was
simply invoking "risk" and "uncertainty" as labels for risk that can
be insured versus risk that cannot (LeRoy and Singell, 1987; Demsetz,
1988b). In this interpretation, Knight was talking about commercial
experimentation, the basis of which is so much inside the head of the
entrepreneur that it cannot be meaningfully assessed by the market
in terms of probabilities (although the entrepreneur himself may be
capable of doing so).

Barzel (1987) interprets Knight's theory of the emergence of the entrepreneurial firm in terms of a standard agency problem: The entrepreneur should assume the roles of manager and residual claimant because his marginal product is the hardest among the complementary inputs to measure. Similarly, LeRoy and Singell (1987) see Knight's main contribution as anticipating the notion of asymmetric information. Kihlstrom and Laffont (1979) reconstruct Knight's theory entirely in terms of differential risk preferences, taking Knight's discussion of firm organization to mean that the "confident and venturesome 'assume the risk' or 'insure' the doubtful and timid" by guaranteeing them a fixed wage (Knight, 1921: 269).

There is considerable textual basis in Knight (1921) for all of the above interpretations. But we agree with Boudreaux and Holcombe (1989) and Langlois and Cosgel (1993) that what LeRoy and Singell (1987: 402) dismiss as "Knight's extended Austrian-style disquisitions on the foundations of human knowledge and conduct and the like" are quite central to Knight's message.[2] They provide the deep foundations for his insistence that what matters for the understanding of probability is the mind's classification of events (i.e., the extent to which events can be meaningfully placed in well-defined, non-trivial categories). Knight's ideas on cognition supply an argument for why many events are truly unique. And they explain why (to use modern terminology) many forward markets are closed, meaning that there are few intertemporal prices that support intertemporal resource allocation, and why judgment in the form of commercial experimentation is therefore necessary.

---

[2] The full passage from LeRoy and Singell (1987: 402) reads as follows: "Even the reader who skips Knight's extended Austrian-style disquisitions on the foundations of human knowledge and conduct and the like – and surely this must include almost all readers – will at times despair of extracting any core of original insight from the overripe fruit of Knight's prose." We are not sure we would take the writing style of the typical neoclassical economist over Knight's, however. Consider this: "The first fact to be recorded is that [economic] reality exists or 'is there.' This fact cannot be proved or argued or 'tested.' If anyone denies that men have interests or that 'we' have a considerable amount of knowledge about them, economics and its entire works will simply be to such a person what the world of color is to the blind man. But there would still be one difference: a man who is physically, ocularly blind may still be rated of normal intelligence and in his right mind." (Knight, 1940: 12).

Knight on probability. Knight's (1921) fundamental contribution is conventionally seen as the risk/uncertainty distinction. However, this particular distinction is only invoked in passing (1921: 21, 233). His fundamental argument, developed in chapter 7 of Knight (1921), involves a tripartite classification of the notion of probability into *"apriori* probability," "statistical probability," and "estimated probability." Situations that can be described epistemically in terms of the two first categories represent risk, while the third condition describes situations involving uncertainty. Thus, *"apriori* probability" refers to situations where probabilities can be ascertained in a purely deductive manner (e.g., the probabilities of either side of a fair coin) and where possible outcomes are entirely well-defined (in Knight's [1921: 224] words, there is an "absolutely homogeneous classification of instances"). In contrast, under "statistical probability" the outcomes are not based on homogeneous (and equally probable) instances. Statistical probability is obtained by identifying and classifying experiential instances (events), lumping heterogeneous together in preselected categories, tabulating the frequencies for the purpose of calculating probability, akin to the frequentist probability interpretation of (Richard) von Mises (1939).[3]

Finally, estimated probability refers to situations where there is "no valid basis of any kind of classifying instances" (Knight, 1921: 225). As Langlois and Cosgel (1993: 459) note: "uncertainty as Knight understood it arises from the impossibility of exhaustive classification of states." In this situation, we are forced to make a "judgment of probability," even though we may be fully aware that our estimate of the set of probable outcomes likely differs from the set of possible outcomes (Jarvis, 2010: 28), and the relevant estimated probabilities are likely to be highly imprecise. This is simply the order that a rational mind seeks to impose on a less orderly universe, and is entirely consistent with man's rational nature.

It is easy to understand why subjective probability theorists (e.g., LeRoy and Singell, 1987) have thought of Knight as a natural ally, indeed precursor. Savage's (1954) derivation of expected utility theory

---

[3] Of course, this also means that there are degrees of statistical probability, depending on how homogenous instances are (Runde, 1998). A priori probability may be seen as one limit of statistical probability (as instances are entirely homogenous) and "estimated probability" as the other limit (instances are highly heterogeneous).

without imposing any objective probabilities may appear close in spirit to Knight's thinking on estimated probability.[4] Indeed, we think Knight clearly accepted the idea of subjective probability, and that he did not claim that it is meaningless to try to assign probabilities to outcomes under uncertainty.[5] However, we also agree with Langlois and Cosgel (1993: 460) that the key to Knight's thought here is the extent to which "categories" can be "estimated" and shared between individuals (rather than the calculation of probabilities). As Langlois and Cosgel (1993: 460) put it: "When the categories of knowledge themselves are unknown, they cannot form the basis of interpersonal agreement and market exchange." Knightian uncertainty is thus primarily about *the ability to articulate and communicate, or transfer, estimates about the future,* rather than the ability of individuals to make these estimates themselves – just as the Hayekian notion of specific knowledge can be described in terms of the ability to transfer information from one person to another (Jensen and Meckling, 1992).

This is the situation of Rumsfeldian unknown unknowns, where judgment becomes the act of resource allocation by an entrepreneur who holds knowledge categories that differ from everyone else's – in other words, entrepreneurs establish firms not because they have no knowledge of the future, but because their beliefs about the future cannot be easily articulated and communicated to existing resource owners. As Casson (1982: 14) notes, "[t]he entrepreneur believes he is right, while everyone else is wrong. Thus, the essence of entrepreneurship is being different – being different because one has a different perception of the situation."

More surprising than the association of Knight with subjective probability theory is the lumping of Knight with Keynes as like-minded proponents of "genuine," "radical," or "deep" uncertainty (e.g., Bewley, 1989: 2). While Keynes invoked uncertainty in the context of

---

[4] This may also suggest the perhaps rather far-fetched suggestion that the Debreu (1959) state-preference approach, in which there are no assignments of probabilities at all, is consistent with Knight's notion of estimated probability or uncertainty.

[5] Richard von Mises (1939: 76), however, held exactly that view: "The peculiar approach of the subjectivists lies in the fact that they consider 'I presume that these cases are equally probable' to be equivalent to 'These cases are equally probable,' since, for them, probability is only a subjective notion."

unique, rare (investor) situations[6] – perhaps the black swans of Taleb (2007) – Knight saw uncertainty as characterizing many, reasonably mundane decisions. To illustrate he asked, "what is the 'probability' of error ... in the judgment" of a manufacturer deciding to expand production? The response (Knight, 1921: 226) is that it is

> manifestly meaningless to speak of either calculating a probability a priori or of determining it empirically by studying a large number of instances ... [T]he "instance" in question is so entirely unique that there are no others or not a sufficient number to make it possible to tabulate enough like it to form a basis for any inference of value about any real probability in the case we are interested in. The same obviously applies to ... most conduct and not business alone.

However, this does not mean that there are no rational grounds for forming beliefs and making decisions.

Kindred spirits: Mises, Shackle, Lachmann

Mises. As noted already, Knight's thinking on probability harmonizes in some key ways with Mises' (1949) thinking on the matter.[7] Mises does not use Knight's terminology, but distinguishes similarly between "class probability" and "case probability." The former describes situations in which an event may be classified as a unique element of a homogeneous class, the properties of which are known. No one can predict whether a particular house in a particular neighborhood will burn down in a given year, but insurance companies know how many similar houses in similar locations have burned in the past, and from this the likelihood of a particular house burning within a particular

---

[6] "By 'uncertain' knowledge, let me explain, I do not mean merely to distinguish what is known for certain from what is only probable. The game of roulette is not subject, in this sense, to uncertainty ... The sense in which I am using the term is that in which the prospect of a European war is uncertain, or the price of copper and the rate of interest twenty years hence ... About these matters there is no scientific basis on which to form any calculable probability whatever. We simply do not know" (Keynes, 1937: 213–214).

[7] See Hoppe (2007) for a comparison of Mises' and Knight's views on probability. There is no evidence that Mises was directly influenced by Knight (1921), but Knight visited Mises' University of Vienna seminar in 1930 (Hülsmann, 2007: 764) and Mises was surely familiar with Knight's work.

period can be estimated. Case probability, by contrast, applies to cases in which each event is unique, such that no general class probabilities can be defined.[8]

Mises builds here on the influential work of his brother Richard von Mises (1939), a developer of the "frequentist" approach to probability. Frequentism defines the probability of a particular event as the limit value of its relative frequency in a series of trials. In this understanding, probabilities can be defined only in cases in which repeated trials are feasible – that is, in situations where each event can be meaningfully compared to other events in the same class. Moreover, and for this reason, probabilities can only be defined *ex post*, as learned through experience, and cannot exist a priori. Hence Mises defines case probability, or uncertainty, as a case in which probabilities, in the frequentist sense, do not exist.[9] This is quite close to Knight's distinction between "statistical probability" and "estimated probability."

However, Mises goes farther than Knight: For Mises, purposeful human behavior *in general* cannot be considered part of a homogenous class, and therefore only case probability applies to economic outcomes (Knight did not make this claim). Of course, as Hoppe (2007) notes, we can define such classes in a technical sense – us writing this chapter is an element of the class "entrepreneurship scholars writing book chapters" – but defining the class is not sufficient for applying class probability to an event. There must also be randomness, or what Richard von Mises (1939: 24) calls "complete lawlessness," within the class. And yet, argues Hoppe (2007: 11), this is not possible with human action:

It is in connection with this randomness requirement where Ludwig von Mises (and presumably Knight) see insuperable difficulties in applying probability theory to human actions. True, formal-logically for every single

---

[8] O'Driscoll and Rizzo (1985) adopt the terms "typical events" and "unique events" to get at this distinction.

[9] Hence the use of the term "case probability," like Knight's term "judgment of probability," is misleading; what Mises really means is "case non-probability," or perhaps "case judgments without probabilities." Confusingly, Mises (1949: 107) also argues elsewhere that "[o]nly preoccupation with the mathematical treatment could result in the prejudice that probability always means frequency." Van den Hauwe (2007) argues, in contrast, that Mises' position is in some ways closer to Keynes'.

action a corresponding collective can be defined. However, ontologically human actions (whether of individuals or groups) cannot be grouped in "true" collectives but must be conceived as unique events. Why? As Ludwig von Mises would presumably reply, the assumption that one knows nothing about any particular event except its membership in a known class is false in the case of human actions; or, as Richard von Mises would put it, in the case of human actions we know a "selection rule" the application of which leads to fundamental changes regarding the relative frequency (likelihood) of the attribute in question (thus ruling out the use of the probability calculus).

Of course, painting Mises as a frequentist, rather than subjectivist, may appear odd given the importance of subjectivism more generally in Austrian economics. As is well-known, Austrians emphasize subjectivity not only of value – an emphasis shared by neoclassical economists – but also subjectivism of knowledge and even expectations (Foss *et al.*, 2008). Langlois (1982), in this vein, argues that probabilities should be interpreted as beliefs about information structures, rather than objective events. "[I]t is not meaningful to talk about 'knowing' a probability or a probability distribution. A probability assessment reflects one's state of information about an event; it is not something ontologically separate whose value can be determined objectively" (Langlois, 1982: 8).

What distinguishes case from class probability, according to Langlois, is the character of the decision-maker's information about the event. Objective probabilities (in the frequentist sense) are simply special cases of subjective probabilities in which the decision-maker structures the problem in terms of classes of events. Entrepreneurship, in Langlois' interpretation, can be described as the act of formalizing the decision problem. To use the language of decision theory, a non-entrepreneur (call him, following Kirzner [1973: 32–37], a Robbinsian maximizer) is presented with a decision tree, a set of outcomes, and the probabilities for each outcome, and simply uses backwards induction to solve the problem. The entrepreneur, as it were, redraws the tree, by noticing a possible option or outcome that other agents failed to see. The key distinction, according to Langlois, is not whether the decision tree is populated with objective or subjective probabilities, but whether the tree itself is exogenous (Knightian risk) or endogenous (Knightian uncertainty).

Shackle. Knight (1921) made a philosophically based distinction between what he called the "ignorance theory of probability" and the "doctrine of real probability," roughly corresponding to whether thinking on probability is based on a deterministic ontology or an indeterminist one. For Knight, this is not merely an epistemically motivated distinction. According to the doctrine of real probability the future is not only unknown, but also "unknowable" (so there are, strictly speaking, no objective probabilities regarding future events), and probability is an epistemic device for handling the resulting indeterminacy. British economist George Shackle (1972) made the unknown and unknowable characteristic of the future the key theme of his thinking on uncertainty (see also Loasby [1976] for an important contribution in this vein). However, he deliberately avoided the terminology of probability, deeming it only appropriate for situations in which the set of possible outcomes is well-defined. To Shackle, the human powers of imagination and innovation and the consequent open-endedness of the economy must imply a situation of what is essentially ignorance: A world where the nature and identity of some non-trivial future states are unknown and unknowable (Shackle, 1979). This gives rise to surprises, or what Taleb (2007) later popularized as "black swans." Shackle even devised a formalism for handling this.[10] The irregular occurrence of major surprising events make the economy "kaleidic," that is, given to major, radical changes that drastically upset the existing pattern of resource allocation.

Lachmann. Ludwig Lachmann (1976, 1977) embraced the importance of imagination and surprise in Shackle's work, but added his own Austrian twist to these arguments: The fundamental reason why the future is unknown and unknowable, and that the economy is given to kaleidic disruptions, relates to the growth of knowledge. We cannot think of time in isolation from a process of the growth of personal knowledge (Lachmann, 1976); the two are inherently intertwined (see also Loasby, 1976). However, future knowledge must be unpredictable; if it weren't, it would be present knowledge.

---

[10] Namely, his "potential surprise" framework, which, however, was argued to be essentially a subjective probability framework (Shackle, 1949, 1955). As Langlois (1986) observes, a radical Bayesian may insist that there is a category of outcomes, namely the unexpected ones, on which a probability number can be placed. The logical meaningfulness of this, as well as of Shackle's potential surprise framework, is clearly open to debate.

In sum, following Knight's lead, a number of economists have argued that when economic change is driven by radical, unpredictable patterns in the growth of knowledge, entrepreneurs use what we call judgment to interpret economic data and anticipate, or "appraise," future market conditions. Entrepreneurship is thus seen as human action that creatively formulates and solves new problems (Mises, 1949).

Modern mainstream treatments

Although Knightian uncertainty crops up most often within heterodox economics and academic management circles, some mainstream economists have dealt with it as well. Bewley (1986, 1989) constructs a "Knightian" decision theory by tweaking Bayesian methods, specifically eliminating the assumption that preferences over lotteries are complete and introducing the possibility of "new alternatives," that is, decision alternatives not present at the time the decision-maker formulates the full contingent program for the whole decision tree. In Bewley's conceptualization the entrepreneur is an agent who starts a project without knowing the precise probabilities of the outcomes of the project, emphasizing ambiguity in the assessment of probabilities.[11] This ambiguity is modeled by assuming that an individual uses many probabilities to evaluate a given (uncertain) outcome of a project. Due to this multiplicity of beliefs – for example, there are many net present values for a given project – situations may arise in which the decision-maker simply cannot compare any two possible outcomes (payoffs), and therefore is unable to calculate the expected utility.

Bewley's ingenious approach to modeling ambiguity (first formulated in two working papers in 1986 and 1989, but not published until 2002 and 2001, respectively) has been picked up by several scholars; Rigotti, Ryan, and Vaithianathan (2011), for example, build a model of an economy with agents who differ in their optimism. Those agents who pick probabilities from the upper part of a distribution or project outcomes are optimists and are likely to form a firm to realize the

---

[11] And the decision problem cannot be modeled as a larger game in which "nature" first chooses which set of probabilities apply, without informing the decision-maker, as in Harsanyi (1967, 1968a, 1968b).

project. They use this characterization to model "innovation-proof equilibria" in which no beneficial opportunities for innovation exist.

Judgment: purposeful behavior under uncertainty

It is a world of change in which we live, and a world of uncertainty. We live only by knowing something about the future; while the problems of life, or of conduct at least, arise from the fact that we know so little.

(Knight, 1921: 199)

Handling uncertainty

As we have seen, many important economists have addressed radical or "deep" uncertainty and its underlying knowledge conditions. They have conceptualized these very differently, however, and have addressed the implications of radical uncertainty for coordination and economic order in very different ways. Thus, Mises (1949, 1951) argued that all actions are essentially shrouded in uncertainty but added, anticipating Alchian (1950), that the market's competitive sorting mechanisms based on the profit-and-loss mechanism and private ownership would successfully discriminate between entrepreneurs with varying abilities to engage in entrepreneurial "appraisal" in the presence of uncertainty (Salerno, 1993). Knight focused on uncertainty because it allowed him to explain the existence of the firm and profits; he did not necessarily deny, however, that many business decisions are entirely routine (in the sense of Cyert and March [1963] and Nelson and Winter [1982]). Based on a "fundamentalist" reading of Keynes, Shackle (1972) developed his "kaleidic" notion of the economy. Ludwig Lachmann followed suit (Lachmann, 1976). Israel Kirzner (1973, 1979a, 1985, 1997), arguably the one who departed the least from the knowledge conditions of the standard model of economics, nevertheless stressed the importance of "sheer ignorance," going beyond the conventional notion of asymmetric information (Kirzner, 1997). These thinkers also drew very different conclusions about how agents handle uncertainty. Lachmann focused on social institutions as entities to reduce uncertainty (Lachmann, 1970; Langlois, 1986; Foss and Garzarelli, 2007). Knight regarded the entrepreneur and the firm as those mechanisms for handling uncertainty.[12] Kirzner conceptualized the entrepreneur as the force that closes "pockets of ignorance" in the market, continuously pushing it towards a kind of equilibrium.

All these scholars recognized that uncertainty poses a fundamental challenge for resource allocation, and at least Mises and Lachmann appealed to higher-level institutions and mechanisms to explain how some measure of order can be maintained in the presence of uncertainty.[13] Both Kirzner and Knight describe the entrepreneur as a coordinating agent, though Kirzner deliberately shies away from addressing the *content* of entrepreneurial decision-making, beyond associating it with alertness to previously unnoticed profit opportunities. Indeed, given Kirzner's refusal to associate such alertness with any opportunity costs, it is hard to describe this as "decision-making" at all. Rather, alertness seems *sui generis*, in between luck and deliberate decision-making. This comes close to Schumpeter's view that entrepreneurship consists of "intuition, the capacity of seeing things in a way which afterwards proves to be true, even though it cannot be established at the moment and of grasping the essential fact, discarding the unessential, even though one can give no account of the principles by which this is done" (1911: 85). Essentially, Kirzner and Schumpeter's characterization of entrepreneurship in terms of alertness and bold intuition puts it in a black box, and, in Schumpeter's case, makes entrepreneurship distinctly extra-economic.

Knight arguably goes farther in his characterization of judgment than Kirzner does in the case of alertness and Schumpeter in the case of intuitive entrepreneurship. Unlike virtually all of the other scholars named above, he grapples directly with the psychology of uncertainty (see in particular Knight, 1921: 241–242), and maintains that

---

[12] As Emmett (2010: 17) explains, for Knight, "those who accept the moral challenge of exercising *responsible judgment* regarding the use of resources in the midst of uncertainty are entrepreneurs. The entrepreneur accepts the challenge of acting even when there is a potential for moral hazard to exist, and backs it up by hazarding his own resources (Knight 1921: 299). But the entrepreneur exercises responsible judgment in doing so. The key judgment the entrepreneur makes, Knight argued, regards his opinion of those with whom he contracts, as suppliers, workers, and clients. In an uncertain world, 'attention and interest shift from the errors in men's opinions of things to the errors in their opinions of men' (Knight 1921: 292)."

[13] See Klein (2008b) for a discussion of the various concepts of equilibrium or coordination that appear in the Austrian literature.

individuals actively and rationally deal with uncertainty by forming (tacit) probability estimates – a different argument from appealing to "intuition," "serendipity," or "understanding." Ironically, those modern scholars who examine the psychological antecedents of entrepreneurship have usually started with Kirzner, rather than Knight. However, Kirzner insists that we "cannot explain how some men discover what is around the corner before others do" (Kirzner, 1976: 121) – although he also admits that the "ability to learn without deliberate search is a gift individuals enjoy in quite different degrees" (1979a: 148).

Elements of judgment

To repeat, we conceive judgment as the crucial entrepreneurial element of making uncertain decisions regarding uses of current or new resources to satisfy future preferences. As Langlois (2007c: 1113) puts it, judgment "is Knight's term for the process of creating frameworks of interpretation and decision." In actuality, judgment therefore is present in a host of decisions related to an entrepreneurial venture (Casson, 1982). This raises the question of whether judgment can in a sense be delegated (as Knight argued). We treat this issue in a later chapter and here provide a characterization of judgment per se.

Economists have generally shied away from theorizing directly about entrepreneurial decision-making (rather than the effects of such decision-making). The main reason is probably the traditional belief that economists per se have nothing to say about such decision-making,[14] or the belief that theorizing about entrepreneurial decision-making is fundamentally self-defeating or pointless as any such theory will immediately become worthless if placed in the public domain or will be privately exploited by a scientist-turned-entrepreneur. However, scholars from other fields and disciplines have been engaged in several decades in examining the constituent components of entrepreneurial decision-making. In the following we rely on some of this work in order to provide a fuller characterization of entrepreneurial

---

[14] Even the recent fascination with neuroeconomics and behavioral economics is essentially about feeding findings from other fields and disciplines into the micro foundations of economic models.

judgment. We are not claiming that a predictive theory of judgment is at hand, merely arguing that judgment may meaningfully be treated as a latent construct, and that we can point to several manifest variables that constitute this construct and which have identifiable antecedents. In the following we treat manifest variables and antecedents under the same heading.

Skills and experience. Entrepreneurial activities have several qualities, involving underlying skills (Casson, 1982: 25). Thus, formulating a decision problem requires specifying potential strategies for dealing with the problem, requiring imaginative skills (Gartner, 2007); deriving decision rules (even if, in the spirit of Knight, highly personal and idiosyncratic ones) requires analytical skills; collecting data requires skills at searching; and so on. Certain firms or types of firms may be particularly good at fostering these stills among their employees (Klepper, 2002; Braguinsky, Klepper, and Ohyama, 2009; Elfenbein *et al.*, 2010). While such skills may be necessary to realizing entrepreneurial ventures, they do not necessarily underlie judgment, even if they are complementary to judgment. Thus, some may argue that judgment is exactly that extra ingredient added to the above more mundane skills that makes an entrepreneurial venture "tick."

While there is much to this view, and while we maintain that judgment is the cognitive faculty that is applied to those unique situations where no obvious or clear decision rule exists, the exercise of judgment may itself be seen as a skilled activity. In turn, skills are, of course, accumulated through experiential learning. Shane's (2000) work clearly points to the important role of experience for entrepreneurship, or, in his case, "opportunity identification." Thus, Shane conducts a series of case studies of entrepreneurs who each seek to exploit a single MIT invention but hold different stocks of experiential knowledge, and demonstrates that different opportunities are perceived by these individuals. Ardichvili, Cardozo, and Ray (2003) specifically point to the role for opportunity identification of special interest knowledge, and general industry knowledge, knowledge of specific markets, knowledge of customer problems, and marketing knowledge.[15]

---

[15] Lazear (2005) famously argues that entrepreneurs are likely to be jacks-of-all-trades, that is, their skill portfolios are broad rather than deep.

Such skills and knowledge play a role in entrepreneurial judgment, but how? As Sarasvathy and colleagues suggest (Sarasvathy, 2008; Dew *et al.*, 2009), such knowledge could in principle be fed into exist- ing analytical frameworks (i.e., frameworks for industry and analysis, procedures for setting up business plans, etc.) to be used in a pre- dictive and analytical way. However, Sarasvathy and her colleagues (e.g., Dew *et al.*, 2009) argue that this is exactly the approach of the "novice" (fresh, presumably, from the MBA), and that experienced, and successful, entrepreneurs follow an altogether different logic, namely that of "effectuation." Effectuation is an incremental and flexible approach, in which goals are often adjusted under the impact of learning about what can be done with available resources and feed- back from the nascent entrepreneur's network.

Sarasvathy's important work harmonizes in significant ways with our perspective.[16] She fully recognizes the importance of uncertainty in entrepreneurial decision-making and details a distinct approach for dealing with it. We see the effectuation approach as detailing some of the elements of judgment, in particular experience (as already indi- cated), but also creativity and ambiguity. Its emphasis on learning and experiential, local knowledge harmonizes with an Austrian per- spective (Hayek, 1945). And its emphasis on the context in which entrepreneurial action take place is consistent with the approach to the entrepreneurial context, namely Austrian capital theory, that we develop in Chapter 5.

Creativity. Influential research (Csikszentmihalyi, 1996) posits that creativity can be understood in five stages: preparation, incu- bation, insight, evaluation, and elaboration. Lumpkin, Hills, and Shrader (2004) argue that prior experiential knowledge underlies the preparation and incubation stages, in a non-deterministic manner. During the insight phase the entrepreneur has his "Aha!" moment (Corbett, 2005: 478). The two last stages refer to market testing and actual opportunity exploitation. In essence, entrepreneurial creativity is about exploring, defining, and redefining the problem space in the pursuit of new opportunities, as memorably captured by Schumpeter's

---

[16] Sarasvathy and Read (in press) are critical of our earlier work. However, we tend to see many more similarities than differences. Both her and our perspective emphasize the basic point that opportunities come into existence only as they are manifested in action.

(1911) notion of "new combinations." In turn, such exploration is positively related to the experience: "Experts not only have a larger mental database of actual experiences to draw from, they also have better access to it than novices do" (Dew *et al.*, 2009: 291).

Uncertainty preferences. A key characteristic of entrepreneurship is often taken to be an above-normal willingness to accept gambles with unclear odds (Bhidè, 2000). This is not the same as having below-normal risk aversion (as in Kihlstrom and Laffont, 1979), but is rather a matter of ambiguity. The once-influential notion that entrepreneurs are less risk averse than the population at large seems now discarded (Caliendo, Fossen, and Kritikos, 2009), and many entrepreneurship scholars argue instead that entrepreneurs tend to come from the ranks of people who are particularly *confident* when they confront ambiguous decisions (Bhidè, 2000; Rigotti *et al.*, 2011) – even irrationally confident (Busenitz and Barney, 1997; Bernardo and Welch, 2001; Forbes, 2005; Koellinger, Maria Minniti, and Schade, 2007).[17] As Coase (1937: 249) argued in his summary of Knight's ideas, "good judgment is generally associated with confidence in one's judgment."

Summing up. Profit, therefore, is a reward to bearing uncertainty, specifically a return that accrues to those entrepreneurs who are particularly optimistic in the face of ambiguity and who succeed with their entrepreneurial ventures (loss, of course, comes to those who are optimistic, but unjustifiably so).

Methods for meeting uncertainty

To Knight, of course, the exercise of judgment, the entrepreneur, the firm, and the delegation of decision-making it allows for are different sides of the same problem of "meeting uncertainty." We treat the role of the firm in greater detail in later chapters, and instead concentrate here on discussing some behavioral aspects of meeting uncertainty.

The entrepreneurship literature features a long-standing tradition of differentiating entrepreneurs and managers based on the degree to which they apply available information and calculative techniques:

---

[17] Ben-David, Graham, and Harvey (2010) argue that a particular form of overconfidence – what they call "miscalibration" – is prominent among corporate managers, suggesting that overconfidence may not be unique to entrepreneurship.

managers do, entrepreneurs don't (e.g., Schumpeter, 1911; Baumol, 1968). Instead, entrepreneurs rely on the "gift" of being able to "learn without deliberate search" (Kirzner, 1979a: 148) and on their "intuition," their "tendency to solve problems without explicit reasoning or analysis" (Mosakowski, 1998: 627). A refinement of this view is Alvarez and Barney's (2007) distinction between "discovery entrepreneurs" (who discover "objectively" existing entrepreneurial opportunities) and "creation entrepreneurs" (who create opportunities *ex nihilo*): While the former can usefully employ the analytical techniques taught in business schools, attempts to construct business plans and the like may be disastrous in the case of creation entrepreneurs.

The problem with these views is that they tend to place entrepreneurial decision-making in an unexplainable black box. However, a number of scholars argue, implicitly or explicitly, that this overly nihilistic conclusion is simply the result of the sway that the classical rational decision-making model holds. In reality, individuals deploy various decision heuristics to deal with uncertainty. Thus, Grandori (2010) draws on the philosophy of science, noting that scientists inherently confront uncertain decision situations, even if they are working within the bounds of normal science (see also Felin and Zenger, 2009). Indeed, many heuristics and procedures of established science are fundamentally procedures for dealing with uncertainty. Grandori argues that those heuristics are not particular to the scientific community, but are the same or close to the heuristics employed by entrepreneurs.[18] Grandori offers several examples of science-based entrepreneurs directly employing their learned heuristics from science to the uncertain situations confronting a new venture and serving to stimulate judgment of new potential opportunities. She finds that these entrepreneurs rely on "systematic observation, questioning and problem reframing by using 'theories' new to the field at hand [that] figure prominently as heuristics in the hypothesis generation phase" (2010: 484), and furthermore argues that these kind of heuristics apply outside of science-based entrepreneurship. For example, Zander (2007) provides an account of how the substitution of incandescent light for gas illumination in New York City was a result of Edison's judgment combined with meticulous market analysis, that is, systematic and

---

[18] Similar arguments have long been made by Brian Loasby (e.g., Loasby, 1986).

disciplined gathering of relevant data, following the formation of an initial hypothesis.

Read and Sarasvathy (2005) argue that because of its incremental and flexible features, an effectuation logic is particularly suited for dealing with uncertainty which tends to nullify the effectiveness of trying to get superior insight in the future, as reflected in detailed business plans, market forecasting, and so on. Effectuation allows the skilled entrepreneur to postpone decisions in order to reduce the ambiguity he faces. Flexibility in the face of uncertainty is the overall message. Similar arguments have been invoked to explain the role of the firm as an institution that exists to reduce uncertainty.

Judgment as ultimate decision-making

In later chapters (7 and 8) we link the firm more directly to judgment and the need for flexibility in the face of uncertainty and ambiguity. Inspired by Knight (1921), we develop the notion of the firm as a *nested hierarchy of judgment*. In this model owners, who possess the ultimate rights to make decisions about resource allocation – akin to Grossman and Hart's (1986) notion of *residual rights of control* – empower subordinates to make decisions on the owners' behalf. These decisions made by employees may be critically important to the viability and profitability of the enterprise, but they are not the "ultimate" decisions about the firm, because these employees were selected and are retained by the firm's owners, and their delegated authority can be taken away. Hence judgment is not simply decision-making under conditions of uncertainty, but decision-making about the resources the decision-maker owns and controls. Judgment, in this sense, represents "ultimate" decision-making (Rothbard, 1962: 602).

Kirzner (1973: 68) makes a similar point about alertness: it can never be fully delegated. "It is true that 'alertness' ... may be hired; but one who hires an employee alert to possibilities of discovering knowledge has himself displayed alertness of a still higher order ... The entrepreneurial decision to hire is thus the ultimate hiring decision, responsible in the last resort for all factors that are directly or indirectly hired for his project." Kirzner goes on to quote Knight (1921: 291): "What we call 'control' consists mainly of selecting someone else to do the 'controlling'."

An important implication is that entrepreneurship, as ultimate decision-making about factors of production, is not itself a factor of production. A passage from the French economist Jean Marchal (1951: 550–551) expresses this nicely:

[E]ntrepreneurs obtain remuneration for their activity in a very different manner than do laborers or lenders of capital. The latter provide factors of production which they sell to the entrepreneur at prices which they naturally try to make as high as possible. The entrepreneur proceeds quite otherwise; instead of selling something to the enterprise he identifies himself with the enterprise. Some people doubtless will say that he provides the function of enterprise and receives as remuneration a sum which varies according to the results. But this is a tortured way of presenting the thing, inspired by an unhealthy desire to establish arbitrarily a symmetry with the other factors. In reality, the entrepreneur and the firm are one and the same. His function is to negotiate, or to pay people for negotiating under his responsibility and in the name of the firm, with two groups: on the one hand, with those who provide the factors of production, in which case his problem is to pay the lowest prices possible; on the other hand, with the buyers of the finished products, from which it is desirable to obtain as large a total revenue as possible. To say all this in a few words, the entrepreneur, although undeniably providing a factor of production, perhaps the most important one in a capitalist system, is not himself to be defined in those terms.

Entrepreneurship, in this sense, is embodied in the firm; the decision to be "entrepreneurial" is not a marginal decision, in the sense of supplying one more or one less unit of entrepreneurial services to the firm.[19] Writing of socialism, fascism, and other forms of government intervention in the economy, Mises (1949: 291) describes the struggle of business owners to operate in deteriorating political circumstances. Despite the threat of expropriation and other hazards, entrepreneurs will continue to act. "In the market economy there will always be entrepreneurs. Policies hostile to capitalism may deprive the consumer of the greater part of the benefits they would have reaped

---

[19] Menger's (1871) treatment of the entrepreneur is similar: "The activity of the entrepreneur is recognized by Menger as being unique in that, unlike other goods of higher order, it is not intended for exchange and therefore does not command a price" (Martin, 1979: 279–280).

from unhampered entrepreneurial activities. But they cannot eliminate the entrepreneurs as such if they do not entirely destroy the market economy." As long as there is private ownership, markets, and prices, there is entrepreneurship – regardless of the numbers of start-ups, patents, and the like.

Part of the reason economists speak of the supply of entrepreneurship and the marginal return to entrepreneurship is that they conceive entrepreneurship as an occupational category such as self-employment. An entrepreneur is a person who starts his own business, as opposed to an employee who works for someone else. In this sense it makes sense to talk about entrepreneurship as a factor of production with an upward-sloping supply curve. As profit opportunities increase, relative to wages, more individuals will choose self-employment over employment. If one conceives entrepreneurship as a function such as judgment, however, it cannot be treated as a factor of production and is exercised, as in the Mises quote above, even in the worst market conditions.

Judgment, complementary investments, and the unit of analysis in entrepreneurship research

To repeat, we conceive judgment as decision-making under uncertainty over the use of scarce resources to satisfy future consumer wants. This typically involves making investments that are complementary to the entrepreneur's idea. For reasons we discuss in greater detail in Chapter 7, the entrepreneur will take ownership of at least some of these complementary resources and will control the undertaking of at least some complementary investments. Thus, the entrepreneurial firm may be characterized as the entrepreneur, his specific judgment, and the assets that he owns or otherwise controls. In this section we explore what this means for the unit of analysis in entrepreneurship research.

First, note that the entrepreneurial firm is organized around an unpriced resource bundle (Lippman and Rumelt, 2003a). Thus, while there are factor markets for many of the resources that the entrepreneur controls, his own judgment is not one of those resources. Judgment, as we shall argue in Chapter 7, is non-tradable. Moreover, factor markets cannot easily ascertain how the entrepreneur's judgment complements other resources. It is conceivable that the entrepreneur may be better off if the market could somehow evaluate the entrepreneur's estimated probability, that is, put a price on his judgment. It is not in general wealth-maximizing to control unpriced resources (Foss and Foss, 2005). However, a potential benefit of controlling non-tradable judgment is that it provides an information advantage with respect to understanding the value of the judgment in combination with other resources (Denrell *et al.*, 2003). In this case, resources can be purchased at a price below their net present value (Rumelt, 1987). Thus, fully understanding the returns to judgment requires understanding how judgment complements other resources. It requires considering a bunch of assets or investments.

Second, note that judgment pertains to a number of interrelated activities. The entrepreneur must decide which inputs to purchase, what investments to undertake, which managers to hire, and so on. Many of these decision situations are uncertain in the sense of Knight. Understanding the exercise of judgment requires considering it in the context of a bundle of assets or investments underlying those activities.

These points have implications for the unit of analysis in entrepreneurship research. Contemporary work tends to take the opportunity as the unit of analysis. Shane and Venkataraman (2000: 220) define entrepreneurial opportunities as "those situations in which new goods, services, raw materials, and organizing methods can be introduced and sold at greater than their cost of production." These opportunities are treated as objective phenomena, though their existence is not known to all agents. For Knight, in contrast, opportunities do not *exist*, waiting to be discovered (and hence, by definition, exploited). Rather, entrepreneurs invest resources based on their expectations of future consumer demands and market conditions, investments that may or may not yield positive return. Here the focus is not on opportunities, but on investment and uncertainty. Expectations about the future are inherently subjective and, under conditions of uncertainty rather than risk, constitute judgments that are not themselves modelable. As explained earlier, this means opportunities are neither "discovered" nor "created" (Alvarez and Barney, 2007), but imagined. They may or may not exist, in an objective sense. Opportunities for entrepreneurial gain are inherently subjective, in the sense that they do not exist until profits are realized.[20]

This implies that treating opportunities as the central unit of analysis may not be optimal, as they are difficult to operationalize and measure. Rather, in a Knightian perspective, the unit of analysis should be the assembly of resources in the present in anticipation of (uncertain) receipts in the future, in other words, investments.[21] One way to capture the Knightian concept of entrepreneurial action is the notion of "projects" (Casson and Wadeson, 2007). A project is a stock of resources committed to particular activities for a specified period of time. (Opportunities are defined as potential, but currently inactive, projects.) Focusing on projects, rather than opportunities, implies an emphasis not on opportunity identification, but on opportunity *exploitation*. In other words, this perspective suggests that the key unit of analysis becomes the execution of business plans.

Making investment the unit of analysis suggests links to the real-options approach to the firm (Tong and Reuer, 2007) and an older literature on firms as investments (Gabor and Pearce, 1952, 1958; Vickers, 1970, 1987; Moroney, 1972). These literatures treat capital as not simply another factor that the entrepreneur can purchase at a price representing its marginal productivity, but as the ultimate, decision-making or controlling factor. Investment resources are allocated not to maximize the level of profit in a given project, but to maximize the (expected) rate of return across projects (just as divisionalized firms allocate internal resources across profit centers). If

---

[20] Confusion over the nature of opportunities is increasingly recognized. As noted by McMullen *et al.* (2007: 273): "a good portion of the research to date has focused on the discovery, exploitation, and consequences thereof without much attention to the nature and source of opportunity itself. Although some researchers argue that the subjective or socially constructed nature of opportunity makes it impossible to separate opportunity from the individual, others contend that opportunity is as an objective construct visible to or created by the knowledgeable or attuned entrepreneur. Either way, a set of weakly held assumptions about the nature and sources of opportunity appear to dominate much of the discussion in the literature."

[21] An analogy with economics may be useful here: the analogy with preferences in microeconomic theory is clear – the unit of analysis in consumer theory is not preferences but consumption. In neoclassical production theory the unit of analysis is not the production function but some decision variable.

the entrepreneur-investor's ability to exercise control is limited, then she will not pursue all positive-net-present-value projects, only those she can supervise effectively. Hence individuals who create or discover opportunities, however defined, may be unable to pursue them without close ties to people willing to commit funds to projects. (We discuss this point further in Chapter 9.)

Conclusions

It is not too unfair to say that until the 1980s (i.e., Bewley [1986] and literature growing from this paper), mainstream economists deliberately shied away from uncertainty in its Knightian sense. The uncertainty theme instead became a hallmark of heterodox approaches in economics, notably post-Keynesian and "radical subjectivist" Austrian approaches (Shackle, 1972; O'Driscoll and Rizzo, 1985; Lachmann, 1986), and was most often used as a critical point against mainstream economics rather than as a building block in positive theorizing. This relative neglect of uncertainty is arguably caused by the belief that under uncertainty "anything goes," indicating either the futility of theorizing uncertainty (the traditional mainstream stance) or, because uncertainty is ubiquitous, the irrelevance of the traditional model of rational decision-making (i.e., the expected utility model) (the heterodox stance).

In contrast, important earlier economists – chief among them Knight and Mises – emphasized uncertainty as a necessary ingredient in explanations of profit, and an important part of theorizing about social organization at large. Knight saw uncertainty as a necessary ingredient in understanding the existence of the firm. Knight and Mises also insisted that while uncertainty is ubiquitous, it does not follow that there are no rational grounds for acting. Thus, Knight emphasized judgment, and Mises entrepreneurial "appraisal" (Salerno, 1990a) as cognitive faculties that deal with uncertainty. Drawing on modern entrepreneurship research and its behavioral foundations, we argue that while there is indeed a significant element of "intuition" and "creativity" to judgment (and entrepreneurial appraisal), judgment can still meaningfully be thought of in terms of certain skilled behaviors, developed through experiential learning, and the confidence that one is capable of dealing with uncertain situations. Thus, judgment is not a mysterious black box. In the following chapter, we discuss some of the important means in the entrepreneurial means-ends structure that judgment relates to. These means are capital assets. We argue that the Austrian approach to capital, updated by means of modern notions of property rights and transaction costs, is a useful complement to the judgment theory of entrepreneurship.

5 | *From shmoo to heterogeneous capital*

In the preceding chapters we have highlighted the entrepreneurial function, arguing that the entrepreneurship literature needs to go beyond its current preoccupation with the discovery and evaluation of opportunities, and consider more fully the exploitation of these opportunities through resource ownership and control. The judgment view explicitly highlights this aspect of entrepreneurship, and therefore points to the role of the entrepreneur as an investor, an owner with skin in the game. But we have not yet explored the *context* in which judgmental decision-making takes place. Some perspectives in entrepreneurship research – notably network perspectives (Greve, 2003; Hoang and Antoncic, 2003; Sorenson and Stuart, 2005) and the effectuation view (Sarasvathy, 2008) – strongly emphasize the contextual aspects of entrepreneurship, albeit in very different ways.

In the previous chapter we discussed the epistemological and ontological contexts of judgment as seen by Knight (1921) and Mises (1949). However, we said little about the more concrete contexts, those of markets for inputs and outputs, and even inputs and outputs themselves. In this chapter we argue that the judgment view is naturally aligned with a specific view of capital, one that is often associated with the Austrian school of economics, but also has a strong similarity to certain key perspectives in modern management research, notably the resource-based view of strategy and, to some extent, transaction-cost economics. These perspectives highlight the heterogeneity of capital assets, the benefits of combining them in complementary bundles that generate competitive advantage, and the hazards associated with investments in assets that depend on particular exchange relationships to maintain their value.

Capital, along with land and labor, is one of the basic factors of production familiar to economists. And yet, "capital theory" has lapsed into obscurity in modern economics. Important debates took place between the Austrians and their American critics in the 1930s

105

about whether capital is best conceived as a stock of heterogeneous capital assets or a fund of homogeneous financial capital,[1] and the 1950s and 1960s brought forth the "Cambridge capital controversy" and controversies about "reswitching" and other issues.[2] The growth theory of the 1950s and 1960s discussed the relative roles of capital accumulation and technological innovation (Solow, 1957). In mainstream microeconomics, and particularly in macroeconomics since the Keynesian revolution of the 1930s and 1940s, there is no "view of capital." Modern economics does not really have a theory of capital per se. It may have various theories of investments and interest, but not a theory of capital in the sense of the classical or the Austrian economists (Lewin, 1999; Garrison, 2001). Similarly, as we discuss below, modern management theory is not explicitly founded upon, or even related to, any particular theory of capital.

We argue, however, that most of economics and large parts of management implicitly adopt the view of capital as a homogeneous blob, what we – with a nod to Paul Samuelson and the classic cartoon Lil Abner – call the "shmoo" view of capital (in the cartoon, shmoos are identical creatures, shaped like bowling pins with legs, that can transform into any shape – the liquid-metal Terminator in James Cameron's *Terminator 2: Judgment Day* may provide a more vivid example for younger readers). In this view, capital is a homogenous mass of inputs. In a world of shmoo, as we explain below, problems of economic organization evaporate, and there is little role for entrepreneurs, as we have described them in previous chapters. To fully articulate the function of the entrepreneur and the role of judgment in a market economy, and the need for an entrepreneurial theory of economic organization, we must break from the shmoo view.

Austrian capital theory (ACT), as represented by Menger (1871), Böhm-Bawerk (1884–1912), Hayek (1941), Mises (1949), Lachmann (1956), Kirzner (1967), Lewin (1999), and others, is uniquely positioned to help make this break. Among many economists, the theory has a mixed reputation, in part because of Böhm-Bawerk's ultimately misguided attempt to measure an economy's aggregate capital-intensity in the form of the "average period of production" (see Blaug,

---

[1] Ironically, Knight (1936) was one of the Austrians' strongest critics.
[2] See Pasinetti and Scazzieri (1987), Lavoie (2000), and Cohen and Harcourt (2003).

1997: chapter 12). However, most Austrian capital theorists reject the idea of characterizing an economy's capital structure with a simple metric (e.g., Hayek, 1941) and focus instead on the complex, intricate latticework of resources or assets that constitute the economy's capital stock, and how these resources fit into entrepreneurs' subjective plans.

We begin by showing why it is necessary to make move beyond the confines of the production-function view of the neoclassical theory of production and the even more extreme world of shmoo. We then show that Austrian capital theory is a natural setting for not only the theory of the firm, but also the judgment view of entrepreneurship.

Entrepreneurship and organization in a world of shmoo capital

The production-function view

Modern (neoclassical) economics focuses on a highly stylized model of the production process. The firm is a production function, a "black box" that transforms inputs (land, labor, capital) into output (consumer goods). As organizational economists have argued (Williamson, 1985, 1996), this model omits the critical organizational details of production, rarely looking inside the black box to see how hierarchies are structured, how incentives are provided, how workers are monitored, how teams are organized, and the like. An equally serious omission is the unrealistic portrayal of production itself. Capabilities theorists of the firm have long drawn attention to this. For example, Richardson (1972: 888) criticized the production-function view for ignoring "the roles of organization, knowledge, experience and skills," and later writers in this tradition have echoed Richardson's misgivings (e.g., Nelson and Winter, 1982; Demsetz, 1988a). For example, Langlois and Foss (1999) argue that the problem with the production function is not so much the functional representation (e.g., Cobb-Douglas functions) as the attendant assumption that the knowledge of production is explicit, easily transferable and imitable – blueprint knowledge, in other words. This makes it difficult to account for firm heterogeneity.

To a certain extent, these critiques all boil down to the basic theme of this chapter, the homogeneity or heterogeneity of the resources that underlie production: If these resources are identical, within and across firms, the problem of organization, and hence the theory of the firm, is trivial, and we have no explanation for systematic differences in firm performance – hence, virtually all of strategic management and large parts of management in general are trivialized. Likewise, more fundamental economic issues, such as the feasibility of central economic planning analyzed by Mises (1920), Hayek (1945), Hurwicz (1972), and many others are rendered moot.

Austrian business cycle theory adds an additional, more specific critique, namely that production unfolds through time, involving a series of temporally specific, causally linked stages and a complex latticework of inputs and intermediate outputs – a radical departure from the conventional, production-function view in which inputs are transformed into final goods in a single stage. The Austrian view implies that heterogeneity is an important aspect of capital, as capital goods differ across (and possibly within) the multiple stages of production that constitute the economy's capital structure. It also translates into an organization problem: Somehow, independently taken decisions that involve relations between complementary capital goods must be coordinated; plan coordination problems that don't arise in a world of homogenous capital become highly important.[3] All these issues disappear in the world of shmoo capital, a particularly simple version of the production-function view.

Shmoo capital and its implications

Following Solow (1957), models of economic growth typically model capital as shmoo – an infinitely elastic, fully moldable factor that can be substituted costlessly from one production process to another. "Capital" is treated as a homogeneous factor of production, the K that appears in the production function along with L for labor.

In a world of shmoo capital economic organization is relatively unimportant. All capital assets possess the same attributes, and thus

---

[3] Foss (1996b) argues that Hayek's recognition of these intertemporal coordination problems was the real driver behind his "transformation" (Caldwell, 1988), that is, his change from a Walrasian to a process view (Hayek, 1937).

the costs of inspecting, measuring, and monitoring the attributes of productive assets is trivial. Exchange markets for capital assets would be virtually devoid of transaction costs. A few basic contractual problems – in particular, principal-agent conflicts over the supply of labor services – may remain, though workers would all use identical capital assets, and this would greatly contribute to reducing the costs of measuring their productivity. Thus, shmoo capital is close to being a substitute for a zero-transaction-cost assumption.

While transaction costs would not disappear entirely in such a world, asset ownership would be relatively unimportant. The possibility of specifying all possible uses of an asset significantly reduces the costs of writing complete, contingent contracts between resource owners and entrepreneurs governing the uses of the relevant assets.[4] Contracts would largely substitute for ownership, leaving the boundary of the firm indeterminate (Hart, 1995).

Similarly, in a world of shmoo capital the entrepreneur is relatively unimportant. It may be that there would be a role of Kirznerian entrepreneurs, equilibrating consumer goods markets. However, if capital were a single "good" with one price, the entrepreneur would only have to choose between capital-intensive and labor-intensive production methods (or among types of labor). Only trivial "calculation problems" (Mises, 1949) and problems of "entrepreneurial appraisal" (Salerno, 1999) would exist in such a world. Thus, in a shmoo world, decision problems would be trivialized as all capital goods possess the same attributes, and thus the costs of inspecting, measuring, and monitoring the attributes of productive assets would be trivial (Barzel, 1997). Finally, a world of homogenous capital is a non-complex world, one in which decision-makers do not reach the bounds of their rationality (Simon, 1955). In contrast, in the world of Austrian capital theory the entrepreneur's primary function is to choose among the various combinations of substitutable and complementary inputs that

---

[4] Contracts might still be incomplete because contracting parties have different, subjective expectations about the likelihood of various contingencies affecting the value of the (homogeneous) capital asset. Agents may also differ in their ability to learn about possible uses of the capital good. In other words, Knightian uncertainty plus bounded rationality could drive contractual incompleteness even in a world without capital heterogeneity. However, the neoclassical world of shmoo capital is characterized by parametric uncertainty, common priors, and hyperrationality.

are suitable for producing particular goods (and to decide whether these goods should be produced at all) based on current prices for the factors and expected future prices of the final goods. It is a complex and uncertain world. As we have argued, building on Knight (1921), it is a world that requires the exercise of judgment.

Heterogeneous capital in the theory of the firm

Implicitly, some of the above points are recognized in extant theories of the firm. Thus, all modern theories of the firm assume (often implicitly) that at least some capital assets are heterogeneous, so that all assets are not equally valuable in all uses. Here we briefly review how capital heterogeneity leads to non-trivial contracting problems, the solutions to which may require the creation of a firm.

Asset specificity approaches. In transaction cost economics (TCE) (Williamson, 1975, 1985, 1996) and the "new" property-rights approach (Grossman and Hart, 1986; Hart and Moore, 1990), some assets are conceived as specific to particular users. If complete, contingent contracts specifying the most valuable uses of such assets in all possible states of the world cannot be written, then owners of productive assets face certain risks. Primarily, if circumstances change unexpectedly, the original governing agreement may no longer be effective. The need to adapt to unforeseen contingencies constitutes an important cost of contracting. Failure to adapt imposes what Williamson (1991a) calls "maladaptation costs," the best known of which is the "holdup" problem associated with relationship-specific investments.

It is obvious that maladaptation costs largely disappear if all assets are equally valuable in all uses. Potential holdup would still be a concern for owners of relationship-specific human capital and raw materials, but disagreements over the efficient use of capital goods would become irrelevant.[5] The scope of entrepreneurial activity would also be severely reduced, since entrepreneurs would have no need to arrange particular combinations of capital assets.

---

[5] Resources that are *initially* homogenous could become heterogeneous over time, through learning by doing or co-specialization of human and physical capital. Here we refer to conditions of permanent homogeneity.

Resource- and knowledge-based approaches. The idea that resources, firms, and industries are different from each other, that capital and labor are specialized for particular projects and activities, that people (human capital), etc. are distinct, is ubiquitous in the theory and practice of management. In particular, resource-based (Barney, 1991; Lippman and Rumelt, 2003a; Wernerfelt, 1984) and knowledge-based (Grant, 1996; Penrose, 1959) approaches emphasize capital heterogeneity. The focus on heterogeneity of resources, including knowledge and managerial ability, in strategy and organization theory stems from heterogeneity being a critical determinant of competitive advantage (Barney, 1991). Superior profitability is seen as emerging from bundles of resources, with different resource bundles associated with different efficiencies. As a consequence, management scholars think of firms as bundles of heterogeneous resources, assets, or activities. These assets have different (economic) life expectancies. Such unique and specialized assets can also be intangible, such as worker-specific knowledge or firm-specific capabilities (Barney, 1986; Dierickx and Cool, 1989). These assets can be specific to certain firms, and "co-specialized" with other assets, such that they generate value only in certain combinations (Teece, 2009). Further, resource- and knowledge-based scholars often emphasize that heterogeneous assets per se do not give rise independently to competitive advantages. Rather, it is the interactions among these resources, their relations of specificity and co-specialization, that generate such advantages (e.g., Teece, 1986; Dierickx and Cool, 1989; Barney, 1991; Black and Boal, 1994). These interactions, coupled with path-dependent outcomes of past strategic investments in heterogeneous resources (Nelson and Winter, 1982), imply that heterogeneity, rather than homogeneity, is the hallmark characteristic of resources and firm organization of these resources.

"Old" property-rights theory. A sophisticated approach to capital heterogeneity can be drawn from the property-rights approach associated with economists such as Coase (1960), Demsetz (1964, 1967), Alchian (1965), and, particularly, Barzel (1997). These writers focus not on individual assets per se, but on bundles of asset attributes to which property rights may be held (Foss and Foss, 2001).

While it is common to view capital heterogeneity in terms of physical heterogeneity – beer barrels and blast furnaces are different because of their physical differences – the old property-rights approach emphasizes that capital goods are heterogeneous because they have different levels and kinds of valued attributes (in the terminology of Barzel, 1997).[6] Attributes are characteristics, functions, or possible uses of assets, as perceived by an entrepreneur. For example, a copying machine has multiple attributes because it can be used at different times, by different people, and for different types of copying work; that it can be purchased in different colors and sizes; and so on.[7] Property rights to the machine itself can be partitioned, in the sense that rights to its attributes can be defined and traded, depending on transaction costs (Foss and Foss, 2001). We later draw on this approach to develop insights into heterogeneity of capital.

Summing up. While capital heterogeneity thus plays an important role in transaction-cost, resource-based, and property-rights approaches to the firm, none of these approaches rests on a unified, systematic theory of capital. Instead, each invokes the needed specificities in an ad hoc fashion to rationalize particular trading problems for transaction cost economics, asset specificity; for capabilities theories, tacit knowledge; and so on. Some writers (Demsetz, 1988c; Langlois and Foss, 1999; Winter, 1988) argue that the economics of organization has shown a tendency (albeit an imperfect one) to respect an implicit dichotomy between production and exchange. Thus, as Langlois and Foss (1999) argue, there is an implicit agreement that the production-function approach with its attendant assumptions (e.g., blueprint, knowledge) tells us what we need to know about production, so theories of the firm can focus on transacting and how transactional hazards can be mitigated by organization. Production issues, including capital theory, never really take center stage. This is problematic if production itself reveals problems of transacting that may influence economic organization.

---

[6] Foss and Foss (2005) link the property-rights approach to the resource-based view, demonstrating how the more "micro" approach of the property-rights approach provides additional insights into resource value. See also Kim and Mahoney (2002, 2005) for similar arguments.

[7] Clearly, this notion of subjectively perceived attributes of capital assets is related to Penrose's (1959) point that physically identical capital assets may yield different *services*, depending on, for example, the nature of the administrative framework in which they are embedded.

Austrian capital theory: an overview

Time and heterogeneity

The Austrian school of economics does have a systematic, comprehensive theory of capital, though it has not generally been applied to the business firm.[8] Instead, most of the substantial literature on Austrian capital theory focuses on the economy's overall capital structure and how money and credit markets affect the allocation of resources across different stages of the production process.[9]

The concept of heterogeneous capital has a long and distinguished place in Austrian economics.[10] Early Austrian writers argued that capital has a time dimension as well as a value dimension. Carl Menger (1871), founder of the Austrian school, characterized goods in terms of "orders": goods of lowest order are those consumed directly. Tools and machines used to produce those consumption goods are of a higher order, and the capital goods used to produce the tools and machines are of an even higher order. Building on his theory that the value of all goods is determined by their ability to satisfy consumer wants (i.e., their marginal utility), Menger showed that the value of the higher-order goods is given or "imputed" by the value of the lower-order goods they produce. Moreover, because certain capital goods are themselves produced by other, higher-order capital goods, it follows that capital goods are not identical, at least by the time they are employed in the production process. The claim is not that there is no substitution among capital goods, but that the degree of substitution is limited; as Lachmann (1956) put it, capital goods are characterized by "multiple specificity." Some substitution is possible, but only at a cost. It is fundamentally because capital in an Austrian world is not shmoo and there

---

[8] Of the several dozen papers on Austrian economics and the theory of the firm (including, for instance, the papers collected in Foss and Klein, 2002), only a few deal with Austrian capital theory (see Yu, 1999; Chiles *et al.*, 2004; Lewin, 2005, and various papers by the present authors).

[9] Hayek's 1974 Nobel Prize in economics was awarded for his technical work on the business cycle and not, as is commonly believed, for his later work on knowledge and "spontaneous order." For a modern restatement of Austrian business cycle theory, see Garrison (2001).

[10] For overviews see Strigl (1934), Kirzner (1966), and Lewin (1999).

are relations of (intertemporal) specificity and complementarity that capital forms a structure in the Austrian view.

Hayek's *Prices and Production* (1931a) introduced the famous "Hayekian triangles" to illustrate the relationship between the value of capital goods and their place in the temporal sequence of production. Because production takes time, factors of production must be committed in the present for making final goods that will have value only in the future after they are sold. However, capital is heterogeneous. As capital goods are used in production, they are transformed from general-purpose materials and components to intermediate products specific to particular final goods. Consequently, these assets cannot be easily redeployed to alternative uses if demands for final goods change. The central macroeconomic problem in a modern capital-using economy is thus one of *intertemporal coordination*: How can the allocation of resources between capital and consumer goods be aligned with consumers' preferences between present and future consumption? In *The Pure Theory of Capital* (1941) Hayek describes how the economy's structure of production depends on the characteristics of capital goods – durability, complementarity, substitutability, specificity, and so on. This structure can be described by the various "investment periods" of inputs, an extension of Böhm-Bawerk's notion of "roundaboutness," the degree to which production uses resources over time.

The development of Austrian capital theory has been marked by the struggle to develop consistent analytical categories and aggregate measures for a class of goods that are fundamentally heterogeneous. In general, Austrian writers have moved away from relatively aggregate concepts emphasized by Böhm-Bawerk (1884–1912) towards increasingly disaggregated ones that are more consistent with Austrian methodological individualism and subjectivism (Lewin, 1999). Böhm-Bawerk tried to characterize the economy's capital structure in terms of its physical attributes. He attempted to describe the temporal "length" of the structure of production by a single number, the "average period of production." This attempt was sharply criticized by John Bates Clark (1893) and by Menger himself (who called Böhm-Bawerk's capital theory "one of the greatest errors ever committed" (Schumpeter, 1954: 847 n8)). Later Austrian approaches (e.g., Kirzner, 1966) avoid these difficulties by defining capital assets in terms of subjective, individual *production plans*, plans that are formulated and continually revised by profit-seeking entrepreneurs. Capital goods should thus be characterized, not by their physical properties, but by their place in the structure of production *as conceived by entrepreneurs*. The actual place of any capital good in the time sequence of production is given by the market for capital goods, in which entrepreneurs bid for factors of production in anticipation of future consumer demands. This subjectivist, entrepreneurial approach to capital assets is particularly congenial to theories of the firm that focus on entrepreneurship and the ownership of assets.

As Lewin (2005) rightly points out, one of the main contributions of post-Böhm-Bawerkian Austrian capital theory, including Hayek (1941), Lachmann (1956), and Kirzner (1966), is the emphasis on the structure dimensions of the capital stock rather than on the aggregate value dimension or notions such as roundaboutness. Lewin makes the case that the doctrinal history of economics demonstrates two very different approaches to capital theory, one structuralist (associated with Smith, Menger, Hayek, and Lachmann) and one quantitative (associated with Ricardo, Böhm-Bawerk, and Solowian growth theory). In the latter approach, capital goods are not necessarily assumed to be homogenous, but there is a claim that they can be made commensurable in value terms, aggregated together, and that this aggregate result has economic significance. There is no particular emphasis on the relations between capital goods.[11]

This understanding of capital as a complex structure formed the basis of the Austrian theory of the business cycle (Mises, 1912; Hayek, 1931a). Monetary injections, by lowering the rate of interest below its "natural rate," distort the economy's intertemporal structure of production. The reduction in interest rates caused by credit expansion directs resources toward capital-intensive processes and early stages of production (whose investment demands are more interest-rate elastic), thus "lengthening" the period of production. Investments in some stages of production are "malinvestments" if they do not help to align

---

[11] In long-run equilibrium or full intertemporal equilibrium (à la Debreu, 1959) the structuralist and the quantitative approaches become identical in their economic implications.

the structure of production to consumers' intertemporal preferences. The boom generated by the increase in investment is artificial; eventually, market participants come to realize that there are not enough savings to complete all the new projects, and the boom becomes a bust as these malinvestments are discovered and liquidated. The concept of "malinvestment" is foreign to neoclassical production theory (as well as mainstream macroeconomics), which usually considers only the *level* of investment. Modern production theory focuses on a single stage of production in which "capital," along with other inputs, is transformed into final goods. As we argue next, this limits the explanatory power of theories, such as modern macroeconomics, that are based on this conception of capital.

Capital heterogeneity: an attributes approach

Understanding capital heterogeneity

The Austrian approach to capital generated considerable controversy, both within the school itself and between the Austrians and rival schools of economic thought. Given the attention devoted to the problem of measuring a heterogeneous capital stock, it is surprising that relatively little analytical effort has been devoted to the concept of heterogeneity itself. The notion of heterogeneous capital is crucial not just for Austrian capital theory, but for (Austrian) economics in general. For example, the Austrian position in the socialist calculation debate of the 1930s (Hayek, 1933; Mises, 1920) is based on an entrepreneurial concept of the market process, one in which the entrepreneur's primary function is to choose among the various combinations of factors suitable for producing particular goods (and to decide whether these goods should be produced at all), based on current prices for the factors and expected future prices of the final goods. If capital is shmoo with one price, then entrepreneurship is reduced to choosing between shmoo-intensive and labor-intensive production methods (or among types of labor), a problem a central planner could potentially solve. The failure of socialism, in Mises' (1920) formulation, follows precisely from the complexity of the economy's capital structure, and the subsequent need for entrepreneurial appraisal. As Lachmann (1956: 16) points out, real-world entrepreneurship consists primarily of choosing among combinations of capital assets:

[T]he entrepreneur's function ... is to specify and make decisions on the concrete form the capital resources shall have. He specifies and modifies the layout of his plant. ... As long as we disregard the heterogeneity of capital, the true function of the entrepreneur must also remain hidden. ◦

Unfortunately, the implications of capital heterogeneity for entrepreneurship have received relatively little attention in the Austrian literature. Böhm-Bawerk's approach to capital theory, which tends to obscure heterogeneity among capital goods *within* given levels of the overall structure of production, focused attention on the characteristics of the aggregate capital stock. Hayek's (1941) more complex (and microeconomic) treatment has remained relatively obscure. However, Kirzner's argument that capital goods are heterogeneous not because of their objective characteristics, but because they play particular roles within the entrepreneur's overall production plan, further developed the link between entrepreneurship and capital heterogeneity.

A generalization of the Kirznerian view is that capital goods are distinguished by their attributes, as discussed above. Entrepreneurs perceive and evaluate attributes as part of their subjective production plans.[12] Property-rights theorists often highlight that most assets have multiple attributes (Coase, 1960; Cheung, 1970; Barzel, 1997; Demsetz, 1988a), including the different functionalities and services or uses (Penrose, 1959) that the resources can offer. For example, a copying machine is a multi-attribute resource in the sense that it can be used in different time periods, by many different persons, for many different types of copying work, can be purchased in different colors, sizes, etc.[13] Specificity and complementarity – key notions in both Austrian capital theory and modern theories of economic organization (Williamson, 1985, 1996; Hart, 1995) – are more

[12] In other words, they go beyond Lancasterian characteristics that are of a more objective character.
[13] Foss and Foss (2005) argue that the understanding of asset value is improved by conceptualizing capital assets or resources as bundles of attributes to which property rights may be delineated, enforced, and exchanged. This builds on the recognition that it is not resources themselves that are valuable, but their attributes. Understanding attributes and the extent to which property rights can be delineated, enforced, and exchanged add increased insight into resource value and value appropriation.

abstract examples of attributes. In our terminology, capital assets are heterogeneous to the extent that they have different, and different levels of, valued attributes. (In contrast, shmoo has the same attributes regardless of the specific shmoo asset one considers.) Attributes may also vary over time, even for a particular asset. In a world of "true" uncertainty, entrepreneurs are unlikely to know all relevant attributes of all assets when production decisions are made. Nor can the future attributes of an asset, as it is used in production, be forecast with certainty. Future attributes must be *discovered* over time, as assets are used in production. As Alchian and Demsetz (1972: 793, original emphasis) note, "[e]fficient production with heterogeneous resources is a result not of having *better* resources but in *knowing more accurately* the relative productive performances of those resources." Contra the production-function view in basic neoclassical economics, such knowledge is not *given*, but has to be created or discovered. In other words, heterogeneity is an endogenous outcome of entrepreneurial activities.

Endogenous heterogeneity

To illustrate some of these notions, consider the following economic history example (see Foss and Foss, 2008). On November 24, 1874 United States Patent #157,124 was granted to Joseph Glidden of DeKalb, Illinois for improved barbed wire fencing. Glidden's patent was only the culmination of a series of nine patents for improvements to wire fencing that were granted by the US Patent Office to American inventors, beginning with Michael Kelly in November 1868 and ending with Glidden's patent (McCallum and McCallum, 1965) which quickly became dominant. To be sure, wire fencing had been used for a very long time. However, property rights over livestock were less secure, as wire fencing would often break under the impact of heavy livestock pressing against the fencing. This would not happen with barbed wire, and the costs at which property rights to livestock could be protected therefore fell dramatically (Dennen, 1976; Anderson and Hill, 2004).

The new fencing innovation set in motion dramatic path-dependent processes of institutional, organizational, and technological innovations throughout the Plains. Indeed, it has been argued that the emergence of barbed wire was as important a factor behind changing the life at the Plains as the rifle, telegraph, and locomotive (Webb, 1931). Arguably, barbed wire was *the* crucial factor underlying the transformation from ranching to farming, as the new fencing protected crops from livestock and meant that fields could be used as pasture after the harvest. Barbed wire ended the great cattle drives and the need for branding. Cattle could be kept at a limited area, which greatly increased the value to agricultural firms (farms) of this resource (Webb, 1931). It prompted experimentation with new, more valuable resources, notably the Shorthorn, Angus, and the Hereford, as substitutes for the tougher, but less valuable Longhorn, as well as with the uses of land.

This example implies that capital assets (e.g., land) hold a number of potential uses, characteristics, etc., and that some of these attributes may not yet have been discovered.

Heterogeneous capital and ownership

Focusing on attributes not only helps sharpen the understanding of the concept of heterogeneous capital, but also illuminates the vast literature on property rights and ownership. Barzel (1997) stresses that property rights are held over attributes,[14] and property rights to *known* attributes of assets are the relevant units of analysis in his work. In contrast, he dismisses the notion of asset ownership as essentially legal and extra-economic. Similarly, Demsetz argues that the notion of "full private ownership" over assets is "vague," and "must always remain so," because "there is an infinity of potential rights of actions that can be owned ... It is impossible to describe the complete set of rights that are potentially ownable" (Demsetz, 1988b: 19). Thus, most assets have unspecified, not-yet-discovered attributes.

We add that an important function of entrepreneurship is to create or discover these attributes. In fact, entrepreneurship creates (contra Demsetz) a distinct role for asset ownership, that is, for holding title to a bundle of existing attributes as well as to future attributes.

---

[14] Barzel (1994: 394; emphasis in original) defines a property right as "an individual's net valuation, in expected terms, of the ability to directly consume the services of the asset, or to consume it indirectly through exchange. A key word is *ability*: The definition is concerned not with what people are legally entitled to do but with what they believe they can do." Thus, property rights are essentially defined in a subjectivist manner, in terms of expectations and self-perceived ability.

Specifically, ownership is a low-cost means of allocating the rights to attributes of assets that are created or discovered by the entrepreneur-owner. Those individuals who create or discover new knowledge have an incentive to use it directly because it is costly to transfer knowledge to others. In a well-functioning legal system, ownership of an asset normally implies that the courts will not interfere when an entrepreneur-owner captures the value of newly created or discovered attributes of an asset he owns. Consequently, the entrepreneur-owner can usually avoid costly negotiation with those who are affected by his creation or discovery. This keeps the dissipation of value at bay. Of course, asset ownership itself provides a powerful incentive to create or discover new attributes, as ownership conveys the legally recognized (and at least partly enforced) right to the income of an asset, including the right to income from new attributes (Littlechild, 1986). Moreover, ownership simplifies the process of entrepreneurial arbitrage (Kirzner, 1973, 1997) – and hence helps to close pockets of ignorance in the market – by allowing entrepreneurs to acquire, in one transaction, a bundle of rights to attributes (i.e., a distinct asset). This means that the parties need not engage in costly bargaining over many rights to single attributes. The dissipation of value is thus minimized.

The idea of heterogeneous capital is thus a natural complement to the Austrian theory of entrepreneurship. Entrepreneurs who seek to create or discover new attributes of capital assets will want ownership titles to the relevant assets, both for speculative reasons and for reasons of economizing on transaction costs. These arguments provide room for entrepreneurship that goes beyond deploying a superior combination of capital assets with "given" attributes, acquiring the relevant assets, and deploying these to producing for a market: Entrepreneurship may also be a matter of *experimenting* with capital assets in an attempt to discover new valued attributes. Such experimental activity may take place in the context of trying out new combinations through the acquisition of or merger with another firm, or in the form of trying out new combinations of assets already under the control of the entrepreneur. The entrepreneur's success in experimenting with assets in this manner may depend on whether his judgment is borne out by the facts, along with secondary factors such as transaction costs in the market for corporate control, internal transaction costs, the entrepreneur's control over the relevant assets, how much of the expected return from experimental activity that he can hope to appropriate, and so on. These latter factors are key determinants of economic organization in modern theories of the firm. As we argue in greater detail in the following chapters, this suggests that there may be fruitful complementarities between the theory of economic organization, which is essentially a theory about the arrangements of property titles that create an efficient employment of capital assets, and Austrian theories of capital heterogeneity and entrepreneurship.

Entrepreneurial judgment in the context of a complex capital structure

Capital as a complex structure

As Lewin (2005) argues, a structure of capital goods becomes a structure rather than just a list of heterogeneous capital goods because it is possible to say something about the overall structure from inspection of a few (possibly typical) capital goods and knowledge of principles of composition. This indicates that a capital structure may have systemic properties. We argue that a natural complement to structural Austrian capital theory is the theory of complex systems associated with Simon (1962) and Kauffman (1993) (for various social science applications, see Levinthal, 1997; Fleming, 2001; Langlois, 2003; Nickerson and Zenger, 2004).

Simon (1962) defines "complexity" as obtaining when a large number of parts "interact in a nonsimple way" (1962: 468). Such complexity frequently takes the form of a hierarchy, that is, as a system that is composed of interrelated (complementary) subsystems. Each one of these subsystems is, in turn, hierarchical in nature, until some elementary subsystem is reached at the lowest level. "In hierarchic systems," Simon explains, "... we can distinguish between the interactions *among* subsystems on the one hand, and the interactions *within* subsystems – i.e., among the parts of those subsystems – on the other" (1962: 473, original emphasis). This forms the basis for the often cited distinction between *decomposable* systems, in which the interactions among the subsystems are negligible; *non-decomposable* systems, in which the interactions among the subsystems are essential; and *nearly decomposable* systems, in which the interactions among the subsystems are weak, but not negligible (1962: 474, original emphasis).[15]

The relevance of these distinctions to Austrian capital theory is indicated by, for example, the reinterpretation of the Böhm-Bawerkian concept of roundaboutness by Hayek (1941) and Lachmann (1956) in which increasing roundaboutness is conceptualized as an increasing number of capital goods with more complex interactions (typically an increasing number of relations of complementarity and specificity). Thus, increasing roundaboutness implies that the overall capital structure becomes less "decomposable," in Simon's terms. Simon's (1962) main aim is to explain an important aspect of the ontology of the social and natural world. However, there is also an epistemological dimension to his discussion. Thus, he points out that an important aspect of what makes the social and natural world comprehensible is that they often involve phenomena that may be represented as nearly decomposable hierarchies; for example, "[s]ubparts belonging to different parts only interact in an aggregative fashion – the detail of their interaction can be ignored" (1962: 477). We can understand the system exactly because we can ignore these "details"; if we also had to comprehend the details it would be "beyond our capacities of memory and computation" (1962: 477) to understand the full system. In other words, the epistemological problem of comprehending a complex system is eased when the system is decomposable or nearly decomposable.

An important implication is that systems, such as capital structures, that are close to the non-decomposable end of the spectrum may be hard to comprehend. In terms of later complexity research (e.g., Kauffman, 1993), the "landscape" of combinations of elements may have multiple peaks. More generally, a landscape is a mapping of how combinations of certain entities perform in terms of some metric. For example, theoretical biologists construct fitness landscapes that map gene combinations into fitness values. One may in an analogous manner think of a landscape of combinations of capital goods that are mapped into (appropriable) monetary values. Finding the optimal (highest) peak in such a landscape may be far from trivial. In general, work on search in complex systems (Levinthal, 1997; Fleming,

---

[15] For an application to the theory of the firm with broadly Austrian features, see Langlois (2002).

2001) demonstrates how the overall performance of the search effort is highly dependent on the characteristics of the system, specifically whether the system is decomposable, non-decomposable, or nearly decomposable. In particular, search in systems that lie close to the non-decomposable end of the spectrum is a tough undertaking, particularly when the search methods are primitive (e.g., gradient search), because in such systems the landscape of combinations of elements has multiple peaks (in extreme cases, this may produce what Kauffman (1993) calls a "complexity catastrophe").[16] This is consistent with the finding that firms often find it difficult to comprehend "architectural" knowledge, that is, knowledge of the multiple links between product components (Henderson and Clark, 1990). On the other hand, in strongly decomposed systems, the landscape may be single-peaked, so that even simple learning modes may quickly reach the peak.

Another related point is the notion that complex relations of complementarity between multiple resources or capital goods may be an important independent barrier to competitive imitation, even if all of the individual resources are perfectly imitable (Rivkin, 2000). A third implication is that there is a distinction between the interdependencies between elements or capital goods in a system or structure that are given to an omniscient observer and those interdependencies that can be seen or imagined by an agent such as a real-world entrepreneur.

Heterogeneous capital and entrepreneurial judgment

In the world of shmoo, landscapes would be entirely flat as any combination of shmoo capital would be as good as any other one. This obviously trivializes entrepreneurship. However, while heterogeneous capital seems to be a necessary condition for the existence of the entrepreneurial function we have described in the preceding chapter, it is not sufficient. As Schumpeter (1911), Knight (1921), and Mises (1949) argued, there would be nothing to do for the entrepreneur in general equilibrium. Indeed, in a full intertemporal equilibrium (Hayek, 1928; Debreu, 1959) whether capital was shmoo or heterogeneous would be irrelevant to the understanding of entrepreneurship. The reason is that in this setting, all possible combinations of capital

---

[16] The height of peaks may here be taken as a measure of the profitability implications of a given combination of capital goods.

goods would be priced, and all prices would perfectly reflect scarcities (Denrell *et al.*, 2003). Imputation would be perfect. Under these circumstances, there would be no need for entrepreneurs who, based on their speculative appraisals, could test alternative combinations of capital goods in the marketplace (Mises, 1949; Salerno, 1999).[17] There would be no need for any search in the landscape of combinations of capital goods, as the highest peaks would be immediately visible to entrepreneurs. This is what Lippman and Rumelt (1982; 2003a) call "full strategic equilibrium" which maximizes surplus across the set of all possible assignments of all possible resources to all possible tasks.[18]

However, with a very different social ontology, one characterized by dispersed knowledge (Hayek, 1948), genuine uncertainty (Knight, 1921; Mises, 1949), bounded rationality (Simon, 1955), and sheer ignorance (Kirzner, 1973), current prices *cannot* reflect all combinations of complementary capital goods, that is, all their "multiple specificities." Some combinations are simply not imagined by anyone (Shackle, 1972). Many forward markets are closed because of the transaction costs implied by dispersed knowledge, bounded rationality, and ignorance (Bewley, 1986; Makowski and Ostroy, 2001).

In such a setting entrepreneurial activity has, in a broad sense, a "search" component. With capital heterogeneity, peaks emerge in the landscape of combinations of capital assets. As the capital structure becomes increasingly complex, the landscape becomes increasingly multi-peaked. Of course, with full information and perfect foresight, all entrepreneurs would enjoy a clear view of the "objectively" existing fitness landscape. In actuality, however, entrepreneurs have only an imperfect model or theory (Choi, 1993; Harper, 1995) of the profitability implications of alternative combinations of capital goods. This is, of course, what is involved in notions of entrepreneurial appraisal and judgment. As Lachmann (1956: 3) notes, "[t]he 'best' mode of

---

[17] There wouldn't be a role for competitive advantage either. Hence, Lippman and Rumelt (2003a: 1085) argue that "the heart of business management and strategy concerns the creation, evaluation, manipulation, administration, and deployment of *unpriced* specialized resource combinations."

[18] Lippman and Rumelt (2003a: 1982) note in passing that "[t]he number of such combinations, in the real world, is literally noncomputable. The idea that firms actually operate at the maximum within this space is not credible."

complementarity is ... not a 'datum.' It is in no way 'given' to the entrepreneur who, on the contrary, as a rule has to spend a good deal of time and effort in finding out what it is."

Thus, the entrepreneur undertakes search in the space of possible combinations of capital assets. Search efforts may or may not give rise to the creation or discovery of valuable capital combinations. In the literature on complex systems, search outcomes (such as valuable capital combinations) are usually said to depend on the mode of search (Levinthal, 1997) – for example, whether search takes place through incremental, trial-and-error search ("gradient search") or whether it takes place based on explicit theories of cause-effect ("heuristic search") – and, as already indicated, on the nature of the landscape over which search takes place. A potential Austrian critique of much of the complexity literature is that it often "dumbs down" human agents, portraying them for example as engaging in trial and error search with virtually no foresight. This is arguably quite true, but a broader conclusion from the literature is that, as a general rule, search modes should be matched to the characteristics of the landscape of combinations of knowledge elements in a discriminating manner. As indicated already, simple search modes will usually not suffice to discover the most valuable combinations of knowledge elements in multi-peaked landscapes. A "simple search mode" may be defined as one that makes no a priori assumptions about which knowledge elements are in the search space, how they may be connected, and the implications in terms of appropriable value. In this mode, search begins at an essentially arbitrary place and proceeds by means of trial and error. Search and learning becomes increasingly sophisticated as decision-makers make explicit assumptions about which elements are relevant and how elements connect.

The role of experience

The search mode that entrepreneurs will apply and the judgments they will form are determined by their theories of the complexity of the problem they face (i.e., the architecture of the landscape of capital combinations) (Choi, 1993). This, in turn, is influenced by the entrepreneur's past experience. Shane (2000) argues and empirically demonstrates that entrepreneurial judgment is influenced by experience because experience influences interpretation of the "facts." In a similar vein, Lachmann argues that experience is the "raw material out of which all expectations are formed" (Lachmann, 1956: 21).

In the management research literature on entrepreneurship, experiential knowledge is taken to include such things as "prior knowledge about markets," "prior knowledge about how to serve markets," "prior knowledge of customer problems," etc. (e.g., Shane, 2000). A parallel research stream emphasizes how experiential knowledge on the firm level gives rise to innovation (e.g., Helfat, 1997; Mosakowski, 1998; Helfat and Raubitschek, 2000; Matsusaka, 2001; Mitchell *et al.*, 2002; Lumpkin and Lichtenstein, 2005). In this literature, experiential knowledge concerns the understanding of the uses, functionalities, services, characteristics, etc. of firm resources, that is, knowledge of resource attributes (Foss and Foss, 2005). Such knowledge emerges from "resource learning" (Penrose, 1959; Mahoney, 1995), that is, human resources learning about the services of other (human and non-human) resources. Experiential knowledge shapes the building of categories and representations that assist entrepreneurs in decision-making (Nisbett and Ross, 1980; Abelson and Black, 1986; Day and Lord, 1992; Gaglio and Katz, 2001). A deep level of expertise within a certain information domain allows people to faster categorize ill-structured problems. Also, deep knowledge may provide an entrepreneur with more detailed ways of understanding and describing his or her resources (Hodgkinson and Johnson, 1994; Rensch *et al.*, 1994), and thereby assist the creation or discovery of new resource attributes. Thus, experiential knowledge from resource learning may underlie path-dependent trajectories of innovative activity in established firms (Helfat, 1994; Helfat and Raubitschek, 2000), and be a source of sustained competitive advantage for such firms (Dierickx and Cool, 1989; Mahoney, 1995).

Transaction costs and the direction of entrepreneurial search

As we noted earlier, individual resources may have a multitude of undiscovered attributes, some of which may be associated with appropriable value (Demsetz, 1988a; Denrell *et al.*, 2003). A determinant of the appropriable value from newly discovered resource attributes is whether the discoverer can delineate and enforce property rights to his new discovery. In turn, this depends on the transaction cost of delineating and enforcing property rights.

A crucial insight of the economics of property rights is that transactions involve the exchange of property rights rather than the exchange of goods per se (Coase, 1960, 1988). Hence, the unit of analysis in this perspective is the individual property right. Property rights consist of the right to consume, obtain income from, and alienate resource attributes (Alchian, 1965). The economics of property rights dissociates property rights from legal connotations, so that an (economic) property right is more about the actual *ability* of an agent to consume, obtain income from, and alienate resource attributes than to whether he is legally entitled to do so, that is, it is about *effective control* (see Barzel, 1997). (Obviously, however, such ability is likely to be influenced by the extent to which property rights are legally enforceable.) In this perspective, transaction costs can be defined in a consistent manner, namely as the costs of delineating, enforcing, and exchanging property rights (Coase, 1960; Barzel, 1997). Property rights may be enforced by the state as well as by private means (Barzel, 1997), as in the case of the barbed wire example. When rights are perfectly enforced, owners can completely hinder non-payers from taking possession of, imitating, or consuming any resource attributes that they hold property rights to. That is, property rights and their enforcement influence the value entrepreneurs can appropriate from exploration of different resource attributes (Bjørnskov and Foss, 2010).

Given that creation or discovery and evaluation of opportunities are closely intertwined processes, transaction costs influence *which attributes* will be subject to creation or discovery. Thus, the perceived cost of delineating and enforcing property rights to newly discovered attributes are likely to influence creation or discovery efforts in predictable directions. As a general matter, "... entrepreneurial energy and innovation are starkly biased towards the creation of those surpluses which can be *appropriated* by the innovator" (Lippman and Rumelt, 2003b: 924, our emphasis; see also Shepherd and DeTienne, 2005).

To illustrate, consider the 1980 Supreme Court decision in Diamond v. Chakrabarty which implied a significant removal of uncertainty with respect to what was the law in biotechnology patenting. This drastically changed the appropriability regime confronting a number of industries (Pisano, 1990), and made

exploring genetic engineering and its uses in these industries substantially more attractive. The space of potential entrepreneurial
opportunities was vastly expanded as a result of the delineation and
enforcement of property rights to biotech research results. Property
rights to resource attributes (or bundles of attributes) are seldom
perfectly enforced, as owners face transaction costs of delineating
and protecting property rights to such attributes. In other words,
the transaction costs of defining property rights to entrepreneurial opportunities help define the space of entrepreneurial opportunities. However, transaction costs also matter to entrepreneurial
opportunities in a different way.

Building the experiential knowledge that much recent entrepreneurship highlights is costly. Resource learning may imply experimenting with resources, combining and recombining them, and learning
about their attributes in the process (Penrose, 1959; Orr, 1996). Thus,
resource learning emerges from mergers and acquisitions (Matsusaka,
2001), the ramp-up and calibration of factory production (K. Foss,
2001; Stieglitz and Heine, 2007), interaction between employees and
managers (Argote, 1999), and other processes that result in the creation or discovery of new resource attributes. These processes are
costly, and some of the relevant costs are transaction costs, such as
the costs of negotiating M&As, contracting (and recontracting) over
resource uses in strategic alliances, delineating decision rights over
corporate resources inside the firm, building information revelation
mechanisms that can reveal the relevant types of human capital, etc.
While no direct estimates of the transaction costs of resource learning appear to exist, there are reasons to believe that such costs are
often substantial; think of expenses on corporate lawyers in connection with M&As or the recruitment costs of hiring new employees. In
sum, transaction costs directly influence resource learning processes,
because the expected gains will be balanced against the (transaction
and other) costs of resource learning.

Conclusions

In this chapter we have linked Austrian capital theory to entrepreneurship and ownership. We began counterfactually by considering
the implications for entrepreneurship and economic organization of
a world of homogenous capital, the world of shmoo. This allowed us

to argue that the Austrian idea of heterogeneous capital is a natural complement to the theory of entrepreneurship[19] and that it connects naturally to ideas on heterogeneous assets in property-rights economics. Entrepreneurs who seek to create or discover new attributes of capital assets will want ownership titles to the relevant assets, both for speculative reasons and for reasons of economizing on transaction costs.

These arguments provide room for entrepreneurship that goes beyond deploying a superior combination of capital assets with given attributes, acquiring the relevant assets, and deploying these to producing for a market. Thus, we argued that entrepreneurship may also be a matter of *experimenting* with capital assets in an attempt to discover new valued attributes. Because entrepreneurs typically lack perfect knowledge of an asset's relevant attributes, it is usually the assets themselves, and not particular attributes, which are traded in capital markets. Ownership of an asset confers the (residual) right to exploit future, as yet undiscovered, attributes of that asset, and entrepreneurs may acquire assets precisely to be in a position to exploit these future attributes.

Such experimental activity may take place in the context of trying out new combinations through the acquisition of or merger with another firm, or in the form of trying out new combinations of assets already under the control of the entrepreneur. The entrepreneur's success in experimenting with assets in this manner depends not only on his ability to anticipate future prices and market conditions, but also on internal and external transaction costs, the entrepreneur's control over the relevant assets, how much of the expected return from experimental activity he can hope to appropriate, and so on.

As we argue in the following chapters these latter factors are key determinants of economic organization in modern theories of the firm, which suggests that there may be fruitful complementarities between the theory of economic organization and Austrian theories of capital heterogeneity and entrepreneurship. Specifically, capital heterogeneity has two important implications for economic organization. First,

---

[19] We note in passing that the understanding of management may also be furthered by beginning from heterogeneous capital assets and the need for coordination they imply. From a resource-based view, Mahoney (1995) argues that an important function of management is the coordination of such assets.

because it is difficult, or perhaps even impossible, to specify all relevant attributes of an asset *ex ante*, ownership rights are assigned to assets, not their attributes. Ownership of an asset gives the owner the rights to exploit attributes unknown at the time ownership rights are conferred. Because firms are defined in terms of asset ownership, this entrepreneurial perspective helps explain the boundaries of the firm. Second, because attributes of assets are costly to measure, and often unknown even to their owners, entrepreneurs must often experiment with different combinations of capital goods.

6 | *Entrepreneurship and the economic theory of the firm*

In Knight's (1921) view, firm organization, profit and loss, and entrepreneurship are inextricably linked. These phenomena arise as an embodiment, a result, and a cause, respectively, of commercial experimentation – a view founded on a particular ontology of the world as essentially open-ended and not deterministic (1921: chapter 7). Few economists have followed Knight in linking the firm, profit and loss, and entrepreneurship,[1] especially from his philosophical starting points. And yet, as we noted in the beginning of this book, there are many good reasons to treat the theory of entrepreneurship and the theory of the firm together. Such a synthesis informs many foundational questions in economics, business strategy, and public policy: Can we meaningfully address entrepreneurship without considering the organization in which such entrepreneurship takes place? How does the structure of the firm influence entrepreneurial actions? How does firm organization (e.g., the allocation of residual income and control rights) affect the quantity and quality of entrepreneurial ideas? And so on. To answer these, we need to bring the theory of the firm and entrepreneurship literatures into close contact. And yet, the important connections between these two bodies of literature have been largely overlooked. We seek to identify and establish some of those connections in this and the next two chapters.

In bringing together entrepreneurship and the theory of the firm we hope to convince scholars in both fields that there are significant gains from trade. We start by reviewing extant theory of the firm, asking why these gains were not recognized, evaluated, and exploited. Economics, and hence the economic theory of the firm, developed throughout the twentieth century in a particular way,

---

[1] Important exceptions are Barzel (1987), Baumol (1994), Casson (1997), and Gifford (1999).

one that effectively excluded the entrepreneur from the organization and the market – not because the insights of Schumpeter, Knight, Mises, and other thinkers on entrepreneurship are unimportant or not subject to clear, precise, systematic presentation and development, but because the increasingly formal and stylized treatment of economic phenomena made it difficult to incorporate judgment and creativity, bounded rationality, unforeseen contingencies, and so on.

We hasten to add that we are not, in this discussion, offering a general critique of modern economics, or tying our call for rehabilitating the entrepreneur's role in economics to some kind of broader reconstruction of the field. On the contrary, the entrepreneur figured prominently in "mainstream" economics until the latter part of the twentieth century, and there is nothing inherently radical or unorthodox in an entrepreneurial theory of the firm and the market.[2] We shall argue that while the substance of much of modern economics allows for a strong entrepreneurial role, the language of formal economic modeling constitutes a barrier. The more formal game- and information-theoretic versions of the theory of the firm, and, more broadly, the economics of organization, build on assumptions and modeling approaches that effectively exclude the entrepreneur. Nonetheless, we think there are opportunities to generate new theoretical insight and provide better explanations for important phenomena in the theory of the firm from adopting a more entrepreneurial perspective.[3]

Likewise, the entrepreneurship literature can benefit from thinking more carefully and systematically about the organizational environment for, and implications of, entrepreneurship. While modern economics has indeed adopted constraining heuristics, this does not mean that insights from contemporary organizational economics cannot be brought to bear on issues of entrepreneurship. In particular, ideas

---

[2] See Salerno (2009a: xxvii–xxxiii) for the case that Murray Rothbard saw his *Man, Economy, and State* (1962), a founding treatise of the modern Austrian school, as a rehabilitation of an older mainstream tradition – the neoclassical economics of Wicksteed (1910), Fetter (1910), and Taussig (1911) – rather than a heterodox reconstruction of economic theory. Our aim here is in the same spirit as Rothbard's.

[3] Hence we disagree with Barreto's (1989) claim that entrepreneurship and the theory of the firm inherently cannot be aligned.

about property rights, transaction costs, relationship-specific assets, and the like are very useful for entrepreneurship research, though perhaps expressed differently from the way they appear in mainstream economic treatments. We also make the case for extending these concepts and theories to the entrepreneurship literature. In other words, our aim in this chapter is to encourage cross-fertilization, not one-directional influence.

Research on the theory of the firm has traditionally been organized around the "classic" Coasean (1937) questions of firm emergence, boundaries, and internal organization. Economic organization, then, is about the distribution of transactions across governance structures and mechanisms, and addressing economic organization means explaining why certain governance structures exist, what explains their boundaries vis-à-vis other governance structures, and what (in the case of firms and hybrids) explains their internal organization. We follow this design in the ensuing three chapters.

Entrepreneurship and the theory of the firm: why so little contact?

The neglect of the entrepreneur by theorists of the firm

As mentioned in Chapter 1, within the last few decades, the theory of the firm has become one of the fastest-growing areas in microeconomics, and has become increasingly influential in management research, though mostly ignored in the entrepreneurship literature (exceptions include Jones and Butler, 1992; Mosakowski, 1998; and Alvarez and Barney, 2005). The economic theory of the firm emerged and took shape as the entrepreneur was disappearing from microeconomic analysis, first in the 1930s when the firm was subsumed into neoclassical price theory (O'Brien, 1984), and then in the 1980s as the theory of the firm was reformulated in the language of game theory and the economics of information (e.g., Holmström, 1979; Grossman and Hart, 1986). The gradual "hardening" of the neoclassical approach in economics (see Leijonhufvud, 1968), including the mainstream approach to the theory of the firm, left little room for entrepreneurship; Baumol (1994: 17) calls the entrepreneur "the specter which haunts economic models." Indeed, the terms "entrepreneur" and "entrepreneurship" do not even appear in the indexes of leading texts on the economics of organization and management such as Brickley *et al.* (2008) or Besanko *et al.* (2010).[4]

Similarly, in modern contributions to the theory of the firm (Williamson, 1975, 1985, 1996; Milgrom and Roberts, 1992; Hart, 1995) reference to entrepreneurship is passing at best. (Spulber [2009] is a conspicuous exception.) As we suggested earlier, we do not think this is because the key insights of the economic theory of the firm are somehow irrelevant or cannot be integrated with ideas on entrepreneurship – our claim is quite the opposite. But the specific *form* in which the economic theory of the firm is increasingly cast makes it difficult to put the entrepreneur back in. For example, large parts of contract theory assume that agreements are "complete," meaning that they specify actions or remedies for all possible contingencies, ruling out the possibility of unanticipated contingencies and fundamental uncertainty in contractual relations. While some aspects of entrepreneurship may be usefully treated in a complete-contracting framework (e.g., Kihlstrom and Laffont, 1979; Barzel, 1987; Lazear, 2005), it flies in the face of the notion, developed in the preceding chapters, that entrepreneurship is exercising judgment about essentially *new* resource uses in the face of uncertainty (see also Boudreaux and Holcombe, 1989; Langlois and Cosgel, 1993).

The constraining heuristics of the theory of the firm

The neglect of entrepreneurship in the theory of the firm has much to do with fundamental heuristics for formal modeling. Theorists of the firm, like most other model-builders in mainstream economics, consistently adopt an "on-off" approach in which, for example, agents are either fully informed about some variable or not informed at all, property rights are either perfectly enforced or not enforced at all, actions are either fully verifiable or not verifiable at all, etc. Subtleties are artificial, as in Bayesian models where "the agent knows the true value of p with probability $\hat{\imath}$." Thus, as a modeling convention extreme values are chosen for many choice variables, because some

---

[4] Two British surveys of economics principles textbooks (Kent, 1989; Kent and Rushing, 1999) confirm a similar absence of the concept. A review of graduate textbooks used in Sweden (largely the same books used in the US and elsewhere [Johansson, 2004]) confirms the absence of the concept of the entrepreneur.

(usually unspecified) information or transaction costs are supposed to prohibit agents from choosing certain actions. Of course, theorists do this to isolate the working of a certain mechanism; for example, how ownership affects investment incentives when it is impossible to contract over investments. The insight derived under extreme conditions, it is argued, may yield insights in investment incentives under less extreme conditions.

But this approach can often lead one astray. Isolating particular mechanisms means suppressing other margins, and thus ignoring entrepreneurship aimed at working around those particular margins. Furubotn (2001: 136) notes, for example, that bounded rationality – a key element of some modern theories of the firm – has important implications for theorizing about the firm:

> [G]iven the cognitive restrictions that constrain each individual and the costly nature of information, a decision maker can have only *partial* knowledge of the full range of options known to the society as a whole. He can no longer be assumed to know everything about existing technological alternatives, the characteristics and availability of all productive inputs, the existence and true properties of every commodity in the system, etc.

In other words, we cannot reduce the relevant decision problem to combining known inputs into known outputs in a transaction-cost-minimizing manner (what Kirzner calls "Robbinsian maximizing"). If decision-makers know only a small subset of the many possible input combinations and cannot perfectly foresee future preferences, "the individual devising the firm's policies has to act as a true entrepreneur rather than as a manager routinely implementing clear-cut marginal rules for allocation" (Furubotn, 2001: 139). For this reason, Furubotn argues, transaction costs cannot be the sole cause of governance and contractual choice; overall profitability must be part of the explanation as well.

In this spirit, we review in the remainder of the chapter the dominant established theories of the firm, to show in more detail how existing theory has had difficulties handling entrepreneurship, and to identify insights that are useful for linking entrepreneurship and economic organization. Subsequent chapters flesh out these insights in greater detail.

Established theories of the firm

The neoclassical theory of the firm

What is usually termed the "neoclassical" theory of the firm emerged in the 1920s and 1930s in the works of Pigou (1928), Viner (1931), and Robinson (1933, 1934) as a parallel effort to the formalization of consumer theory (Hicks and Allen, 1934; Loasby, 1976). (Just as consumers maximize utility subject to a budget constraint, so firms maximize profit subject to a given production function and input prices.) These writers also sought to make precise Marshall's price-theoretic apparatus, particularly his notion of the "representative firm." It has been argued, however, that the result was something that was very far from Marshall's intentions (Foss, 1994). Indeed, one unfortunate result was that the Marshallian entrepreneur was squeezed out of price theory (Loasby, 1982). The neoclassical production theory underlying the new theory of the firm, with its attendant assumption that all knowledge is exogeneously given blueprint knowledge that is immediately applicable in production, makes the entrepreneur at best a *deus ex machina*. The theory furnished by Pigou, Viner, and Robinson survives in microeconomics textbooks in the form of the well-known cost apparatus, and it appears – in even more abstract form – in the characterization of producers in competitive general equilibrium models (Debreu, 1959).

In today's economics textbooks, the "firm" is a production function or production possibilities set, a black box that transforms inputs into outputs. The firm is modeled as a single actor, facing a series of decisions that are portrayed as uncomplicated: what level of output to produce, how much of each factor to hire, and the like. These "decisions," of course, are not really decisions at all; they are trivial mathematical calculations, implicit in the underlying data. In the long run, the firm may choose an optimal size and output mix, but even these are determined by the characteristics of the production function (economies of scale, scope, and sequence). In short: the firm is a set of cost curves, and the "theory of the firm" is a calculus problem. There is nothing for an entrepreneur to do.

While descriptively vacuous, the production-function approach has the appeal of analytical tractability along with its elegant parallel to neoclassical consumer theory (profit maximization is like utility maximization, isoquants are like indifference curves, and so on). Nonetheless, many economists, and most management scholars, find this "production function view" (Williamson, 1985) increasingly unsatisfactory, as unable to account for a variety of real-world business practices: vertical and lateral integration, mergers, geographic and product-line diversification, franchising, long-term commercial contracting, transfer pricing, research joint ventures, and many others. Of course, the theory was never designed to explain such phenomena; it was merely an intermediate step toward explaining market prices (see Machlup, 1967). Still, the silence of the traditional theory of the firm towards questions of comparative economic organization explains much of the recent interest in agency theory, transaction-cost economics, the property-rights view, and other approaches that hark back to Coase's landmark 1937 article, "The Nature of the Firm."

Coase

Coase (1937) introduced a fundamentally new way to think about the firm. In the world of neoclassical price theory, he noted, firms have no reason to exist. If firms emerge in a market economy, he reasoned, it must be that there is a "cost to using the price mechanism" (Coase, 1937: 390). Market exchange entails certain costs, such as identifying trading partners, negotiating terms, and writing and enforcing contracts. The "most obvious cost of 'organising' production through the price mechanism is that of discovering what the relevant prices are" (Coase, 1937: 390). A second type of cost is that of executing separate contracts for each of the multifold market transactions that would be necessary to coordinate some complex production activity. These costs can be avoided by organizing activities within a firm. Inside the firm, the entrepreneur may be able to reduce these "transaction costs" by coordinating these activities himself. However, internal organization brings other kinds of transaction costs, namely problems of information flow, incentives, monitoring, and performance evaluation. The boundary of the firm, then, is determined by the trade-off, at the margin, between the relative transaction costs of external and internal exchange.

In a single, short paper, Coase laid out the basic *desiderata* of the economic theory of the firm, namely accounting in a comparative-institutional manner for the allocation of transactions across alternative governance structures. Perhaps the most striking aspect of Coase's article is its programmatic character: Coase calls for a research agenda incorporating incomplete contracts and transaction costs ("the costs of using the price mechanism"), and he argues in favor of a basic contractual conceptualization of the firm and uses an efficiency approach. Most importantly, he defines the main tasks of a theory of the firm, namely to "discover why a firm emerges at all in a specialized exchange economy" (i.e., the *existence* of the firm), to "study the forces which determine the size of the firm" (i.e., the *boundaries* of the firm) and to inquire into, for example, "diminishing returns to management" (i.e., the *internal organization* of the firm). All this, Coase explains, can be reached by incorporating the "costs of using the price mechanism" into ordinary economics. Although terminology and specific insights may differ, most modern theories of the firm are Coasean in the sense that they adhere to this program. But what about the entrepreneur in Coase's thought?

Coase, Knight, and the entrepreneur

Coase's position on the entrepreneur is somewhat ambiguous. He uses the word, defining the entrepreneur as "the person or persons who, in a competitive system, takes the place of the price mechanism in the direction of resources" (Coase, 1937: 388 n2), but his "entrepreneur" seems to be engaged primarily in the exercise of comparing the costs of organizing specified transactions in given governance structures rather than forming judgment under uncertainty, exercising Kirznerian alertness, or being innovative in the Schumpeterian sense.[5] On the other hand, Coase stresses certain aspects of economic organization that are best understood in the context of entrepreneurial activities. Notably, his discussion of the employment contract makes appeal to unpredictability and the need for qualitative coordination in a world of uncertainty (Langlois and Foss, 1999). This provides ample room for the entrepreneur as a speculating and coordinating agent. However, this potential was not fulfilled, neither in Coase's

---

[5] This was in keeping with the post-Marshallian tradition of taking "manager" and "entrepreneur" as synonymous (e.g., Kaldor, 1934; Robinson, 1934). Some writers outside the Marshallian tradition, such as Fetter (1905) and Davenport (1914), used words like "enterpriser," "adventurer," and "imprenditor" to distinguish the entrepreneur from the manager.

own thought, nor, as we shall see, in later post-Coasean contributions to the economic theory of the firm.

Coase dismissed Knight's (1921) entrepreneurial explanation of the firm. Arguably, Coase misunderstood Knight (Foss, 1996b). Coase criticizes Knight for making the "*mode of payment* the distinguishing mark of the firm," with entrepreneurs insuring risk-averse workers by assuming full residual claimancy themselves. This can't be a definition of the firm, for Coase, because one "entrepreneur may sell his services to another for a certain sum of money, while the payment to his employees may be mainly or wholly a share in profits" (Coase, 1937: 392). Coase seems to miss that the whole point of Knight's analysis is that the "entrepreneur's services" represent uninsurable risks or genuine uncertainty, and are too costly to trade. (We return to this discussion in the next chapter.)

This does not mean that Coase's analysis is opposed to Knight's, however. In some dimensions, the two approaches are complementary. Coase's explanation for the firm's existence, in terms of relative transaction costs, focus on the *employment* boundaries of the firm. The key distinction for Coase, in other words, is whether the entrepreneur will contract with independent suppliers and distributors or will hire employees. Langlois (2007c) argues that Knight does not provide a compelling reason why the entrepreneur-owner must hire employees, so Knight's approach does not constitute a theory of the firm in the Coasean sense. This may be true, but for Knight, the firm is defined in terms of ownership of assets, not employment of people. Knight's theory – like the incomplete-contracting or property-rights view that would emerge in the 1980s and 1990s – focuses on the *ownership* boundaries of the firm, not the employment boundaries.[6] Still, Langlois is correct that to explain the use of employees

---

[6] Spulber (2009) defines the firm in terms of Fisher's (1930) "separation theorem," which argues that the neoclassical firm's optimal investment decision is independent of the owner's preferences (and independent of the financing decision). For Spulber (2009: 63), the firm "is defined to be a transaction institution whose objectives differ from those of its owners. The separation is the key difference between the firm and direct exchange between consumers." In our Knightian framework, as in the property-rights approach, the firm is defined in terms of asset ownership, not independent preferences – indeed, the owner's preferences represent an ultimate constraint on the firm's activities, even for publicly traded firms. See Hart (2011) for further discussion.

rather than independent contractors as the entrepreneur's associates, a Knightian approach must also incorporate Coasean, transaction-cost considerations.

Modern organizational economics

Lacking the appropriate "analytical technology" that could render his ideas acceptable to mainstream economists, Coase's seminal analysis was neglected for more than three decades. (For a detailed discussion, see Foss and Klein, 2011.) Coase's theory was known and acknowledged, but not *used*, as Coase (1972) later pointed out. However, at the time of Coase's lamentation, serious work on the theory of the firm had begun to take off, thanks to four seminal contributions that defined the central streams of modern research in the theory of the firm: transaction cost economics (Williamson, 1971), the nexus-of-contracts view of the firm (Alchian and Demsetz, 1972), agency theory (Ross, 1973), and team theory (Marschak and Radner, 1972).

Taken together, post-Coasean theories of the firm have followed Coase in conceptualizing the firm as a contractual entity whose existence, boundaries, and internal organization can be rendered intelligible in terms of economizing on (various types of) transaction costs. This is not to say that any one theory in modern organizational economics has addressed all three of these key issues in a unified framework involving the same kind of transaction costs. Instead, there seems to be a division of labor: principal-agent models (Holmström and Milgrom, 1991) and team theory (Marschak and Radner, 1972) are interested mainly in internal organization, while transaction cost economics (Williamson, 1985) and the property-rights approach (Hart, 1995; Hart and Moore, 1990) deal with firm boundaries. Likewise, these approaches stress different kinds of transaction costs, with the principal-agent models emphasizing monitoring costs, the property-rights approach emphasizing costs of writing (complete) contracts, and transaction cost economics focusing on the enforcement and haggling costs that arise after contracts are signed.[7]

---

[7] This is a rational reconstruction on our part; formal contract theorists, such as principal-agent or property-right theorists, are generally not comfortable with the notion of "transaction cost." See Gibbons (2005) for further discussion.

Among these approaches, only transaction cost economics and the property-rights approach are conventionally seen as theories of the firm per se (Hart, 1995). Principal-agent and team theories deal with productive relationships, but do not address asset ownership; that is, they do not talk about the boundaries of the firm. To explain boundaries, one must presuppose that contracts are incomplete, for otherwise everything can be stipulated contractually and there is no need for ownership, understood as the "residual right" to make decisions that are not specified by contract. Team theory and principal-agent models assume complete contracts, whereas transaction cost economics and property-rights theory work from an incomplete contracting foundation. Accordingly, our main emphasis will be on the latter two approaches.

While the various branches of modern organizational economics contain diverse theories, approaches, and emphases, they share the understanding – sometime implicit – that to explain the *raison d'être* of firms, one must move beyond the perfectly competitive model (of Debreu, 1959). This clearly unites all economic theories of the firm from Knight (1921) (where the argument is set very clearly out) to Coase (1937) and his transaction-cost successors (Williamson, 1996) to modern contract theory (Salanié, 1997; Laffont and Martimort, 2002). While the relevant frictions come in many forms, from (genuine) uncertainty (Knight, 1921), imperfect foresight or bounded rationality (Coase, 1937; Kreps, 1996; MacLeod, 2002), small-numbers bargaining (Williamson, 1996), haggling costs (Coase, 1937), private information (Holmström, 1979), cost of processing information (Marschak and Radner, 1972; Bolton and Dewatripont, 1994), costs of inspecting quality (Barzel, 1982, 1997), or imperfect legal enforcement (Hart, 1995; Williamson, 1996), all these approaches allow deviations from the complete, contingent contracting model of perfectly competitive general equilibrium theory (Debreu, 1959).

One result of imperfect contracting is that created value ("welfare," "wealth," "surplus," etc.) falls short of some hypothetical maximum. That first-best situation is taken, however as a benchmark – despite Coase's (1964) and Demsetz's (1969) methodological strictures against this "Nirvana approach." Typically, modern theories of the firm take as the benchmark some notion of the value that would have been created if agents had been interacting in a world entirely free of the sorts of frictions listed above. Such settings may be represented by the conditions underlying the Coase theorem (Coase, 1960) or the First Welfare Theorem of neoclassical economics (Debreu, 1959). Under these conditions maximum value creation obtains; thus, it is not possible to rearrange resource uses, coalitions, etc. so that more economic value is produced. Notably, these situations are, to a large extent, institutionally and organizationally neutral, meaning that unconstrained market competition based on privately held property rights will implement the optimal allocation (as will full-scale socialism!). Similarly, whether resources are primarily allocated by firms or by markets does not, strictly speaking, matter for resource allocation.[8]

Of course, such first-best efficiency never obtains in reality, and institutional and organizational arrangements, using different mechanisms for governing inputs, affect the allocation of resources, depending on what is assumed about transactions, property rights, information, and so on. Indeed, a key heuristic underlying all economic theories of the firm is that the relevant units of analysis (transactions, activities, inputs) can be matched to particular alternatives (governance structures such as vertical integration or contracts) to satisfy some efficiency criterion (what Williamson [1985] calls "discriminating alignment"). It is typically assumed, often using "as if" reasoning, that decision-makers are rational optimizers and that any Pareto-improving (or potential Pareto-improving) changes in alignment between transactions and governance structures will be undertaken (e.g., Milgrom and Roberts, 1992). If agents are unwilling or unable to make these changes, competitive selection forces should still weed out inefficient organizational choices (Williamson, 1985, 1988; Lien and Klein, 2009). (If transition costs prevent adaptation, then the inefficiency may not be "remediable" [Williamson, 1996: chapter 8], and hence the previous alignment is not really inefficient.)

The argument that firms emerge when markets for certain transactions or activities "fail," and that organizations are superior means of governing these transactions or activities, does not in itself tell us what mechanisms are involved, and without specifying such mechanisms

---

[8] Nevertheless, it is usually argued that with perfect and costless contracting, there is no room for anything resembling organizations. Even one-person firms would not exist under such conditions, because consumers could contract directly with owners of factors services and would not need the services of the intermediaries (i.e., firms) (e.g., Cheung, 1983).

the argument is simply a tautology. Consequently, a lot of effort has gone into identifying and theorizing the relevant mechanisms. The *Leitmotiv* of the relevant work over the last three decades has been incentive conflicts emerging from situations like the prisoners' dilemma.[9] To see incentive conflicts in a market, or, more precisely, small-numbers bargaining context, and how governance can remedy particular kinds of incentive conflicts, consider a simple example.

An example

The example (which is borrowed from Wernerfelt, 1994) lays out the basic logic of "incomplete contracting" theory, one of the dominant theories current in organizational economics. The specifics do not automatically translate to other approaches, but the fundamental reasoning and assumptions are quite similar. The example is illustrated by the strategic-form games shown in Figure 6.1.

Following Hurwicz (1972), one can imagine economic agents choosing game forms, and the resulting equilibria, for regulating their trade. Although the example only highlights two agents (players), "B" can initially be taken as representative of a number of potential agents (e.g., firms) that might want to cooperate with A. That is, "large numbers" conditions obtain, and we can think of the situation as taking place, at least initially, in a market setting.

Assume that agents initially want to regulate such trade under conditions where they maintain their independence (i.e., they are distinct legal persons). Efficiency requires that agents choose the game form and equilibrium that maximizes the gains from trade. The two players begin by confronting Game 1. In this game, the Pareto criterion is too weak to select a unique equilibrium, since both {up, left} and {down, right} may be equilibria on this criterion. However, the {down, right} equilibrium has a higher joint surplus than the {up, left} equilibrium, so that it will be in A's interest to bribe B to play {right}. Surplus maximization

[9] Some work has drawn from team theory (Marschak and Radner, 1972; Aoki, 1986; Radner, 1986; Bolton and Dewatripont, 1994) or started from pure common-interest games (Camerer and Knez, 1996) and has downplayed incentive issues. However, while this approach can further the understanding of those aspects of internal organization that relate to information processing, it cannot explain the existence and boundaries of organizations (Williamson, 1985; Hart, 1995; Foss, 1996a).

Game 1

B

	left	right
up	2, 2	0, 0
down	0, 0	4, 1

A (for the rows)

Game 2

B

	left	right
up	2, 2	0, 0
down	0, 0	$4 - u$, $1 + u$

A (for the rows)

Figure 6.1 Two game forms

suggests that this equilibrium is the agents' preferred one. Their problem then is to design a contract that will make agents choose strategies such as these equilibrium choices. Note that this problem captures the spirit of work on specific investments (Klein *et al.*, 1978; Williamson, 1985; Hart, 1995) in which an agent (or possibly both agents) has to choose a strategy (in this case {right}) that, while surplus maximizing (when the other agent plays his best-response strategy), is not necessarily attractive to the agent (he only gets 1).

The apparent solution is to choose a side payment, u, which can be chosen ($1 < u < 2$) to implement the equilibrium where A plays {down} and B plays {right}. If the contracting environment is such that this contract can be (costlessly) written and enforced, then agents will choose the efficient strategies. Apparently, there is no need for a firm as defined here, and the small-numbers bargaining situation poses no inefficiency.

However, different contracting environments may give different results. For example, it may be too costly to describe all contract stipulations in a comprehensive manner (e.g., u may be intangible, such as goodwill, and hard to describe precisely). This may be due to information costs, the limitations of natural language, the unavoidable emergence of genuine novelties, and the like. The contract ends up incomplete. Alternatively, the parties may be sufficiently smart to write down all the manifold possible aspects of their relationship, but a third party is unable to verify and enforce this agreement (Hart, 1990). Or, the costs of contracting may outweigh the gains (Saussier, 2000). In all these cases, it may not be possible to sustain the first-best outcome, that is, the one that unambiguously maximizes joint surplus. In the context of the example, A may be confronted with a contingency that is not covered by the contract, refuse to pay B the bribe, and B may have no recourse. However, B may well have the foresight to anticipate this possibility. Thus, the contract stipulating the side payment may not be sustainable in equilibrium (i.e., the outcome where the agents get $[4 - u, 1 + u]$ may not be subgame perfect). Value is lower than in the optimal outcome, because B will not rationally choose {right}.

Whether an efficient or an inefficient outcome occurs will in many situations be critically sensitive to the structure and timing of the game. However, in the specific example, timing doesn't really matter if the contracting environment is such that the promise to transfer u in return for B playing {right} is, for whatever reason, unenforceable. Thus, if A gives B the bribe *before* the game begins, B will not play {right}, which means that A will decide not to give B any bribe. And if A promises B to pay the bribe *after* the game, B will realize that this will not be in A's interest, and will still play {left}. This captures the idea that agents who anticipate opportunism on the part of their contractual partner will refrain from taking efficient actions or making efficient investments. The bottom line is that contracts cannot completely safeguard against the reduction of surplus or loss of welfare stemming from incentive conflicts (given risk preferences).

The analytical enterprise is therefore one of comparing alternative contracting arrangements, all of them imperfect (Coase, 1964). A specific contracting arrangement is represented by the authority relation. This obtains when one of the players becomes an employee, accepting the other player's *orders* to play a specific strategy (e.g., {right}) in return for some specified compensation. In other words, the underlying idea is that transferring a transaction or activity from a market to an organization context means that the agreement will be honored. According to Williamson (1985), for example, the reason is a change of incentives: When an agent changes his status from independent entrepreneur to employee, he becomes less of a residual claimant. His incentives to engage in behavior that results in suboptimal equilibria are correspondingly attenuated. In terms of the example, B (or A) may have nothing to gain from playing {left} (rather than {right}) once he has assumed employee status, and will therefore obey A's (B's) orders. The law regulating labor transactions may reinforce such "docility" (Masten, 1988), to use Simon's (1991) expression. Or, reputation effects from the ongoing employer-employee relationship may be sufficient to constrain opportunistic behavior (Kreps, 1990, 1996).

The modern theory of the firm and entrepreneurship

The normal-form game representation shown in the preceding section illustrates a number of the crucial assumptions underlying the modern theory of the firm – assumptions that may not square easily with the phenomenon of entrepreneurship. These are discussed in the following.

Cognition

Most modern theories of the firm make very strong cognitive assumptions about the cognitive powers of agents. Like virtually all of formal, mainstream economics, these theories assume cognitive homogeneity, correctness, and constancy: agents hold the same, correct, model of the world, and that model does not change. These assumptions are built into formal contract theory (i.e., agency theory and property-rights theory) through the assumption that payoffs, strategies, the structure of the game, and so on are common knowledge. Bounded rationality is occasionally invoked as a necessary part of the theory of the firm, particularly by Williamson (1985, 1996);[10] but most of the contracting problems studied in the modern theory of the firm require only asymmetric information (Hart, 1990). Indeed, bounded rationality seems to serve little function beyond justifying the assumption that contracts are incomplete (K. Foss, 2001). Likewise, because of the Bayesian underpinning of game-theoretic contract theory, Knightian uncertainty, or any notion of open-endedness or indeterminacy, has no role to play. In the above representation, players can never be *surprised*.[11]

---

[10] "But for bounded rationality," he argues (1996: 36), "all issues of organization collapse in favor of comprehensive contracting of either Arrow–Debreu or mechanism design kinds." "Comprehensive contracting" does not allow for "governance structures" in the Williamsonian sense of mechanisms that handle the coordination and incentive problems that are produced by unanticipated change (Williamson, 1996: chapter 4).

[11] Some contributions to contract theory have invoked unanticipated contingencies (e.g., Grossman and Hart, 1986), but such contingencies are never a source of new benefits to the agents, nor do they change the

Clearly, this modeling approach makes little room for entrepreneurship and the characterization of an entrepreneurial market setting that we have described so far. As Phelps (2006: 13) observes:

[W]ork on contracts has posited, explicitly or implicitly, that the parties to a contract share identical "rational expectations," since they have the identical model of the world. Work in that vein does not fit in a theory of capitalist economies, in which views are never homogenous and may be wildly diverse.

Thus, entrepreneurs may not make optimal use of all available information (Sarasvathy, 2001), their judgments may be biased (Busenitz and Barney, 1997), and rational expectations simply aren't well-defined under conditions of Knightian uncertainty.[12]

Everything is given

Because of these strong assumptions about agents' cognitive powers, decision situations are always unambiguous and all decision alternatives are given (Furubotn, 2002). The choice of efficient economic organization is portrayed as a standard maximization problem in the case of contract design or as a choice between given "discrete, structural alternatives" in the case of the choice among governance structures (Williamson, 1996). There is no need for experimentation, no learning, and no place for the introduction of novel contractual or organizational forms. In terms of the game-theoretic representation above, strategies and game forms are given, and a host of questions simply are not addressed: How do players come to know the payoffs? Or each other? Or the available strategies? Will they hold the same

distribution of benefits across agents. Thus, agents are posited to know their final utilities even if unanticipated contingencies impact their trading relationship. For some acerbic comments on this assumption, see Kreps (1996).

[12] As Furubotn (2002: 89) argues, "since Knightian uncertainty prevails, the firm is not in a position to adjust its structure optimally for operation over time. In particular, decision-makers cannot rely on probabilistic calculations … it can be argued that the New Institutional Economics requires analysis to be very clear in explaining how the boundedly rational entrepreneur makes decisions and acquires information, and in indicating how much information he can reasonably be expected to acquire in any given situation."

views of the payoffs? Of each other? Of the available strategies? How do they know which game, and type of game, they are playing?[13] In the economics of organization (and in most of game theory), these kinds of questions are suppressed by assuming common knowledge: players have identical, shared beliefs about other players' strategies and these beliefs are consistent with some equilibrium in the game. For some purposes, suppressing ignorance and ill-structured decision situations (Simon, 1973) is entirely legitimate. However, for other purposes, such as understanding the link between entrepreneurship and organization, it is a big problem.[14]

Motivation

Modern theories of the firm focus on "high-powered" incentives – rewards and punishments that are explicit, measurable, and extrinsic. While not denying that intrinsic motivation plays a role, for instance, in agents' choice of occupation, extrinsic incentives is the main determinant of actions and behaviors on the margin (e.g., the choice of effort, how much to invest in relationship-specific capital, whether to misrepresent information, and so on). Lower-powered incentives, such as fixed wages, promotions by seniority, or reliance on subjective performance evaluation, are used only in situations where high-powered incentives have undesirable side effects – e.g., an agent who works hard in response to a piece rate but shirks on quality. (This problem features prominently in multi-task agency models such as Holmström and Milgrom, 1991.)[15]

---

[13] Obviously, trying to solve this problem by adding a "supergame" in which nature first chooses (with known probabilities) which game the agents are playing, with the agents subsequently acting according to the expected values of the various outcomes, taking nature's prior move into account, simply shifts the problem back a step. How do the agents know the set of possible games among which "nature" can choose? Where do the (typically shared) prior beliefs about the probabilities of various games being played come from? Etc.

[14] As Loasby (1976: 134) puts it: "The firm exists because it is impossible to specify all actions, even contingent actions in advance; it embodies a very different policy to emergent events. Incomplete specification is its essential basis: for complete specification can be handled by the market."

[15] Bénabou and Tirole (2003) try to incorporate intrinsic motivation in the context of an agency model.

Today's critics worry about the standard treatment of motivation, not because it assumes opportunism – the *bête noire* of earlier critics – but because it focuses so strongly on extrinsic motivation (e.g., Osterloh and Frey, 2000). Behavior is almost wholly understood as a response to some external force, such as expectation of a tangible. Agents never undertake a task for its own sake. These critics do not necessarily deny the reality of opportunism, moral hazard, and so on, but assert that there are other ways to handle these problems besides reliance on explicit monetary incentives, sanctions, and monitoring. The arguments are often based on social psychology (notably Deci and Ryan, 1985) and experimental economics (e.g., Fehr and Gächter, 2000).

Social psychology research based on "self-determination theory" (Deci and Ryan, 1985) suggests that people have an innate desire for exercising their competences, maintaining a measure of autonomy, and engaging in relationships with other people. Intuitively, these characteristics sound like those that motivate entrepreneurs, and there is indeed some evidence that intrinsic motivation is particularly important to entrepreneurs (e.g., Delmar, 1996; Stenmark, 2000; Guzmán and Santos-Cumplido, 2001; Segal Borgia, and Schoenfeld 2005; see also Phelps, 2006). This is not to deny, of course, that entrepreneurs pay attention to material rewards (Kirzner, 1982, 1985; Baumol, 1990), particularly on the margin. As we explained in Chapter 4, the entrepreneurial act itself, from the judgment-based perspective, is an intellectual, and not a marginal decision; we do not speak of a supply curve for entrepreneurship as with capital or labor. But within the set of entrepreneurial actions, decisions to invest in one line of business or another, to acquire these or those resources, to write particular contracts or hire particular employees, are affected by marginal rewards and punishments, both extrinsic and intrinsic (Douglas and Shepherd, 1999). And creative, entrepreneurial efforts inside firms may be particularly driven by intrinsic motivation (Osterloh and Frey, 2000). The neglect of intrinsic motivation in theories of the firm may help explain their uneasy relationship with entrepreneurship.

Neglect of heterogeneity and capabilities

Many heterodox economists, notably evolutionary economists, along with strategic management scholars, have criticized the neglect of firm heterogeneity, or differential capabilities, in the theory of the firm (e.g., Winter, 1988; Langlois, 1992; Kogut and Zander, 1992; Jacobides and Winter, 2005). In contrast, they favor a capabilities or "knowledge-based" view of the firm that starts from the empirical generalization that firm-specific knowledge is sticky and tacit and develops through path-dependent processes, implying that organizations are necessarily limited in what they know how to do well.[16] Much of this work builds on Penrose's (1959) insights about resources, organizational capabilities, and firm growth.

Differential capabilities imply differences in entrepreneurs' abilities to combine and recombine resources efficiently. Skill at exercising entrepreneurial judgment may be considered a capability, and other forms of capabilities may generate Ricardian or Marshallian rents. Beginning perhaps with Kogut and Zander (1992) and Langlois (1992), knowledge-based scholars have also argued that the characteristics of capabilities that make them relevant for the study of competitive advantage are also crucial for the main issues in economic organization. Thus, knowledge-based writers argue for a theory of the firm derived from knowledge-based considerations rather than incentives, opportunism, and transaction costs.

We agree with the basic thrust of the critique, that the modern theory of the firm unduly homogenizes what should not be homogenized. And we appreciate the connections between capabilities and knowledge-based views and Austrian ideas about tacit knowledge.[17] Indeed, in many ways, the notion that mainly industries matter, and that within-industry differences among firms are

---

[16] Large parts of the knowledge-based view implicitly and sometimes explicitly subscribe to methodological collectivism (Felin and Foss, 2005; Abell, Felin and Foss, 2008).

[17] Several Austrian writers have been particularly attracted to the knowledge-based view as it appears to take seriously the Hayekian notions of tacit, dispersed knowledge and rule-following behavior (Malmgren, 1961; O'Driscoll and Rizzo, 1985; Loasby, 1991; Langlois, 1992, 1995, 1998; Foss, 1997; Dulbecco and Garrouste, 1999; Foss and Christensen, 2001). Exploring the Austrian roots of capabilities theory has become a virtual cottage industry in recent years. The connection between Penrose and the Austrian school – both indirect and directly through Penrose's dissertation advisor, Mises's student Fritz Machlup – has also been examined (Connell, 2007; Foss *et al.*, 2008). However, these explorations have produced few distinctive insights and refutable implications, limited mainly to exploring similarities between the two bodies of thought.

relatively unimportant, resembles the portrayal of productive activities based on shmoo that we criticized in the previous chapter. As Demsetz (1991) points out, much of the modern theory of the firm treats knowledge needed for production as essentially free, while knowledge needed for exchange is costly. Capabilities theories, by contrast, acknowledge that both production and transaction knowledge are costly. In many ways, we clearly side with the capabilities approach in this regard: If capital assets (including knowledge assets) are heterogeneous (Chapter 5), the knowledge needed for production should be costly to acquire. Furthermore, if the transaction costs of combining these assets differ across firms (Coase, 1992), firms will grow and develop in different directions. Finally, judgment is obviously heterogeneous across entrepreneurs and different judgment will give rise to different initial resource assembly in starting a firm and in different boundaries and structures of internal organization as firms grow. For these reasons, firms do not possess the same "capabilities."

We thus concur with the capabilities view's emphasis on firm-level heterogeneity. However, an appreciation for heterogeneous capabilities does not mean that contractual considerations are unimportant. Thus, as other researchers have noted (e.g., Silverman, 1999; Nickerson and Zenger, 2004), capabilities and contractual approaches are complements, rather than substitutes; firm-specific knowledge and capabilities affect what an entrepreneur does, but transaction costs may determine how he does it – for instance, whether he works with hired labor or independent contractors, whether he owns or rents his facilities, and so on. We would go further, however, and argue that entrepreneurial judgment and the transaction costs of resource assembly are antecedents of heterogeneous capabilities. Capabilities emerge as a result of resource assembly and experimentation with asset combinations (see Chapter 5). Thus, entrepreneurial and transaction-cost perspectives are logically prior to capabilities.

Neglect of process

The explanation of economic organization in terms of efficiency and maximization has been a frequent target for critics of the theory of the firm. If agents are boundedly rational, how can they reason through efficient contractual, governance, and organizational arrangements

(Dow, 1987; Furubotn, 2002)?[18] Moreover, how does the implicit view of the firm as a highly plastic entity, easily reconfigured in response to exogenous shocks, square with more realistic notions of inertia and path dependence? If firms are composed of heterogeneous, but complementary capital assets, with entrepreneurial judgment required to determine the best combinations, then firms are formed and reformed as processes of experimentation and learning, not moment-by-moment optimization. According to Winter (1988: 178),

the size of a large firm at a particular time is not to be understood as the solution to some organizational problem. General Motors does not sit atop the Fortune 500 ... because some set of contemporary cost minimization imperatives (technological or organizational) require a certain chunk of the US economy to be organized in this manner. Its position at the top reflects the cumulative effect of a long string of happenings stretching back into the past.

One way to interpret this critique is that the theory of the firm seeks to explain the governance of individual transactions (Williamson, 1996), or clusters of attributes (Holmström and Milgrom, 1994), without identifying how the governance of a particular transaction depends on governance decisions about other transactions. Argyres and Liebeskind (1999) term this dependency "governance inseparability." In the face of governance inseparability, firms may rely on governance structures that appear inefficient at a particular time, but which make sense as part of a longer-term process.[19] Changes in governance structure affect not only the transaction in question, but the entire temporal sequence of transactions. This may make organizational form appear more "sticky" than it really is.

---

[18] As a first approximation, efficient economic organization is supposed to be consciously chosen by well-informed, rational agents. If pressed on the issue, economists of organization may also invoke evolutionary selection processes. Williamson (1988: 174), for example, notes that applied work in transaction-cost economics "relies in a general, background way on the efficacy of competition to perform a sort between more and less efficient modes and to shift resources in favor of the former." Thus, explanation is either fully "intentional" or "functional-evolutionary" (Elster, 1983; Dow, 1987). See Lien and Klein (2011) for further discussion.

[19] Governance inseparability refers both to connections between transactions over time, and to connections among transactions within an organization at a moment in time (Argyres, 2010).

These criticisms sound somewhat familiar to Austrian and evolutionary economists, who have long argued for a "process" view of economic activity that takes time seriously (Hayek, 1948; Kirzner, 1973; Dosi, 2000). Hayek (1948) distinguished between the neoclassical economics notion of "competition," identified as a set of equilibrium conditions (number of market participants, characteristics of the product, and so on), and the older notion of competition as a rivalrous process. Practices that appear inefficient or even anticompetitive at a given moment are better understood as part of a process of competition through time; it is the process that should be evaluated in welfare terms, not the conditions that obtain at a particular moment in the process (Matsusaka, 2001; Klein and Klein, 2001).[20]

Relatedly, it does not make much sense to cast the entrepreneur in an atemporal setting. Entrepreneurship is not best understood as an instant flash of insight; nor should we compress processes of judgment or discovery or innovation into a single *Gestalt*. These are processes that extend over time, as entrepreneurial conjectures are revised as information is revealed. Moreover, as we argue below, this process understanding of entrepreneurship is central to economic organization.

Suppressing margins

Besides the issues mentioned so far there are other, more subtle reasons for the disconnect between entrepreneurship and the modern theory of the firm.[21] In the standard models, particularly in contract theory (agency theory and the incomplete-contract approach), assumptions about what agents can do go too far in some respects, while not going sufficiently far in others. Put differently, many theorists of the firm adopt an "on-off" approach to theory-building in which, for example, agents are either fully informed about some variable or not informed

---

[20] Williamson (1996), recognizing the need to incorporate history into transaction cost economics, has introduced the notion of remediableness as a welfare criterion. The outcome of a path-dependent process is suboptimal, he argues, only if it is remediable – that is, an alternative outcome can be implemented with net gains. Merely pointing to a hypothetical superior outcome, if it is not attainable, does not establish suboptimality. This, however, is not a process theory *per se*.

[21] For a fuller analysis of the issues treated in these paragraphs, see Foss and Foss (2000).

at all, property rights are either perfectly enforced or not enforced at all, actions are either fully verifiable or not verifiable at all, and so on.[22] As a modeling convention, extreme values are chosen for many decision variables, with the explanation that some (usually unspecified) information or transaction costs prevent agents from choosing certain actions.

Some of the critiques of the theory of the firm addressed in the preceding section are, in essence, critiques of the arbitrary suppression of certain margins. In other words, the particular "isolations" chosen in many theories of the firm mean that margins that would be relevant to real-world decision-makers are suppressed.[23] Notably, agents are not allowed to exercise entrepreneurship to somehow circumvent the interaction problems caused by the suppression of margins (Makowski and Ostroy, 2001).

Perhaps the best-known example of the isolation procedures of suppressing margins and entrepreneurship is Keynesianism of the Hicks–Hansen–Modigliani type (what was once called "the neoclassical synthesis"). This type of macroeconomic modeling was designed to produce Keynesian results by introducing arbitrary frictions into an otherwise perfect "classical" model – for example, assuming that money wages were rigid downwards (Leijonhufvud, 1968). Indeed, in Hutt's (1939) reading, Keynes produced his results by simply assuming away any optimizing and entrepreneurial behaviors on specific markets, namely labor markets.

---

[22] This is captured by the notion of "theoretical isolation" that has been developed by Uskali Mäki (1992, 1994), and applied to specific economic debates by Mäki (2004) and Kyläheiko (1998). "Isolation" broadly refers to which items are included or excluded in the attempt to comprehend economic reality, something accomplished through "idealizing assumptions." Mäki argues that isolation plays an important role in theoretical disputes in economics, many of which revolve around charges that a given theory isolates too little, too much, or wrongly.

[23] Isolation may be defined as the procedure under which "a limited set of items is *assumed* to be isolated from the involvement or influence of the rest of the world" (Mäki, 2004: 4, original emphasis). As Mäki (2004) further clarifies, along one dimension theoretical isolation may be *vertical* (i.e., the particularities of items are abstracted away so that something resembling a universal emerges) and/or *horizontal* (i.e., isolation at a given level of abstraction). Along another dimension, it may be *internal* (i.e., the system is isolated from influences from within the system) and/or *external* (i.e., the system is isolated from items outside the system itself).

Other well-known examples concern the public-good nature of lighthouses (Coase, 1974), the externalities involved in decentralized production of apples and honey (Cheung, 1973), and the collective goods of fisheries and other non-exclusive resources (Cowen, 1988). In the lighthouse case, the standard argument that lighthouses are pure public goods stemmed from an unexamined assumption that enforcement of property rights for this particular type of good would be prohibitively costly. In contrast, careful consideration of the full set of options available to suppliers of lighthouse services revealed that sufficiently low-cost means of enforcing (at least a significant subset of) the relevant property rights did in fact exist – and were historically employed by alert entrepreneurs (Coase, 1974).[24] The moral of this story is that categories like "public goods" make sense only within particular arrangements of property rights (Demsetz, 1964; Cowen, 1985) and – more important – these arrangements are endogenous, defined by alert entrepreneurs through contractual innovations, innovations in enforcement methods, and the like (Makowski and Ostroy, 2001). Therefore, neglecting entrepreneurship easily leads to erroneous conclusions about which margins are in play.

Relatedly, modern formal theorists of the firm, such as Hart (1995), suppress margins in order to explain a certain institutional solution (e.g., a certain type of ownership pattern), without considering alternative institutional solutions that may keep interaction problems at bay (e.g., alternative contractual solutions).[25] As these models are set up, agents are not allowed to surpass the problems caused by suppressed margins by creating new institutional solutions. In other words, *entrepreneurship* is suppressed. As stated, suppressing margins means prohibiting the agent from knowing or doing certain things within a given interaction structure (typically, by choosing extreme values for some variables); "suppressing entrepreneurship" refers to prohibiting the agents from going beyond given interaction

---

[24] This is not to say that the British lighthouses were totally private, as Coase's analysis is often thought to have demonstrated. Rather, they were a kind of public-private hybrid in which the properties were privately owned but licensed by the state, and duties were collected under public supervision (van Zandt, 1993; Bertrand, 2006).

[25] Moreover, to these economists it seems completely legitimate to suppress *any* margin if it can somehow throw light on some contractual phenomenon.

structures in an attempt to remedy the problems caused by suppressed margins.[26] Suppressing entrepreneurship implies that agents are not allowed to imagine and implement new institutional solutions, for example to externality problems. Such restrictions imply unexploited profit opportunities (Barzel, 1997), but agents are prohibited from exploiting them as a matter of modeling convention (or lack of imagination on the part of the modeler). In this way, entrepreneurship is suppressed. However, as we argue next, suppressing entrepreneurship is costly, in terms of our understanding of important organizational and strategic phenomena. Incorporating entrepreneurship into the theory of the firm generates substantial insight.

Entrepreneurship as an unrealized potential in the theory of the firm

Ontological commitments

Consider the basic view of the economy adopted by both Austrian and new institutionalist writers. In our reading, they stress that economic actors never possess perfect knowledge and that transacting is not costless, but that active, profit-seeking entrepreneurs are continually adjusting and readjusting the economic structure of production in pursuit of profit, including devising new and less costly ways to transact and to acquire information. Now, theorists of the firm may also accept such an ontology, and most likely they do. The real difference lies in the sort of commitments about how economic modeling should be carried out that are believed to flow from such an ontology (O'Driscoll and Rizzo, 1985).

On this issue, many positions are possible, and the history of economics witnesses many different ontological commitments. Different extremes are defined by Shackle (1972), who came close to denying the possibility of virtually any modeling for the reason that such modeling would inherently misrepresent the nature of human choice, and

---

[26] This is another way of expressing Kirzner's (1973) distinction, discussed in Chapter 3 above, between "Robbinsian maximizing" – optimizing within a given means-ends framework – and the creation of a new means-ends framework ("entrepreneurship").

Debreu (1959: viii), who from a mathematical formalist point of view stressed that his theory be "logically entirely disconnected from its interpretations." In a highly pertinent context, Barreto (1989: 115, 141) argues that

The confrontation between the basic axioms [of mainstream economics] and the entrepreneur leaves two possibilities: to accept the entrepreneur and reject the modern theory of the firm, or to reject the entrepreneur and maintain allegiance to the modern theory of the firm ... Simply put, entrepreneurship is above "formalization" – it cannot be neatly packaged within a mechanistic, deterministic model. Importantly, the choice is an "either-or" proposition; there is no happy medium. The corner solution, which economic theory has chosen, is consistency, and for this reason the entrepreneur disappeared from economic theory.

While we agree with Barreto's link between the squeezing out of the entrepreneur and the hardening of economics as a research program, we disagree with the drastic conclusion that "there is no happy medium." Our critique of the modern theory of the firm does not concern all of its basic insights and constructs; rather, we are concerned mainly with the specific *form* that these insights and constructs take. For example, while modern contract theory uses specific game-theoretic (Bayesian) equilibrium concepts that assume that coordination takes place by means of pure ratiocination,[27] this is a specific form in which more fundamental, "intuitive" insights are cast for the purposes of ease of mathematical modeling and tractability; it is not *essential* to the theory as such.

Putting entrepreneurship into the theory of the firm

In a number of ways, modern organizational economics applies an analytical apparatus that is potentially capable of illuminating important aspects of entrepreneurship, particularly the judgment-based view we are developing here. For example, the emphasis on asset ownership in TCE and the property-rights view as a crucial

---

[27] Thus, agents are assumed to be able to coordinate on any desired game form and equilibrium thereof, subject to constraints such as attitudes to risk, incentive trade-offs, bargaining power, and asymmetric information.

aspect of firm organization accords well with Knight's (1921) and Mises' (1949) views. So does the emphasis on incomplete contracting. And notions of asymmetric information help to illuminate what is distinctive about entrepreneurship relative to other kinds of decision-making. Still, the modern economics of organization is in many ways a direct descendant of the neoclassical theory of the firm that it supplanted. For example, as capabilities theorists have pointed out, the modern economics of organization has not made a break with the neoclassical theory of production, but merely a grafted super-structure of asymmetric information, transaction costs, and other "frictions" onto the neoclassical theory (Langlois and Foss, 1999). Moreover, the modern economics of organization has the same deterministic and "closed" feel as the neoclassical theory of the firm: although notions of uncertainty, ignorance, and surprise are occasionally invoked, these serve mainly as rhetorical devices to justify the assumption of contractual incompleteness (Foss, 2003). Such notions are not themselves addressed, explained, and explored, and they are certainly not invoked to make room for process and entrepreneurship. Still, key insights from organizational economics may be usefully applied to an extended theory of economic organization, one that makes room for entrepreneurial judgment.

Specifically: An entrepreneur needs to transact with other agents – owners of heterogeneous physical and human capital – to realize his judgment as embodied in a business plan, or, more narrowly, a business model.[28] The relevant transactions can be organized by multiple contractual institutions. Transaction cost economics therefore seems to be well-positioned to shed light on the economic organization of key aspects of entrepreneurship, notably how can an entrepreneur safeguard his investments into a business plan against the appropriation by other contracting parties. Williamson's (1985, 2000) simple contracting schema suggests that contracting parties match the governance mode to the transaction attributes to safeguard investments. The entrepreneur becomes tied to a resource

---

[28] We are using the term "human capital" here loosely, in the conventional sense of valuable knowledge, skills, experience, etc., while recognizing that human capabilities are not, strictly speaking, "capital," as they do not exist as discrete, marginal units that can be bought and sold and priced, the way a factory or a machine or a piece of land can be exchanged in a market.

coalition if the investment into a business plan is relationship-specific. The exploitation of the business idea then requires access to other resources, leading to bilateral or multilateral dependency between contracting parties. Dependency not only increases the need for continuous adaptation, but also creates a possible holdup situation for the entrepreneur. Other resource owners may block the pursuit of the business idea, unless they receive a larger share of the generated income. Thus, the entrepreneur must also decide on contractual safeguards to protect entrepreneurial returns in designing the business model.

Human agents may be boundedly rational, but, in the transaction cost perspective, they are far from myopic in designing a business model. Rather, contracting is assumed to be far-sighted (Williamson, 1996, 2000; see N. Foss, 2001). When entering a contractual relationship, the parties consider possible contractual hazards that may emerge and try to structure the safeguards accordingly. Without safeguards, a contracting party may be reluctant to invest into specific assets, since it may suffer from the holdup problem after making the investment. Thus, an entrepreneur may be keenly aware of problems of safeguarding possible entrepreneurial gains before devoting resource to researching and developing a business idea. He will attempt to protect himself against opportunism by others and structure the business model around these hazards.

However, transaction-cost economics does not assume that there always is an optimal match between transaction characteristics and contractual safeguards (Williamson, 1985). Contracting parties may fail to identify a hazard when entering a relationship; safeguards may not work effectively. Disappointments are bound to happen. Appropriate safeguards may emerge only over time, as parties learn from their mistakes (Mayer and Argyres, 2004; Argyres and Mayer, 2007.) Thus, contracting may be far-sighted, but it is far from perfect or comprehensive. Contracting partners do not form rational expectations of the (net) benefits (utilities) that may flow from a relation (Kreps, 1996), although they can be assumed to form rough estimates and "confidence intervals" of these. Viewed from this angle, the simple contracting schema offers a process perspective on economic organization. It suggests that how a given transaction is governed may change over time, as the contracting parties learn and adapt the modes of governance (Furubotn, 2006). In turn, contracting partners may revise their estimates of such benefits. These actions are manifestations of entrepreneurship. Such straightforward application of a key organizational economics theory suggests the potential fruitfulness in linking established work in this broad research stream to ideas about entrepreneurial judgment.[29]

Existing attempts at integration

We are not the first to call for a closer integration between the theory of entrepreneurship and the theory of the firm, though our approach is more "mainstream" than most, as we build primarily on contractual, rather than capabilities, views of organization. As Langlois (2007c) points out, the existing literature consists of two types of studies: "entrepreneurial theories of the firm" and "theories of the entrepreneurial firm." The latter category includes most of the extant literature, and focuses on the economic organization of new ventures. Much of the literature on venture capital and the contractual relationships between venture capitalists and firm founders (Gompers, 1995; Kaplan and Strömberg, 2003) can be considered part of this literature.

Our approach, by contrast, falls into the former category; that is, we seek to show how concepts of the entrepreneurial *function* (in the sense described in Chapter 2 above) can be incorporated into economic and managerial theories of the firm. Other scholars have built on the resource-based and knowledge-based theories of the firm to argue that particular firm capabilities should be understood in an entrepreneurial context. Langlois and Robertson (1995), for

---

[29] While the simple contracting schema suggests a comparative-static, optimization approach, Williamson has always emphasized the process aspects of economic organization through his emphasis on adaptation. The choice between "market" and "hierarchy" can be seen as the choice among mechanisms to facilitate particular types of adaptation: decentralized, market governance supports "autonomous" adaptation, while the key advantage of internal organization is its ability to effect "bilateral" adaptation (Williamson, 1991b: 163–164). See also Gibbons (2005) for the case that there are two theories of the firm in Williamson's writings, the asset specificity and holdup theory associated with Williamson and Klein *et al.* (1978) and a distinct adaptation theory that receives greater emphasis in Williamson's earlier work.

example, conceive the firm's "dynamic capabilities" as its ability to respond to opportunities for rent creation in a changing landscape – a sort of firm-level version of Kirznerian alertness (see, more broadly, Zahra, Sapienza, and Davidsson [2008] for the dynamic capabilities link to entrepreneurship). Kor, Mahoney, and Michael (2007) focus on Penrose's (1959) concept of the firm's "productive opportunity set," explaining how the set of opportunities facing the firm is not given, exogenously, but created through team dynamics and other organizational attributes, attributes which can be interpreted as entrepreneurial characteristics (see also Foss *et al.*, 2008). Witt's (1998a, 1998b, 2007) theory of entrepreneurship as cognitive leadership, described in Chapter 2, represents another way to link entrepreneurship to organizational design. However, as we noted above, the leadership approach helps us understand what teams do, but does not explain how these activities should be structured, contractually. Diffuse networks, such as open-source communities, members of professional associations, and the like, share many of the characteristics of Witt's cognitive teams, but do not share ownership of tangible assets or relate through each other through employment contracts. Understanding the boundaries of the firm per se requires some kind of contractual explanation.

Conclusions

In summary, while various economists and management scholars have suggested links between the economics of the firm and entrepreneurship (Foss, 1993a; Langlois and Cosgel, 1993; Casson, 1997; Foss and Klein, 2005; Alvarez and Barney, 2007), analysis of these links are few, highly preliminary, and mainly based on ideas on capabilities and resources rather than on the more mainstream, Coasean, contractual approach to the firm. We suspect that entrepreneurship scholars and "heterodox" organizational economists have been turned off by the formal, static, "closed" characteristics of contractual theories that seem to have little room for entrepreneurship and bounded rationality, ignore the possibility that mental models differ across entrepreneurs, emphasize risk rather than Knightian uncertainty, and treat opportunity discovery as solely a function of past learning and experience. Large parts of the modern theory of the firm (transaction cost economics excepted) rest on game theory (Gibbons, 1999), which seems particularly unsuited for exploring these broader issues.

We share many of these frustrations with modern, "mainstream," contractual approaches to the firm. However, we see much potential for incorporating entrepreneurship into the contractual approach. This is further pursued in the following two chapters.

7 | Entrepreneurship and the nature and boundaries of the firm

In the previous chapter we discussed a number of currents in the modern theory of the firm, explaining why they struggle to come to terms with the entrepreneurship phenomenon. In this and the next chapter we rely more constructively on select insights from these theories to piece together a theory of the entrepreneurial firm. We organize our discussion around the three classic themes in the theory of the firm: existence (or emergence), boundaries, and internal organization. The present chapter deals with existence and boundaries.

Coase (1937) explained the firm as a means for economizing on transaction costs, a theme elaborated by Williamson (1975, 1985, 1996). Alchian and Demsetz (1972) viewed the firm as an (albeit imperfect) solution to the free-rider problem in team production (see also Holmström, 1982), and agency theorists have subsequently provided important contributions to the understanding of contracts within the firm (e.g., Holmström and Milgrom, 1991; Roberts, 2004). The "new" property-rights approach of Oliver Hart and his colleagues and students adopted the emphasis on specific assets and investments of Klein *et al.* (1978) and Williamson (1985) and gave it a new twist by showing how incentives to invest in relationship-specific assets vary with ownership arrangements (Grossman and Hart, 1986; Hart and Moore, 1990). Resource-based theories emphasize the need to generate and internalize tacit knowledge, and while they are mainly theories of firm performance (financial-market returns, innovation, etc.), they do have implications for economic organization (Kogut and Zander, 1992; Langlois and Robertson, 1995; Conner and Prahalad, 1996).

All of these theories deal, in some way, with transaction costs (Foss and Klein, 2011). In each theory, firms emerge in a market economy as agents (we'll call them entrepreneurs) seek to economize on a particular type of transaction cost, such as *ex ante* search and bargaining costs (Coase), costs of *ex post* contractual bargaining costs related to opportunism (Williamson), *ex ante* misalignment of investments (Hart), specific agency costs (Alchian and Demsetz), or costs of aligning differential capabilities (Langlois and Robertson). It is not obvious where entrepreneurial judgment fits into these approaches, however.

In the following we develop the argument that from an entrepreneurial perspective, the firm emerges as the entrepreneur's means of maximizing the returns from his judgment. This overall idea can explain not only the emergence of firms, but also their boundaries and internal organization.

The emergence of the firm

The role of non-contractible judgment

As we argued in Chapter 2, entrepreneurship should not be regarded as a distinct factor of production or an occupational category but as an aspect of human action and of the market mechanisms that can never be absent. At the same time, as discussed in Chapter 4, entrepreneurial profit can be interpreted as the reward for successful judgment, a reward that tends to accrue to particular individuals with particular types of knowledge, skills, and experience. In general, agents may realize returns from their human capital through three means: (1) selling labor services on market conditions; (2) entering into employment contracts; or (3) starting a firm. Barzel (1987) argues that moral hazard implies that options (1) and (2) are often inefficient means of realizing these returns. In other words, entrepreneurs know themselves to be good risks but are unable to communicate this to the market. For this reason, firms may emerge because the person whose services are the most difficult to measure (and therefore are most susceptible to moral hazard and adverse selection) becomes an entrepreneur, employing and supervising other agents, and committing capital of his own to the venture, thus contributing a bond.

The judgment-based explanation is somewhat different. Bewley (1989) interprets Knight as providing an explanation of why markets are incomplete that is not quite the same as, while complementary to, explanations based on moral hazard, adverse selection, and transaction costs (see also Foss, 1993a; Langlois and Cosgel, 1993). A key point in Knight (1921) is that entrepreneurs are those individuals "who undertake investments with unevaluatable risks" (Bewley, 1989: 32).

These risks are therefore uninsurable. Casson (1982: 14) takes a more Schumpeterian position, arguing that "[t]he entrepreneur believes he is right, while everyone else is wrong. Thus the essence of entrepreneurship is being different because one has a different perception of the situation" (see also Casson, 1997). This still results, however, in the view that entrepreneurial judgment is non-contractible. Rothbard (1962: 602) identifies judgment (implicitly) with ownership and argues that entrepreneur-owners cannot delegate their own authority over the production process. Kirzner (1979a: 181) takes an even more radical approach and stresses ignorance rather than ambiguity: "entrepreneurship reveals to the market what the market did not realize was available, or indeed, needed at all."

In all these cases, non-contractibility arises because "[t]he decisive factors ... are so largely on the inside of the person making the decision that the 'instances' are not amenable to objective description and external control" (Knight, 1921: 251). A nascent entrepreneur may be unable to communicate his "vision" of a commercial experiment as a specific way of combining heterogeneous capital assets to serve future consumer wants in such a way that other agents can assess its economic implications. In such a case, this nascent entrepreneur cannot be an employee, but will instead start his own firm. The existence of the firm can thus be explained by a specific category of transaction costs, namely, those that close the market for entrepreneurial judgment.

Is judgment non-contractible?

The argument that markets for judgment are incomplete may seem to be contradicted by the existence of markets for advice-giving. Isn't a strategy consultant essentially in the business of offering judgment to the market regarding resource allocation decisions that are highly uncertain? (Hence, the frequent resort to non-probabilistic scenario analysis.) Aren't businesspeople frequently hired for company boards exactly because their judgment is valued and aren't they often paid handsomely for this?[1] Aren't business school professors – particularly

---

[1] As Zeckhauser (2006: 9) notes: "A number of [Warren] Buffet's investments have come to him because companies sought him out, asking him to make an investment and also to serve on their board, valuing his discretion, his savvy, and his reputation for rectitude – that is, his [judgment]."

those teaching in entrepreneurship programs – primarily in the business of selling judgment to students? (Not paid quite as handsomely, but still ...)

Coase (1937) criticized Knight's argument that the attempt to capture the returns to judgment is the fundamental feature of the firm. Thus, Coase (1937: 249) argues that Knight does not, in modern parlance, sufficiently cast the problem in terms of comparative contracting:

[T]he fact that certain people have better judgment or better knowledge does not mean that they can only get an income from it by themselves taking part in production. They can sell advice or knowledge. Every business buys the advice of a host of advisers. We can imagine a system where all advice or knowledge was bought as required. Again, it is possible to get a reward from better knowledge or judgment not by actively taking part in production but by making contracts with people who are producing.

Foss (1996b) argues that Coase missed the crucial point of Knight, namely that while much can be "imagined," the "system where all advice or knowledge was bought as required" cannot include entrepreneurial judgment – in particular, the entrepreneur's judgment about whether to accept or reject the teachings of his "host of advisers." Coase therefore did not recognize that Knight's theory of why the price mechanism is "superseded" is simply different from his own. Costs of moral hazard or of trying to communicate entrepreneurial judgments close markets for judgments, for the same reasons that judgment is uninsurable. As a result, the entrepreneur has to start a firm to capture the returns to his judgment. Such a firm consists as a minimum of the entrepreneur and the assets he owns. It may, or may not, include employees.

As we argued in Chapter 3, it seems virtually impossible to meaningfully conceive of the "poor and penniless" entrepreneur of Kirzner who literally owns nothing but his own human capital. What about the young Steve Jobs and Steve Wozniak, tinkering in Jobs' father's garage, eventually creating Apple Computer? Were they not Kirznerian pure entrepreneurs, simply discovering opportunities without putting assets at risk? We don't think so. Even the Steves needed access to resources to create their first computer. And note that in using Jobs' father's garage, the father, in choosing to let Jobs and Wozniak use the space for their tinkering rather than allocating it to some other potentially valuable use, was putting his own resources at risk – acting as an entrepreneur! If, however, the garage had no alternative use, and, for the sake of argument, the computer parts used by Steve and Steve were surplus parts, then what they were doing wasn't really entrepreneurship, but merely play. It only became entrepreneurship at the point where productive resources were put at stake, and those resource owners were the entrepreneurs.

Langlois (2007b: 1114) argues that the argument from judgment is too hasty (depending on what exactly is meant by a "firm"), and that Coase has an important point in his critique of Knight: "To say that the entrepreneur cannot sell judgment is not to say that the entrepreneur cannot make use of markets to profit from that judgment." An entrepreneur with a great idea for a new widget can make use of markets to commercialize that idea, contracting with assemblers for building the widget, with ad agencies for marketing and with Amazon.com for the selling it. There is no need for an employment contract, and, hence, no need for a firm in the Coasean sense, although the entrepreneur's one-man operation is indeed a firm. Thus, while judgment may indeed not be tradable, exploiting Knightian judgment does not, according to Langlois, require the exercise of the control rights that ownership confers (whether over alienable or non-alienable assets).

Langlois therefore contrasts the Knightian firm, which may be only a one-person firm that exploits a certain entrepreneurial judgment using market relations, with the Coasean firm which per definition consists of more than one person (as Coase makes the employment relation the hallmark of the firm). Now, Langlois also stresses Coase's (1937: 391–392) point that the incomplete employment contract has important options-features in an uncertain world. "It may be desired to make a long-term contract for the supply of some article or service," Coase writes, and goes on to observe that

owing to the difficulty of forecasting, the longer the period of the contract is for the supply of the commodity or service, the less possible, and indeed, the less desirable it is for the person purchasing to specify what the other contracting party is expected to do. It may well be a matter of indifference to the person supplying the service or commodity which of several courses of action is taken, but not to the purchaser of that commodity or service. But the purchaser will not know which of these several courses he will want the supplier to take. Therefore, the service which is being provided is expressed in general terms, the exact details being left until a later date ... The details of what the supplier is expected to do is not stated in the contract but is decided later by the purchaser. When the direction of resources (within the limits of the contract) becomes dependent on the buyer in this way, that relationship which I term a "firm" may be obtained.

Langlois suggests that Coase's point about the flexibility afforded by incomplete contracts may complement Knight's emphasis on uncertainty. Thus, it is quite clear from Knight that he, too, stressed the firm's role as a "method of meeting uncertainty," stressing that the "true uncertainty in organized life is the uncertainty in an estimate of human capacity, which is always a capacity to meet uncertainty" (Knight, 1921: 309). However, Langlois's point needs to be addressed. Specifically, how to get from the entrepreneur with some non-tradable judgment to the entrepreneur as an owner of capital, and even an employer. The following section addresses this.

Judgment and the multi-asset, multi-person firm

While the notion that an entrepreneur can profit from judgment by relying on market forces in the way described by Coase and Langlois cannot be dismissed out of hand, it would seem to presuppose that a number of conditions hold true: the entrepreneur can coordinate the many other firms in his network at reasonably low cost; that either no changes to inputs and downstream assets like production, marketing, and sales channels are required (Teece, 1986) or that the necessary changes can easily be communicated (Langlois, 1992; Hellman, 2007); that input markets are "thick" and there are plenty of suppliers of downstream assets (to stall potential opportunism; Williamson, 1996); and so on. Absent these conditions, the entrepreneur will have incentives to acquire other assets and to employ personnel.

Of course, such idealized conditions are almost certainly absent in a world of Knightian uncertainty and heterogeneous capital. Judgment and its embodiment in business plans and their execution typically pertain over multiple decision domains, because the services of several heterogeneous assets (including multiple skills and capabilities) need coordination (Chapter 4). We have also characterized capital assets as nearly always possessing undiscovered attributes (Chapter 5). The entrepreneurial process of combining and recombining heterogeneous resources plays out continually, through time, as new attributes are created or discovered (and as consumer preferences and technological capabilities change). In our framework, the entrepreneurial act is not restricted to new venture formation; entrepreneurial judgment is necessarily exercised on an ongoing basis.[2]

The idea of incomplete markets for judgment helps us understand the one-person firm. However, similar ideas may also be useful for understanding the multi-person firm. As discussed in Chapter 5, when capital is homogenous it is easy to conceive, coordinate, and implement plans for producing, marketing, and selling goods and services. The decision problem is one of choosing the intensities with which shmoo is applied to various activities. In the real world of heterogeneous capital assets, by contrast, production plans are much more difficult to conceive, coordinate, and implement. It is not necessarily obvious to which activities capital goods are most profitably applied and account has to be taken of complex relations between capital goods. As Lachmann (1956: 16, original emphasis) notes: "[T]he entrepreneur's function ... is to *specify* and make decisions on the concrete form the capital resources shall have. He specifies and modifies the layout of his plant ... As long as we disregard the heterogeneity of capital, the true function of the entrepreneur must also remain hidden. In a homogenous world there is no scope for the activity of specifying."

Matching heterogeneous assets as a process of experimentation. Given that the optimal relationships among assets is often shrouded in uncertainty *ex ante*, and often so complex that entrepreneurs cannot resort to analytical methods (Galloway, 1996), some kind of experimental process is typically required. "Experiments" should be understood in a wide sense, ranging all the way from setting up and fine-tuning an assembly line to designing and implementing organizational architectures to inventing and commercializing new product. In other words, experimental activity in this sense covers much of "the main activity of a firm, running a business" (Coase, 1991: 65).[3]

---

[2] An important implication is that the effectual logic described by Sarasvathy (2008) does not apply only in the process of forming a venture, but also describes the operations of ongoing ventures, large and small, old and new.

[3] The need for firm-wide (and smaller-scale) experimentation of this kind is generally recognized in the change management literature, but not in the theory of the firm more broadly.

Such broadly experimental activity is suppressed within the production-function approach, which assumes that all factors are placed in their optimal uses within the firm (Nelson and Winter, 1982; Leibenstein, 1987). As new institutional economists (e.g., Furubotn, 2001) argue, this representation of productive activity entirely disregards the manifold problems of information, coordination, and the alignment of incentives that characterize real production activities. Kirsten Foss (2001) adds an additional layer of detail. She argues that what seemingly are purely technological problems of optimizing production processes in the context of heterogeneous assets and coordinating the division of labor inside the firm are really about specifying property rights, specifically use rights (Alchian, 1965). This is based on the notion, discussed in Chapter 5, that assets should be seen as bundles of attributes, including uses and functionalities (Barzel, 1997) and on linking the division of labor to the specification of tasks (attributes). The division of labor, in other words, proceeds from the discovery and specification of new tasks (attributes).[4]

In a world of perfect information, all rights to all attributes could conceivably be delineated and allocated in complete, state-contingent contracts. In a world of Knightian uncertainty, costly information, and heterogeneous assets, attributes are instead created or discovered through processes of entrepreneurial experimentation (Nelson, 1981). More, ongoing changes of the division of labor, as entrepreneurs experiment with dividing production tasks, introduce more complexity to the extent that more interdependencies are introduced, which in turn introduce more uncertainty. Thus, it may be difficult for the entrepreneur to specify all valued dimensions of assets *prior to* specialization, since many of the valued dimensions of assets only become apparent from experimenting with the uses of assets and discovering the best uses of those assets.[5] Given the interdependence that typically exists in a complex production system spanning several stages of production and involving myriads of inputs and numerous tasks, the best

---

[4] Bylund (2011) also emphasizes the division of labor as the impetus for firm formation, independent of transaction costs.

[5] Even if important dimensions can be specified, it may be difficult to allocate these rights in ways that ensure the best use of assets. This may, for example, be the case with the time and place dimension of assets where suboptimal allocations result in excess stocks of intermediate products or in idle assets.

time and place to use an asset depend on the specification of the uses of all other assets that are needed in production (Hayek, 1941).[6]

This creates costs of specialization due to coordination problems. In firms, such coordination problems emerge as, for example, problems of bottlenecks. These are problems where complexity and interdependent activities make it difficult to specify how best to sequence various activities, or where the introduction of more specialized tools and equipment creates capacity utilization problems due to technical indivisibilities, or where innovations in individual activities result in an uneven development of tools, equipment, and components.[7] Basically these problems arise when those who deliver parts or carry out activities are not aware of the need for mutual adjustment, or do not have the incentive to make their activities mesh with those of others. Reducing them through the specification of means of coordination (planning, standard operation procedures, liaison mechanisms, and so on) is, of course, paramount. However, designing such means of coordination already presupposes considerable knowledge about the process of production – and it is just this knowledge that is lacking.

In the context of optimizing a production system (e.g., Galloway, 1996), and absent templates that can be copied exactly (Winter and Szulanski, 2001), an experimental approach may proceed in the following manner. First, one must isolate the system boundaries, that is, where the relevant relationships among assets are most likely to be. Second, the process of adjusting assets to each other must be organized like a controlled experiment (or a sequence of such experiments) to isolate the system from outside disturbances. Third, there must be some sort of guidance for the experiment. This may take many forms, ranging from centrally provided instructions to negotiated agreements to shared understandings of where to begin experimenting, how to avoid overlapping experiments, how to revise the experiment in light of past results, and so on. While the analogy is

---

[6] As noted previously, this idea of complex relations among heterogeneous assets, applied to an economy-wide scale, is at the heart of Mises' position in the socialist calculation debate (Salerno, 1990b).

[7] Note that the problem here is not what Hayek (1948) calls the "coordination of plans" across individuals, but the technical coordination of activities even under the control of a single entrepreneur. For critiques of Hayek's concept of plan coordination see Kirzner (2000) and Klein (2008a).

inexact, problem-solving activities in firms have many of the features of experimental activity. For example, iteration between the problem-solving efforts of distributed, but highly interdependent, teams often characterizes major development efforts, such as the Boeing 777 development effort and Microsoft Windows (Cusumano, 1997). In the Boeing project, the team working on a 20-piece wing flap found 251 interferences where parts occupied the same coordinates in space, which gave rise to constant iteration between design efforts in different subproblems (Sabbagh, 1995).[8] The following quotation from a software developer is illustrative:

> A lot of time people don't realize that they are dependent on something. It's just not obvious. For example, you don't realize that you have a dependency because you are not familiar with that part of the code. Or a dependency just sort of materializes out of thin air because of a need and is tracked informally. Or instances where the solution to one dependency creates problems for a third party. The real problems with the hidden interdependencies – the ones that no one thought about – pop up at the last minute.
>   (quoted by Staudenmayer and Cusumano, 1998: 18–19)

The developer goes on to stress the need for carefully managing the process of iteration. Such management often mimics a controlled experiment in which all connected developments efforts, except for a few whose exact links need to be further investigated, are temporarily halted.

Organizing the experimental process. The central problem is how a problem-solving experimental process is best organized. Does the need for experimentation help explain the existence of the firm, or can such experimentation be organized efficiently through markets? Nickerson and Zenger (2004) address this using a problem-solving perspective derived from Simon (1962) and Kauffman (1993). In their approach, "problems" come well-defined. However, solutions to problems (which may relate to virtually any business activity, e.g., a problem of setting up a greenfield investment, reducing production costs with a certain percentage, marketing new products, etc.) do not exist in ready-made form and need identification and exploration. Similar

---

[8] The need for iteration between subproblems and succeeding design changes follows from the impossibility of getting the decomposition of the problem right initially (see Simon 1973: 191).

to the way we described the entrepreneur's search over a landscape in Chapter 5, Nickerson and Zenger argue that firms search and that such search depends on the characteristics of the problem (its degree of decomposability, Simon, 1962) as well as the search heuristics employed by the firm. Search for problems that are highly decomposable may take place in the market; however, less decomposable problems are best solved within the hierarchy. This is partly because the latter involves deep knowledge sharing, which thrives best inside hierarchy. But it is also a matter of coordinating heterogeneous assets.

In a world of heterogeneous assets with attributes that are costly to measure and foresee, complete contracts cannot be drafted. The resulting set of incomplete contracts may constitute a firm, a process of coordination managed by the entrepreneur's central direction. If relationship-specific assets are involved, and contractual relations must be frequently renegotiated, then the holdup problem becomes a serious concern. This is what Williamson (1996: 102–103) means when he writes:

Some [unanticipated] disturbances … require coordinated responses, lest the individual parts operate at cross-purposes or otherwise suboptimize. Failure of coordination may arise because autonomous parties read and react to signals differently, even though their purpose is to achieve a timely and compatible combined response …

More generally, parties that bear a long-term bilateral dependency relation to one another must recognize that incomplete contracts require gapfilling and sometimes get out of alignment. Although it is always in the collective interest of autonomous parties to fill gaps, correct errors, and effect efficient realignments, it is also the case that the distribution of the resulting gains is indeterminate. Self-interested bargaining predictably obtains. Such bargaining is itself costly. The main costs, however, are that transactions are maladapted to the environment during the bargaining interval … Lest the aforementioned costs and delays associated with strategic bargaining be incurred, the relation is reconfigured by supplanting autonomy by hierarchy. The authority relation (fiat) has adaptive advantages over autonomy for transactions of a bilaterally (or multilaterally) dependent kind.

Williamson does not use the metaphor of the laboratory experiment, but the idea is similar: namely that "coordinated adaptation" may be necessary in complex, interdependent systems surrounded by Knightian uncertainty.

We would add, however, that asset specificity may itself be an outcome of an experimental process. To be sure, Williamson (e.g., 1985, 1996) clearly allows for intertemporal considerations relating to what he calls the "fundamental transformation" (i.e., the transformation of large-numbers to small-numbers situations, and therefore the emergence of asset specificity). However, Williamson doesn't describe this process in much detail. In our approach, as experimental activity provides information about how to organize the "system," assets will be increasingly specific in time and location.[9] Temporal and site specificity will tend to increase as assets become more efficiently coordinated. This provides one rationale for organizing the experiments inside firms. Firms may also be justified by problems associated with the dispersion of knowledge across agents. Production systems may exhibit multiple equilibria, and it may not be obvious how to coordinate on a particular equilibrium or even which equilibria are preferred.

In principle, an experimenting team could hire an outside consultant who guides the experimental activity, giving advice on the sequence of actions and asset uses, initiating the experiments, drawing the appropriate conclusions from each experiment, determining how these conclusions should influence further experimentation, and so on. However, such an arrangement is likely to run into serious bargaining costs (see the Williamson quote above). Under market contracting any team member can veto the advice provided by the consultant, and submitting to authority may be the least costly way to organize the experimental activity. "Authority" here means that the entrepreneur has the right to redefine and reallocate decision rights among team members and to sanction team members who do not use their decision rights efficiently. By possessing these rights, entrepreneur-managers can conduct experiments without continuously having to renegotiate contracts, saving bargaining and drafting costs. Such an arrangement then provides a setting for carrying out "controlled" experiments in which the entrepreneur-manager changes only some aspects of the relevant tasks to trace the effects of specific rearrangements of rights.

---

[9] This is like the idea, in Austrian business-cycle theory, that general-purpose assets become specialized to a particular place in the economy's intertemporal structure of production as they are used, leading to misallocations of resources when interest rates change (Klein, 1999b: 185–187).

Establishing these property rights is tantamount to forming a multi-asset, multi-person firm.

The boundaries of the firm

The boundaries of firms in an entrepreneurial perspective

In the mainstream theory of the firm (see Chapter 6), the boundaries of the firm are explained in comparative-static terms. For Coase (1937), optimum boundaries exist where the transaction costs of organizing a transaction internally are exactly equal to costs of the relevant contractual alternative, on the margin. When this marginal equality is established for all transactions that the firm is involved in the firm's optimum boundaries are defined. Later theories (e.g., Hart, 1995; Williamson, 1991a) cast the analysis in more discrete, rather than marginal, terms, but in these analyses boundaries still result from well-specified optimization problems. Although Williamson (1985, 1996) explicitly allows for process considerations, uncertainty, and unexpected events, the governance ramifications of these can be anticipated at the time of contracting and folded into the choice and design of efficient governance structures. New property-rights theory (Grossman and Hart, 1986; Hart and Moore, 1990) explicitly assumes that parties to a relation can anticipate (probabilistically) the distribution of payoffs associated with various ownership structures (essentially, they have rational expectations). Given this, they choose the efficient structure of ownership (since the payoffs are common knowledge – i.e., uncertainty is ruled out). However, in spite of these features we can make use of new property-rights theory to illuminate the boundaries of the firm from an entrepreneurial perspective.

In Hart's incomplete-contracting approach, parties anticipate their bargaining positions after entering a contractual relationship and adapt the incentives to make relationship-specific investments accordingly. The stronger the *ex post* bargaining position, the higher the *ex ante* incentives to make relationship-specific investments. Obtaining ownership rights over tangible and intangible assets strengthens the bargaining position. Ownership rights include the residual rights to control over an asset – the right to "fill in the blanks" of a contract – and allow the owner to exclude others from accessing an asset. In the new property-rights approach, acquiring ownership rights is thus seen to be an overarching instrument to strengthen the bargaining position. Moreover, the allocation of ownership rights influences the incentives to invest in the development of a business idea.

Consider a version of the property-rights story with an entrepreneurial twist. Assume there are two aspiring entrepreneurs, Bill and Mary, whose activities are vertically related.[10] Bill is active upstream from Mary, producing an intermediate product with the help of a resource A. Mary produces and sells the final product, using the resource B. Both could invest into searching for a business idea – that is, forming a judgment – that makes their stage of production more efficient or enhances its quality. We assume that the business ideas lead to a higher quality of the final product in the following. Both Bill and Mary are interested in making the final product more competitive through quality benefits, thereby allowing them to charge a higher price than their competitors. That is, the vertical structure and the existing resources A and B provide guidance in the entrepreneurial search. The implementation of a business idea requires access to both assets A and B. The investments into a business idea are therefore relationship-specific.

For the sake of simplicity, assume that the relationship only exists for two periods. In t_0, Bill and Mary separately decide on investments into searching and developing business ideas that increase the price of the final product. However, in t_0, there is uncertainty about the exact specification of the intermediate product to be delivered to Mary, so the two contracting parties are unable to write a complete contract. Uncertainty about the specification of the intermediate product is resolved in t_1, when the final product is produced and sold. Under those conditions, both contracting parties may be reluctant to make substantial investments into a business idea, since they anticipate a possible holdup by the other contracting party. For example, after Bill makes substantial investments into a quality-improving idea, Mary might demand a much higher quality from Bill for the agreed-upon price. Since Bill's business idea requires access to both resources A and B, Bill grudgingly has to accept a much lower share of profit to cover his initial investment costs. This reasoning corresponds to the analysis in transaction cost economics (Williamson, 1985). By investing into a relationship-specific business idea, the

---

[10] This follows Stieglitz and Foss (2010).

contractual relationship undergoes a fundamental transformation, making both parties bilaterally dependent on each other. The suggested remedy is vertical integration – placing the resources A and B under common ownership – to safeguard the specific investments. However, transaction cost economics does not address who should acquire whose assets, and, thereby, who will be the entrepreneur with a business idea.

The answer provided by the new property-rights approach is that ownership of resources influences the incentives to make specific investments. Ownership of a resource is defined in terms of having the residual control rights over a resource, especially the right to exclude others from a resource. The allocation of ownership rights thereby shapes the bargaining positions of contracting parties. If Mary owns resources A and B, she can exclude Bill from accessing the resources and implementing his business idea. Due to her ownership position, she can hold Bill up and appropriate most of the value created by Bill's business idea.

The benefits of vertical integration and placing both resources under common ownership are therefore the increase in bargaining power by the owner and the strengthening of the owner's incentive to invest money into the search for a business idea. It also implies that there are costs to vertical integration, the weaker incentives to engage in entrepreneurial search by non-owners. If Mary owns both resources, Bill does not have a high-powered incentive to search for business ideas for these, since Mary can appropriate much of the value created simply by threatening Bill with exclusion from the needed resources. Ownership over resources thus influences the ability to appropriate entrepreneurial rents, and thereby shapes the incentives to engage in forming entrepreneurial judgment in the first place. It also implies that the *identity* of the entrepreneur matters. From a new property-rights perspective, who develops and implements judgment and acquires ownership rights to assets critically depends on the respective potential for value creation. Mary acquires ownership rights over A and B if she expects that the added value outweighs the surplus created by Bill. Under those conditions, Mary is ready to offer a higher price for acquiring the resources and placing them under common ownership. In sum, the argument that judgment and asset ownership are complementary also makes sense from the perspective of holdup and underinvestment.

Overall, the new property-rights approach adds important insight
into entrepreneurship by highlighting the importance of the *ex post*
bargaining position for the *ex ante* incentives to forming and refining judgment (conceived here as entrepreneurial search). The primary way to secure prospective entrepreneurial rewards, according
to the new property-rights approach, is to acquire ownership rights of
complementary resources. Ownership rights contain residual rights
of control over a resource and especially the right to exclude others
from accessing a resource. They increase the bargaining position of
the owner vis-à-vis other resource owners. In addition, the resources
currently under common ownership guide entrepreneurial search in
the vast space of possible resource combinations. However, the new
property-rights approach at best allows for a stark, somewhat limited
picture of entrepreneurship; only owners engage in entrepreneurial
search and make substantial investments into relationship-specific
resources. It is unclear how non-owners may be motivated to engage
in entrepreneurial search. We examine this in Chapter 8. Here we go
beyond the static perspective of the new property-rights economics
and address the dynamics of firm boundaries.

The dynamics of firm boundaries

The notion of judgment, as elaborated in Chapter 4, as well as recent
theoretical and empirical research on search, suggests that agents use
specialized mental models to navigate the vast space of combinations
of heterogeneous resources (see Nickerson and Zenger, 2004; Gavetti,
2005; Gavetti and Rivkin, 2007).[11] Using a simulation model, Gavetti
and Levinthal (2000) show that effectiveness of entrepreneurial
search may be substantially enhanced by cognitive representations of
the resource space. A cognitive representation is a simplified picture
of the resource space. A well-informed cognitive representation is part

---

[11] In contrast, Denrell *et al.* (2003) take a more Kirznerian stance, arguing
that entrepreneurs stumble upon resource combinations by serendipity.
Entrepreneurial search or discovery is guided by prior access to idiosyncratic
resources, but not by entrepreneurial cognition: "What is the role of
strategizing and intentionality in this story? According to the argument it
is unlikely that the firm acquired most of the components based on some
vision of the value of the eventual combination. In this sense, the process of
opportunity recognition is serendipitous" (Denrell *et al.*, 2003: 986).

of the entrepreneur's judgment and allows him to identify attractive regions in a problem space. Because the cognitive representation is just a coarse-grained depiction of the resource space, an entrepreneur engages in local technical and commercial experimentation to refine the initial business idea. Thus, the overall conception of entrepreneurial search emerging from this stream of research is that the initial identification of an opportunity is initially guided by a coarse representation of possible resource combinations. After the discovery of a potential business idea, the entrepreneur proceeds to its refinement and modification (Siggelkow and Levinthal, 2003). Hence, what the cognitive representation fundamentally represents is the entrepreneurial expectation and speculation about more attractive regions in the resource space.

Above we argued that the notion of making use of local experimentation to fine-tune a business idea may cast light over the existence of the multi-person firm. It may also be fruitfully applied to the boundaries of the firm. Entrepreneurs also form cognitive representations about which assets they need to secure the services from, the major contractual hazards associated with such procurement, and the most effective ways of protecting against such hazards. This suggests that the same transaction might be governed very differently, as human agents may hold heterogeneous cognitive representations (see Argyres and Liebeskind, 1999; Furubotn, 2002; Mayer and Argyres, 2004). Cognitive representations and the viability of resulting business models get tested in the marketplace, and they get updated and revised by feedback (Stieglitz and Heine, 2007).

Explicitly accounting for the heterogeneity of the mental models of management teams and entrepreneurs introduces an evolutionary twist that so far has been absent from transaction cost economics. In the context of different governance modes existing for managing similar transactions, Williamson (1985) refers to "mistaken integration." However, in an entrepreneurial setting with fundamental uncertainty and heterogeneity, it is not necessarily obvious what is and what isn't "mistaken" economic organization (Furubotn, 2002). In particular, because managers and entrepreneurs hold different mental models, they will value resources differently (Barney, 1986; Denrell *et al.*, 2003). Firm boundaries, and boundary changes, may be understood in this light.

Consider also boundary changes through mergers, acquisitions, divestitures, and other reorganizations. The academic literature clearly suggests that corporate restructurings do, on average, create value (Jarrell, Brickley, and Netter 1988; Andrade, Mitchell, and Stafford 2001). A recurring puzzle, however, is why so many mergers are later "reversed" in a divestiture, spin-off, or carve-out. From a static, equilibrium perspective, reversals indicate error, mendacity, or both, and cast doubt on the efficiency of the market for corporate control (Ravenscraft and Scherer, 1987). In this view, entrenched managers make acquisitions primarily to increase their own power, prestige or control, producing negligible efficiency gains, and acquisitions by manager-controlled firms are likely to be divested *ex post*. Most important, because the acquiring firm's motives are suspect, such acquisitions are *ex ante* inefficient; neutral observers can predict, based on pre-merger characteristics, that these mergers are unlikely to be viable over time. (Moreover, by permitting these acquisitions, capital-market participants are also guilty of systematic error.)

A process-oriented, entrepreneurial view recognized instead that unprofitable acquisitions may be "mistakes" *ex post*, but argues that poor long-term performance does not indicate *ex ante* inefficiency (Klein and Klein, 2001). In this perspective, a divestiture of previously acquired assets may mean simply that profit-seeking entrepreneurs have updated their forecasts of future conditions or otherwise learned from experience. They are adjusting the structure of heterogeneous capital assets specific to their firms. As Mises (1949: 252) puts it, "the outcome of action is always uncertain. Action is always speculation." Consequently, "the real entrepreneur is a speculator, a man eager to utilize his opinion about the future structure of the market for business operations promising profits. This specific anticipative understanding of the conditions of the uncertain future *defies any rules and systematization*" (1949: 585, emphasis added).

Klein and Klein (2001) discuss empirical evidence that the long-term success or failure of corporate acquisitions cannot, in general, be predicted by measures of manager control or principal-agent problems. However, significantly higher rates of divestiture tend to follow mergers that occur in a cluster of mergers in the same industry. As argued by Mitchell and Mulherin (1996), Andrade *et al.* (2001), and Andrade and Stafford (2004), mergers frequently occur in industry clusters, suggesting that mergers are driven in part by industry-specific factors, such as regulatory shocks. When an industry is regulated, deregulated, or reregulated, economic calculation becomes more difficult, and entrepreneurial activity is hampered. It should not be surprising that poor long-term performance is more likely under those conditions.

This notion of entrepreneurial decision-making under uncertainty squares with recent theories of acquisitions as a form of experimentation (Mosakowski, 1997; Boot, Milbourn, and Thakor, 1999; Matsusaka, 2001). In these models, as in the above discussion of the emergence of the multi-person firm as an experimental process, profit-seeking entrepreneurs can learn their own capabilities only by trying various combinations of activities, which could include diversifying into new industries. Firms may thus make diversifying acquisitions even if they know these acquisitions are likely to be reversed in a divestiture. This process generates information that is useful for revising entrepreneurial plans, and thus an acquisition strategy may be successful even if individual acquisitions are not. In these cases, the long-term viability of an acquisition may be systematically related to publicly observable, pre-merger characteristics associated with experimentation, but not characteristics associated with managerial discretion.

Economic calculation, judgment, and the limits of organization

What about the firm's upper bound? In the judgment-based perspective, the limits to firm size can be understood as a special case of the arguments offered by Mises (1920) and Hayek (1937, 1945) about the impossibility of rational economic planning under socialism (Klein, 1996). Kirzner (1992: 162) adopts this approach in interpreting the costs of internal organization in terms of Hayek's knowledge problem: "In a free market, any advantages that may be derived from 'central planning' ... are purchased at the price of an enhanced knowledge problem. We may expect firms to spontaneously expand to the point where additional advantages of 'central planning' are just offset by the incremental knowledge difficulties that stem from dispersed information."

What, precisely, drives this knowledge problem? The mainstream literature on the firm focuses mostly on the costs of market exchange, and much less on the costs of governing internal exchange. It has yet to produce a fully satisfactory explanation of the limits to firm size (Williamson, 1985: chapter 6). Existing contractual explanations rely on problems of authority and responsibility (Arrow, 1974); incentive distortions caused by residual ownership rights (Grossman and Hart, 1986; Holmström and Tirole, 1989; Hart and Moore, 1990); and the costs of attempting to reproduce market governance features within the firm (Williamson, 1985: chapter 6). Rothbard (1962: 544–550) offers an explanation for the firm's vertical boundaries based on Mises' claim that economic calculation under socialism is impossible. Rothbard argues that the need for monetary calculation in terms of actual prices not only explains the failures of central planning under socialism, but places an upper bound on firm size.

As summarized by Klein (1996), Rothbard's account begins with the recognition that Mises' position on socialist economic calculation, as noted above, is not about socialism *per se*, but the role of prices for capital goods. Entrepreneurs allocate resources based on their expectations about future prices, and the information contained in present prices. To make profits, they need information about all prices, not only the prices of consumer goods but the prices of factors of production. Without markets for capital goods, these goods can have no prices, and hence entrepreneurs cannot make judgments about the relative scarcities of these factors. In any environment, then – socialist or not – where a factor of production has no market price, a potential user of that factor will be unable to make rational decisions about its use. Stated this way, Mises' claim is simply that efficient resource allocation in a market economy requires well-functioning asset markets. To have such markets, factors of production must be privately owned.

Rothbard's contribution is to generalize Mises' analysis of this problem under socialism to the context of vertical integration and the size of the organization. Rothbard writes in *Man, Economy, and State* that up to a point, the size of the firm is determined by costs, as in the textbook model. However, "the ultimate limits are set on the relative size of the firm by the necessity for *markets* to exist in every factor, in order to make it possible for the firm to calculate its profits and losses" (Rothbard, 1962: 536). This argument hinges on the notion of "implicit costs." The market value of opportunity costs for factor services – what Rothbard calls "estimates of implicit incomes" – can be determined only if there are external markets for those factors (1962:

542–544). For example, if an entrepreneur hires himself to manage the business, the opportunity cost of his labor must be included in the firm's costs. Yet without an actual market for the entrepreneur's managerial services, he cannot know his opportunity cost; his balance sheets will therefore be less accurate than they would if he could measure his opportunity cost.

The same problem affects a firm owning multiple stages of production. A large, integrated firm is typically organized into semi-autonomous profit centers, each specializing in a particular final or intermediate product. The central management of the firm uses the implicit incomes of the business units, as reflected in statements of divisional profit and loss, to allocate physical and financial capital across the divisions. To compute divisional profits and losses, the firm needs an economically meaningful transfer price for all internally transferred goods and services. If there is an external market for the component, the firm can use that market price as the transfer price. Without a market price, however, the transfer price must be estimated, either on a cost-plus basis or by bargaining between the buying and selling divisions; such estimated transfer prices contain less information than actual market prices.

The use of internally traded intermediate goods for which no external market reference is available thus introduces distortions that reduce organizational efficiency. This gives us the element missing from contemporary theories of economic organization, an upper bound: the firm is constrained by the need for external markets for all internally traded goods. In other words, no firm can become so large that it is both the unique producer and user of an intermediate product; for then no market-based transfer prices will be available, and the firm will be unable to calculate divisional profit and loss and therefore unable to allocate resources correctly between divisions.[12] Of course,

---

[12] Note that in general, Rothbard is making a claim only about the upper bound of the firm, not the incremental cost of expanding the firm's activities (as long as external market references are available). As soon as the firm expands to the point where at least one external market has disappeared, however, the calculation problem exists. The difficulties become worse as more and more external markets disappear, as "islands of noncalculable chaos swell to the proportions of masses and continents. As the area of incalculability increases, the degrees of irrationality, misallocation, loss, impoverishment, etc., become greater" (Rothbard, 1962: 548).

internal organization does avoid the holdup problem, which the firm would face if there were a unique outside supplier; conceivably, this benefit could outweigh the increase in "incalculability" (Rothbard, 1962: 548).

Like Kirzner (1992), Rothbard viewed his contribution as consistent with the basic Coasean framework. In a later elaboration of this argument (Rothbard, 1976: 76), he states that his own treatment of the limits of the firm

serves to extend the notable analysis of Professor Coase on the market determinants of the size of the firm, or the relative extent of corporate planning within the firm as against the use of exchange and the price mechanism. Coase pointed out that there are diminishing benefits and increasing costs to each of these two alternatives, resulting, as he put it, in an "'optimum' amount of planning" in the free market system. Our thesis adds that the costs of internal corporate planning become prohibitive as soon as markets for capital goods begin to disappear, so that the free-market optimum will always stop well short not only of One Big Firm throughout the world market but also of any disappearance of specific markets and hence of economic calculation in that product or resource.

"Central planning" within the firm, then, is possible only when the firm exists within a larger market setting. Ironically, the only reason the Soviet Union and the communist nations of Eastern Europe could exist at all is that they never fully succeeded in establishing socialism worldwide, so they could use world market prices to establish implicit prices for the goods they bought and sold internally (Rothbard, 1991: 73–74).

The impossibility of selective intervention

Of course, firms have the great advantage relative to socialist planning boards that they can to a much larger extent rely on the prices of outside markets. Thus, the Misesian calculation problem, while helping to explain the sizes of firms, does not imply that firm organization itself, unlike socialism, is "impossible." However, some of the property-rights insights into socialism also apply to firms. In particular, a good deal of recent analytical energies have been devoted to the commitment problems of delegation in firms (e.g., Williamson, 1985; Miller, 1992; Baker, Gibbons, and Murphy 1999). Williamson (1996) refers to these kinds of problems with his concept of the "impossibility of (efficient) selective intervention." The main problem is that incentives are diluted. This is because the option to intervene "can be exercised both for good cause (to support expected net gains) and for bad (to support the subgoals of the intervenor)" (Williamson, 1996: 150–151). Promises only to intervene for good cause can never be credible, Williamson argues, because they are not enforceable.

A main conclusion in this literature is indeed that credible delegation may be very hard to sustain, since reneging on a promise to delegate will in many cases be very tempting and those to whom rights are delegated anticipate this.[13] An immediate implication of this kind of reasoning is that emulating market organization inside firms, for example, by radically decentralizing the firm and allocating far-reaching decision rights to employees may be hard to accomplish in a successful manner. Unlike independent agents in markets, corporate employees never possess ultimate decision rights. They are not full owners. This means that those who possess ultimate decision rights can always overrule employees. Thus, there are incentive limits to the extent to which market mechanisms can be applied inside firms, and

---

[13] The problem can be stated in the following way (see Baker *et al.*, 1999). Assume that a subordinate initiates a project, where a "project" may refer to many different types of decisions or clusters of decisions. Assume further that the manager has information that is necessary to perform an assessment of the project, but that he decides upfront to ratify *any* project that the subordinate proposes. Effectively, this amounts to full informal delegation of the rights to initiate and ratify projects – "informal," because the formal right to ratify is still in the hands of the manager and because that right cannot be allocated to the subordinate through a court-enforceable contract (see Williamson, 1996). Because the subordinate values being given freedom, this will induce more effort in searching for new projects (Aghion and Tirole, 1997). The expected benefits of these increased efforts may overwhelm the expected costs from bad projects that the manager has to ratify. However, the problem is that because the manager has information about the state of a project ("bad" or "good"), he may be tempted to renege on a promise to delegate decision authority, that is, intervene in a "selective" manner. But if he overrules the subordinate, the latter will lose trust in him, holding back on effort. Clearly, in this game a number of equilibria are feasible. The particular equilibrium that emerges will be determined by the discount rate of the manager, the specific trigger strategy followed by the subordinate (e.g., will he lose trust in the manager for all future periods if he is overruled?), and how much the manager values his reputation for not reneging relative to the benefits of reneging on a bad project (for details and extensions, see Baker *et al.*, 1999).

delegation, while not exactly a rare flower, is certainly a very delicate one.

Other means of introducing market mechanisms inside firms are also problematic, if for somewhat different reasons. Thus, multi-task agency theory suggests that there are quite rational reasons for the "low-powered" incentives one typically observes inside firms (in contrast to the "high-powered" incentives of the marketplace) (Holmström and Milgrom, 1991). This is because managers wish employees to undertake multiple tasks, some of which may be very costly to observe and measure, but which may nevertheless be vital to the firm (e.g., sharing knowledge with colleagues, handling calling customers in a polite manner, etc.). Providing incentives that are only tied to those tasks that can be measured (at low cost) risks twisting efforts away from the costly-to-measure tasks. These problems would appear to be particularly acute in Hayekian settings, because of dispersed knowledge.

Conclusions

In summary, while the mainstream Coasean, contractual approach to the firm – particularly when dressed in formal, mathematical garb – is tied closely to neoclassical economics notions of static efficiency, there is room for incorporating ideas about entrepreneurship, ideas that generate alternative perspectives on the basic issues of the firm's nature and structure. Firms exist not simply to economize on given transaction costs, or to mitigate hazards caused by exogenous conditions of asset specificity. Rather, firms exist as manifestations of entrepreneurial judgment – to realize their visions, entrepreneurs must take possession of resources and, in a world of heterogeneous assets and Knightian uncertainty, they are continually combining and recombining these resources. Doing so as a network of independent contractors, each possessing residual income and control rights over his own resources, would be prohibitively costly. Hence it makes sense for entrepreneurs to own complementary resources.

And yet, resource bundles are not chosen "optimally," in the neoclassical economics notion of optimality. Entrepreneurs exercise judgment about these combinations – not only in the small, owner-operated firm, but in the large, complex, multi-person enterprise, and hence they are continually readjusting their structure, boundaries, and (as we discuss in the next chapter) internal organization. What Schumpeter called the "perennial gale of creative destruction" applies not only to creation and dissolution of entire firms and industries, but the continual changes in firm boundaries that occur in a competitive market economy – to the benefit of consumers.

8 | *Internal organization: original and derived judgment*

The entrepreneurship literature in economics and management is biased towards start-up firms. And yet, profit opportunities are imagined, evaluated, and captured by existing firms. Employees often play a key role for developing and pursuing business opportunities (Baumol, 1994; Bhardwaj, Camillus, and Hounshell 2006). In fact, modern firms increasingly encourage "intrapreneurship," "autonomous strategic initiatives," and "corporate venturing" at all levels of the organization (e.g., Day and Wendler, 1998; Yonekura and Lynskey, 2002; Covin and Miles, 2007; De Clercq, Castaner, and Belausteguigoitia 2007). Clayton Christensen's *Innovator's Dilemma* (1997), one of the most influential business books of the last two decades, deals with the difficulties facing established firms that try to innovate.

To foster entrepreneurial attitudes and behavior, managers must give employees significant discretion. The need for such entrepreneurial attitudes is partly driven by deep-seated changes, sometimes placed under the rubric of the "knowledge economy" (Foss, 2005). Thus, greater variability in the environments firms confront, more emphasis on innovation as a competitive tool, an increased need to source heterogeneous knowledge inputs, and so on call for an increased reliance on decision-making within firms that is not only fast, but also adaptive and intelligent.[1] This amounts to an increase of delegation of discretion to employees at all levels in order to make them exercise responsible judgment. Cowen and Parker (1997: 28) cogently summarize this line of thinking:

Market changes are moving manufacturing farther and farther away from steady-state, low variety, long-batch production runs, relevant to Taylorist

---

[1] For example, Foss, Laursen, and Pedersen (in press) show that firms engaged in interaction with users for the purpose of leveraging their knowledge in the context of innovation have a high level of delegation/decentralization.

methods, to high variety and small runs ... Organizations are adopting new forms of decentralization to cope with the instability, uncertainty, and pace of change of the market-place ... In clusters of network working, employees of undifferentiated rank may operate temporarily on a certain task or tasks in teams. The clusters are largely autonomous and engage in decentralized decision-making and planning ... They are conducive to individual initiative ("intrapreneurship") and faster decision-taking. They facilitate organizational flexibility.

A parallel argument asserts that the increased importance of knowledge in production tends to erode authority-based definitions of the boundaries of the firm, because authority increasingly shifts to expert individuals who control crucial information resources and may not be employees of the firm.[2] To the extent that important knowledge assets are increasingly controlled by employees ("knowledge workers") themselves, traditional authority relations are fading into insignificance. This is partly a result of the increased bargaining power on the part of knowledge workers (stemming from the control over critical knowledge assets), and partly a result of the increasingly specialist nature of knowledge work (Hodgson, 1998; Rousseau and Shperling, 2003). The latter implies that principals/employers may not know the full set of actions open to agents/employees, thus making the exercise of authority through direction increasingly inefficient (Minkler, 1993a, 1993b).

While systematic empirical evidence on delegation and decentralization is sketchy, several studies document increased use of high-powered incentives and broad-based decision authority in particular firms and industries. Rajan and Wulf (2006) document an increase in breadth (more managers reporting to CEO) and decrease in depth (fewer managers between CEO and division heads) in a cross-industry sample of US companies in the 1980s and 1990s. The literature on organizational complementarities finds that the diffusion of information technology inside the workplace during this period

---

[2] As Zucker (1991: 164) argues: "While bureaucratic authority is by definition located within the firm's boundaries, expert authority depends on the information resources available to an individual, and not on the authority of office. Thus, authority may be located within the organization ... but when an external authority market can provide information that leads to greater effectiveness, then authority tends to migrate into the market."

was accompanied by increased use of delegation, performance-based pay, and teams (Milgrom and Roberts, 1995; Ichniowski, Shaw, and Prennushi, 1997; Bresnahan, Brynjolfsson, and Hitt, 2002). Foss and Laursen (2005) find that firms in "dynamic" industries are more likely to delegate decision rights, make use of performance pay, and let employees multitask. In an earlier study (Laursen and Foss, 2003) they find that firms making extensive use of "new organizational practices" – delegation, bonuses, quality circles, job rotation, and the like – are more innovative than firms using only a few of such practices, or none at all.

The combined effect of the increased importance of knowledge assets that are controlled by knowledge workers themselves and of the increasingly specialist nature of knowledge work is to challenge the traditional economist's criterion of what distinguishes market transactions from hierarchical transactions (Zingales, 2000). Thus, whether direction by means of giving orders (Coase, 1937; Simon, 1951; Williamson, 1985; Demsetz, 1991) and backed up by the ownership of alienable assets (Hart and Moore, 1990) takes place is increasingly irrelevant for understanding the organization of economic activities in a knowledge economy (Grandori, 2001). Or so the argument goes.

In this chapter, we develop a framework for analyzing entrepreneurship within firms. We then use this framework to evaluate claims that authority and "traditional" firm organization are fading under the impact of delegation of decision rights to entrepreneurial employees who control critical knowledge. We find these claims suspect on theoretical grounds, and note while there are many anecdotes about flattening hierarchies, "starfish" organizations (Brafman and Beckstrom, 2006), "wikified" firms (Tapscott and Williams, 2008), there is little systematic empirical evidence that authority is a vestige of the "old economy."

We start from the fact that delegated rights can be used in both beneficial and harmful ways, presenting managers with a challenge between encouraging beneficial entrepreneurship and limiting harmful entrepreneurship inside the firm. Building on key ideas from earlier chapters, we develop a framework for analyzing this trade-off. We link this analysis to issues of the employment relation and asset ownership, arguing that our entrepreneurial perspective provides a fresh look on these classic issues in the economic theory of the firm.

As we argued in Chapter 7, when entrepreneurial judgment is complementary to other assets, these assets or their services are not traded in well-functioning markets, and refining the entrepreneur's business plan requires local experimentation, it makes sense for entrepreneurs to hire labor and own assets. The entrepreneur's role, then, is to arrange and rearrange the human and capital assets under his control. This role becomes particularly important in a dynamic economy in which agents face unforeseen changes so that sequential decision-making, such as revising business plans that embody entrepreneurial judgment, is necessary (Coase, 1937; Hayek, 1945; Lachmann, 1956; Williamson, 1996). Contrary to the argument that such conditions render the exercise of authority based on ownership inefficient (Hodgson, 1998; Carson, 2008), we argue that asset ownership plays a critical role in facilitating the entrepreneurial revision of such plans.

The claim we've been making throughout the book that entrepreneurial judgment is manifest in ownership is straightforward for small firms with one or few owners. It is harder to see the entrepreneurial element in ownership within large, complex organizations with fragmented ownership and decentralized decision-making. We argue that a type of Knightian entrepreneurship – what we term *original judgment* – is inseparable from resource ownership, and is exercised by owners even if they delegate most day-to-day decisions to subordinates. In firms with decentralized organizational structures, employees have considerable latitude but, as non-owners, their discretion is limited (Holmström and Milgrom, 1990). In our framework, employees holding decision authority act as "proxy-entrepreneurs," exercising delegated or *derived judgment* on behalf of their employers. Such employees are asked not to carry out routine instructions in a mechanical, passive way, but to apply their own judgment to new circumstances or situations that may be unknown to the employer. This type of arrangement is typically seen in the management literature as a form of empowerment, encouraging employees to utilize the knowledge best known to them and giving them strong incentives to do so (e.g., Osterloh and Frey, 2000; Gagné and Deci, 2005). Such discretion is ultimately limited, because owners retain the rights to hire and fire employees and to acquire or dispose of complementary capital goods.[3]

The precise manner in which employees' discretion is limited is given by the firm's organizational structure – its formal and informal systems of rewards and punishments, rules for settling disputes and renegotiating agreements, means of evaluating performance, and so on. Under some organizational structures, the employment relation is highly constrained, giving employees few opportunities to engage in proxy-entrepreneurship – exercising a form of judgment derived from the primary, or original, judgment of the entrepreneur-owner. In other firms the employment relation may be much more open. Granting such latitude to employees brings benefits and costs. As agents become less constrained, they are likely to engage in both "productive" proxy-entrepreneurship – activities that increase firm value – and "destructive" proxy-entrepreneurship, meaning activities that reduce firm value. One important function of contracts and organizational design is to balance productive against destructive proxy-entrepreneurship by selecting and enforcing the proper contractual constraints. The optimal organizational structure encourages employees to use derived judgment in ways that increase firm value while discouraging unproductive rent-seeking, influence activities, and other forms of proxy-entrepreneurship that destroy value. The allocation of ownership rights and the characteristics of the employment relation thus matter for the efficient exercise of judgment.

Original and derived judgment

"Original judgment" is the kind of judgment we have discussed in earlier chapters: the entrepreneurial formation and execution of a business idea. The idea may be anything from a loose, overall concept

---

[3] To state the problem differently: decentralized decision rights and outcome-based compensation approximate the high-powered incentives of private property and the price mechanism, but not perfectly (Foss, 2003). *De facto* discretion is not a perfect substitute for *de jure* discretion: a line worker may have effective control of "his" machine, for example, but – unlike an actual owner – cannot sell or give away the machine. We thus stand with Coase (1937), Williamson (1985, 1996), and Hart (1995) and against Alchian and Demsetz (1972) and Jensen and Meckling (1976) in seeing firm and market as alternative mechanisms for resource allocation, rather than simply different sets of contractual relations.

of how to combine inputs into outputs to a carefully specified, detailed business plan. A business plan involves the identification and coordination of inputs and activities designed to make the business profitable.

An entrepreneur with a potentially valuable business plan will often need employees so that he delegates parts of its implementation to agents, such as salaried managers.[4] Moreover, as Rajan and Zingales (1998) point out, the entrepreneur will often wish those employees to make relationship-specific human capital investments to increase the total value of the plan. Since he cannot own these human resources, he needs to find contractual or organizational mechanisms to induce relationship-specific investments by safeguarding employees and protecting them against *ex post* recontracting. Giving employees access to his business idea may provide incentives to undertake such investments because it raises the bargaining power of the employee. For example, assume that the entrepreneur's idea rests on a new technology that the employee has to develop further. The employee needs access to the technology to work with it. However, gaining access to the technology also means that the employee may learn about the business idea, and then walk away with it to start his own venture, sell it to rivals, or otherwise seek to extract rents from the entrepreneur. Clearly, allowing employees to access the business plan gives rise to trade-offs, and not surprisingly Knight (1921: 297, emphasis in original) stressed that "in organized activity the *crucial* decision is the selection of men to make decisions."

For Knight (1921: 296), the hierarchy is one in which managers placed at different levels judge managers below them, because what matters is "knowledge of a man's capacity to deal with a problem, not concrete knowledge of the problem itself." This differs from the notion that the hierarchy may be described as hierarchically nested agency relations (as in Tirole, 1986), because Knight explicitly does not make the agency-theoretic assumption that the principal knows

---

[4] We assume here a single entrepreneur-owner, but an individual or group could have an idea, then seek additional investor-partners to be joint owners of the venture, prior to (or in conjunction with) hiring employees. In that case, the members of the ownership group jointly exercise original judgment. This raises, of course, a host of issues related to collective action, preference aggregation, and the like. We discuss these in Chapter 9 below.

the set of decisions that may be made relative to a concrete problem; he assumes instead that the principal can judge the agent's general ability to solve a problem. Knight (1921: 276) also clearly recognized that in delegating discretion to employees in order to carry out his entrepreneurial plan (giving them access in the sense of Rajan and Zingales, 1998), the entrepreneur makes his employees entrepreneurs themselves, what we call "proxy-entrepreneurs": "When, however, the managerial function comes to require the exercise of judgment, involving *liability to error,* and when in consequence the assumption of *responsibility* for the correctness of his opinions becomes a condition prerequisite to getting the other members of the group to submit to the manager's direction, the manager becomes an entrepreneur."

However, the entrepreneur will limit the employees' entrepreneurial behavior as the overall, essential actions to be taken are already laid out in the plan. These place constraints on the set of behaviors the employees can engage in. If the entrepreneur recognizes a need for ongoing adjustment of the business plan, and wishes to take advantage of specific knowledge he himself does not possess, he will delegate the right to exercise derived judgment to employees.[5]

The hierarchy of delegation may be deep and nested. Owners may choose to exercise original judgment directly, in the day-to-day management of assets, or to delegate some or all proximate decision rights to subordinates. Owners may be represented by a board of directors that decides which decision rights to delegate to managers, who exercise derived judgment over resource uses (and try to communicate such judgments to the board). Managers may then further delegate their own derived judgment rights to lower-level employees. As Knight (1921) argued, corporate governance is a nested hierarchy of judgment. In an important sense, however, original judgment remains with the owner, because as a minimum, even the most "passive" owners must choose someone to manage the asset. Rothbard (1962: 538) puts it this way:

Hired managers may successfully direct production or choose production processes. But the ultimate responsibility and control of production rests

---

[5] Note that the notion of "derived judgment" does not imply a subordinate position in economic or legal significance; the notions of original and derived judgment are hierarchical (and temporal).

inevitably with the owner, with the businessman whose property the product is until it is sold. It is the owners who make the decision concerning how much capital to invest and in what particular processes. And particularly, it is the owners who must choose the managers. The ultimate decisions concerning the use of their property and the choice of the men to manage it must therefore be made by the owners and by no one else.[6]

The claim that owners make the "ultimate" decisions about resource use does not imply that owners supply the complete *content* of the firm's entrepreneurial plans. Instead, the owners, or the board of directors on behalf of the owners, may rely on plans and proposals developed by hired managers or outside consultants. In this situation, the board's judgment consists of deciding whether to commit resources to implement the business plan presented by the manager or consultant. In Fama and Jensen's (1983) terminology, owners exercise *decision control* while delegating *decision management* to non-owners.

In large, complex organizations, judgment is delegated across many levels. As the success of the business plan likely depends on the actions of top managers, the board delegates considerable discretion to them. These managers in turn delegate discretion to their own subordinates, and so on throughout the organization. Thus, all levels below the owners exercise judgment that is derived from the original judgment of the owners. For ease of exposition, in the following we focus on a simple model of a single entrepreneur-owner holding original judgment and an employee who can exercise derived judgment. This employee exercises derived judgment in the sense that the entrepreneur delegates discretion to him but constrains his entrepreneurial activities, where the relevant constraints are derived from the original business plan and relate to, for example, the type of activities and the means of coordination described in that plan.

Lachmann (1956: 97–98), in the context of his broader analysis of the economy's capital structure, expresses a very similar notion:

---

[6] Kirzner (1973: 68) argues similarly that entrepreneurial alertness cannot be fully delegated: "It is true that 'alertness' ... may be hired; but one who hires an employee alert to possibilities of discovering knowledge has himself displayed alertness of a still higher order ... The entrepreneurial decision to hire is thus the ultimate hiring decision, responsible in the last resort for all factors that are directly or indirectly hired for his project." Kirzner goes on to quote Knight (1921: 291): "What we call 'control' consists mainly of selecting someone else to do the 'controlling'."

We hear it often said that in the modern industrial world the managers who make decisions about investment, production, and sales are "the entrepreneurs," while capital owners have been reduced to a merely passive role. ... But the argument appears to be based on a fundamental praxeological misconception. No doubt, he who decides on action is "active"; but so is he who creates the conditions in which the decision-maker acts. We have endeavored to explain that the asset structure of the enterprise is a complex network of relationships, transmitting knowledge and the incentive to action from one group to another. The notion of the capital owner as a merely passive recipient of residual income is clearly incompatible with that view.

Lachmann (1956: 98–99) goes on to analyze delegation, using the terms "capitalist-entrepreneur" and "manager-entrepreneur" to describe something very close to our "entrepreneur" and "proxy-entrepreneur," the key being the hierarchy of "specification" in which the capitalist-entrepreneur establishes the conditions under which the manager-operator acts, and so on down the line.

For the sake of terminological clarity it is desirable to call an "entrepreneur" anybody who is concerned with the management of assets. ... [A]s regards capital, the function of the entrepreneur consists in specifying and modifying the concrete form of the capital resources committed to his care.
    We might then distinguish between the capitalist-entrepreneur and the manager-entrepreneur. The only significant difference between the two lies in that the specifying and modifying decisions of the manager presuppose and are consequent upon the decisions of the capitalist. If we like, we may say that the latter's decisions are of a "higher order."
    Thus a capitalist makes a first specifying decision by deciding to invest a certain amount of capital, which probably, though not necessarily, exists in the money form, in Company A rather than in Company B, or rather than to lend it to the government. The managers of Company A then make a second specifying decision by deciding to use the capital so received in building or extending a department store in one suburb rather than another suburb, or another city. The manager of this local department store makes further specifying decisions, and so on, until the capital has been converted into concrete assets.
    All these decisions are specifying decisions.

In our terminology, these "specifying decisions" are the set of formal and implicit contracts by which the entrepreneur delegates judgment to subordinates in the multi-person organization. In deciding what decision rights to delegate, what monitoring and reward systems to implement, what evaluation schemes to use, and so on, the entrepreneur must recognize that – contrary to some of the popular management literature – more delegation is not necessarily better.

Derived entrepreneurship: productive and destructive

The productive/destructive distinction

The general, often implicit claim in the mainstream entrepreneurship literature, both in economics and in management, is that all entrepreneurial activity is socially beneficial (e.g., Mises, 1949; Kirzner, 1973; Yonekura and Lynskey, 2002; Shane, 2003). However, as Baumol (1990) points out, entrepreneurship may be socially harmful: individuals can exercise judgment, alertness, creativity, innovation, etc. in attempts to direct resources or authority to themselves, at the expense of a larger group. Rent-seeking, influence activities, and even fraudulent or criminal behavior, both inside and outside organizations, can be modeled as "entrepreneurial." The creative use of "special-purpose entities" by Enron accountants,[7] the increased reliance by governments on private security firms like Blackwater, the aggressive marketing of mortgage-backed securities by Countrywide Financial, the US Treasury's Troubled Assets Relief Program, the US Federal Reserve System's novel attempts at "quantitative easing" – all can be described as forms of entrepreneurship, but with questionable social benefit.

It thus makes sense to distinguish between productive and destructive entrepreneurship. Consider the distinction in the context of derived entrepreneurship. For employees to exercise derived judgment they must have some discretion. When employees use their discretion to expend effort creating or discovering new attributes and taking control over these in ways that reduce firm value, we will call this destructive entrepreneurship. Thus, discovering new forms of moral hazard (Holmström, 1979), creating holdups (Williamson, 1996),

---

[7] See Bradley (2008) for the case that Enron represented the triumph of "political capitalism," with CEO Ken Lay excelling in regulatory (entrepreneurial) arbitrage.

and inventing new ways of engaging in rent-seeking (Baumol, 1990) are examples of destructive entrepreneurship. Productive entrepreneurship, by contrast, refers to judgment, alertness, creativity, or innovation by employees that increases firm value. In the attributes perspective developed above, productive entrepreneurship consists of the creation or discovery of new attributes that lead to value creation. For example, a franchisee may discover new local tastes that form the basis for new products for the entire chain; an employee may figure out better uses of production assets and communicate this to the TQM team of which he is a member; etc. In the following we use this distinction to sketch an entrepreneurial approach to internal organization.

As a reminder, we assume that employees, while not exercising the original judgment, exercise derived judgment through decision rights that are delegated to them. As proxy-entrepreneurs, they make decisions about the use of resources owned by others.[8] These decisions may be value creating (productive) or value destroying (destructive). Although original judgment cannot be assigned a marginal product, owners can form expectations about the costs and benefits of employees' derived judgments.

Managing derived judgment

Many firms operate on the presumption that beneficial effects can be produced by giving employees more rights to work with company assets, monitoring them less, and trusting them more. We will call this "reducing constraints on employees" in various dimensions. For example, firms such as 3M give research employees free time to pursue their own experimental projects, in hope of encouraging serendipitous discoveries (and as a perquisite that can attract and retain high-quality researchers). Many consulting firms have adopted similar practices. Industrial firms have long known that employees with many decision rights – senior industrial researchers, for example – can be monitored and constrained more loosely than employees charged

---

[8] Of course, to the extent that the proxy-entrepreneur's decisions affect the value of his own personal reputation, human capital, and so on, he is acting as an entrepreneur-owner, exercising original judgment with regard to these intangible, personal assets.

only with routine tasks. More broadly, the increasing emphasis on "empowerment" during recent decades reflects a recognition that employees derive a benefit from controlling aspects of their job situation (Osterloh and Frey, 2000; Gagné and Deci, 2005). The total quality movement emphasizes that delegating various rights to employees motivates them to find new ways to increase the mean and reduce the variance of quality (Jensen and Wruck, 1998). Foss *et al.* (2009) find that highly autonomous job designs (i.e., strong delegation, allowing employees to control significant parts of a work process) increase creativity and encourage knowledge sharing. To the extent that such activities create value, they represent productive entrepreneurship.[9]

Stimulating the productive creation and discovery of new asset attributes by reducing constraints on employees and tying pay to performance results in principal-agent relationships that are open-ended, as agents have opportunities to exercise their own judgment in expanding the set of potential actions beyond those envisioned by the principal. While this open-endedness could bring the principal unanticipated benefits, reducing the constraints that agents face introduces potentially destructive proxy-entrepreneurship. Managing the trade-off between productive and destructive proxy-entrepreneurship thus becomes a critical management task.

Note that we are agnostic here about the precise form the compensation for productive proxy-entrepreneurship should take. It could be bonuses tied to specific outcomes (profit, market value, patents or other innovation measures, introduction of new products, etc.), direct equity stakes, stock options, or something else. (Note that to the extent that employees hold equity stakes in the enterprise, they are acting as entrepreneurs, exercising original judgment, rather than proxy-entrepreneurs exercising derived judgment.) Manne (2010) argues that allowing employees to trade on inside information is a

[9] Our notion of "more constrained" and "less constrained" employment relations includes, but is broader than, the notion of contractual completeness in the transaction-cost literature (e.g., Crocker and Masten, 1991; Crocker and Reynolds, 1993; Saussier, 2000). Crocker and Reynolds (1993) define completeness as the probability that a contingency not covered by prior contractual agreement arises. Under Knightian uncertainty, all contracts are incomplete, meaning that it is impossible to specify all contingencies *ex ante*. The firm's organizational structure, governing the employment relation more broadly, can constrain employee opportunism even when formal contracts are highly incomplete in the Crocker and Reynolds sense.

more effective mechanism for encouraging proxy-entrepreneurship than direct ownership stakes or performance bonuses.[10] Permitting insider trading is a highly general mechanism: unlike bonuses, gains from insider trading can be realized without the need for management to identify and measure individual employees' marginal contributions to firm-level outcomes and, unlike equity stakes, go directly to the employee possessing the information, rather than being shared across all equity holders.

[A]n entrepreneurial compensation system must possess some unusual characteristics if it is to successfully attract the sought-after services. It must appeal to the personality of the entrepreneurial type; it must avoid valuation and attribution issues post hoc; and it must ideally motivate any prospective employee – and possibly even outsiders – to act as an entrepreneur. It is hard even to imagine a system that will meet all these requirements other than the right of corporate employees with valuable new information to trade on that news in advance of public disclosure. (Manne, 2010: 14).

Of course, insider trading is illegal in most jurisdictions, so firms must rely on more conventional forms of incentive-based pay.

However proxy-entrepreneurship is compensated, firms will seek to reduce the chance that derived judgment will be used in ways harmful to the firm. How, though, can destructive proxy-entrepreneurship be minimized? Firms may delimit employees' use of assets, such as telephone and internet, by specifying use rights over the relevant assets, instructing employees to act in a proper manner towards customers, to exercise care when operating the firm's equipment, and the like. However, firms are unlikely to succeed entirely in their attempt to curb value-destroying activities in this way, given the open-endedness described above. Not only is it costly to monitor employees (including costs of reducing intrinsic motivation; see Gagné and Deci, 2005), but employees may creatively circumvent constraints, for example by finding ways to hide their behavior, or inventing behaviors that are not formally prohibited (employment law in many countries stipulates that firms must explicitly define banned behaviors before more drastic sanctions, such as termination, can be imposed on employees).

---

[10] See also Manne (1966a, 1966b).

Although firms may know that such destructive entrepreneurship takes place, they may prefer not to try to constrain it further; the various constraints that firms impose on employees (or, more generally, that contracting partners impose on each other) to curb destructive entrepreneurship may have the unwanted side effect that productive entrepreneurship is also stifled (see Kirzner, 1985). More generally, imposing (too many) constraints on employees may reduce their propensity to create or discover new attributes of productive assets within the limits set by the business plan.

In this context, the employment relation and asset ownership are important because they give owner-entrepreneurs the rights and the ability to define formal and informal contractual constraints, that is, to choose their own preferred trade-offs. Ownership by conferring authority allows the employer-entrepreneur to establish his preferred organizational structure – and therefore a certain combination of productive and destructive entrepreneurship – at lowest cost. This function of ownership is particularly important in a dynamic world (Schumpeter, 1911; Kirzner, 1973; Littlechild, 1986; D'Aveni, 1994), where the trade-offs between productive and destructive entrepreneurship inside the firm are likely to change as the entrepreneur-owner revises his judgment.

An example

Consider a relation between two actors, Jack and Jill. Cooperation between Jack and Jill generates gains from trade because their services are complementary. Each can exercise either original or derived judgment. Assume that the relation is an employment relation and that it involves the use of an asset. The relation is only productive if the asset is used. This asset has multiple attributes in the sense defined in Chapter 5, that is, multiple functions, uses, and characteristics. Jack and Jill do not know all relevant present and future attributes of the asset. Instead, attributes must be created or discovered, over time, as the asset is deployed in production. The relation can be organized so that Jack is employer and Jill employee, or vice versa. The asset may be owned by Jack or by Jill. What allocation of ownership and assignment of roles of employer and employee maximizes value?

The employer exercises original judgment by conceiving and implementing a business plan. The employee exercises derived judgment in executing all or elements of that plan. The employer puts the plan in place by instructing and monitoring the employee in accordance with the plan; for example, by monitoring whether the employee maintains the value of the business plan by keeping the required quality levels of the product or service, physical assets, suppliers, etc. The employer not only forms original judgment, but also revises the business plan in the course of the relation as he discovers new uses of the assets in the project. As the employee is also equipped with entrepreneurial abilities, she may discover hitherto undiscovered attributes of the asset in the relation. Some of these discoveries will add to the value of the business plan, either by adding elements to the plan or increasing the effectiveness of the implementation of the plan. For example, in a restaurant chain, the discovery by a local manager of a new dish may add value to the overall chain.

The employment relation is constrained in several dimensions. There are limits to what the employee can do, as well as when, how, with whom, etc. In other words, the decision (property) rights held by the employee are circumscribed by the employer (see Jones, 1983). The number, scope, and character of such constraints are choice variables (imposing them on the employee obviously requires bargaining power; we deal with this later). The employer may issue more or less detailed instructions. At one end of the spectrum, the employer instructs the employee about everything, and no scope is left for derived judgment. At the other end, the employee has very considerable discretion; she has virtually full scope for exercising derived judgment. Here we use the terminology that the relation can be made more or less "incomplete."[11] Less complete relations are those that give the employee more discretion. To abstract from enforcement issues (which are well-treated in the modern economic theory of the firm) we assume in the example that all constraints that the employer specifies can be costlessly enforced, once implemented. What may require bargaining power, however, is the implementation of the employer's preferred constraints.

---

[11] As explained in footnote 9, we have in mind a broader notion of "completeness" than what is found in modern contract theory.

Value creation as a function of entrepreneurship

As suggested above, there are costs as well as benefits associated with the relaxation of employment constraints, and, hence, an optimum level of incompleteness that is larger than zero. The diagram depicted in Figure 8.1 maps Jack and Jill's expectations (we assume these coincide) about the effect on firm value of the employee's productive and destructive proxy-entrepreneurship. These expectations are functions of the incompleteness of the relation combined with the employer's original judgment, as embodied in the business concept. The trade-off may be regulated by means of the constraints that are placed on the employee, for example, by determining the budgets to which employees have access (Jensen and Meckling, 1992), the activities they can engage in (Holmström, 1989), the people with whom they can work (Holmström and Milgrom, 1990), the type of equipment to which they have access, and how they are allowed to operate that equipment (Barzel, 1997).[12] Such specifications of decision rights are simultaneously specifications of incompleteness. To simplify, one may think of "the degree of incompleteness" in terms of the time that the employee is allowed to use corporate resources (including their own work time) to conduct "research," that is, activities that are not directly prescribed by the employer-owner, as in the above example of 3M allowing its research personnel very considerable discretion.

The solid upward-sloping curves show the benefits that may result from such *productive* proxy-entrepreneurship as a function of the free time the agent is given. These curves thus map those new discoveries of the employee that when implemented complement the employer's original judgment. The claim is that, as the employee is given more freedom, there is a greater probability that she will discover more beneficial attributes of the productive asset she operates. For example, the probability increases that she may discover new ways of making the asset more effective or new markets to which the asset's services may be deployed. The relation between total benefits and more free time is a strictly concave one. The decreasing marginal returns

---

[12] For example, regulating with whom an employee is allowed to interact clearly influences destructive as well as productive entrepreneurship; on the one hand, it may lead to destructive collusion among agents (as in Holmström and Milgrom, 1990), on the other hand it may lead to the generation of new ideas as the TQM literature emphasizes (Jensen and Wruck, 1998).

from new discoveries may be caused by the increasing difficulties of implementing the new discoveries, given that the employer and the employee are constrained in terms of the time that is available for productive activities. Alternatively, the employee's attention is more focused on making valuable discoveries when she has less free time than when she has more.

Because of differential entrepreneurial capabilities, and the complementarities between Jack and Jill's judgments, it matters for the joint gains from trade (i.e., the joint value created from the relation) who assumes the role of principal and who is the agent (and as we argue later, who owns the asset). As drawn in the figure, joint gains from trade are higher when Jill is employee and Jack is employer.

However, there are also costs to giving the employee more free time for discovery, namely destructive entrepreneurial activities. The upward-sloping dashed curve shows the costs from *destructive* proxy-entrepreneurship as a function of the free time the employee is given.[13] The claim is that as the employee is given more freedom, there is a greater probability that she will discover new ways of destroying value. For example, the probability increases that she may discover new ways of misusing equipment, engaging in wasteful new projects, etc. Thus, with increased discretion over the multi-attribute asset, the employee will discover more new ways of controlling attributes, which increases the employee's own benefit, but reduces expected joint surplus.

The parties' preferred constraints

Although the different degrees of incompleteness represent differences in created value for the different teams (i.e., {Jack as employer, Jill as employee}, {Jill as employer, Jack as employee}), we cannot identify the preferred points of the parties until we have taken full account of their costs and benefits, that is, their opportunity costs and the way in which they share the joint gains from trade from the relation. We assume the employee realizes relationship-specific private benefits (i.e., a non-transferable utility) of engaging in entrepreneurial activities and

---

[13] Of course, one may not envision only different joint benefit curves but also different cost curves.

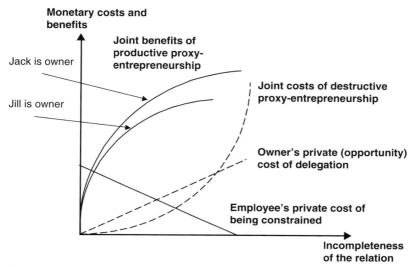

Figure 8.1 Monetary surplus as a function of entrepreneurship

that this provides her sufficient motivation.[14] Because of these benefits, the employee suffers opportunity costs of being constrained.

The downward-sloping solid line in Figure 8.1, assumed to be linear, represents the employee's opportunity costs of being constrained. These costs are inversely related to the degree of incompleteness. The employer suffers opportunity costs (the upward-sloping dashed line) of letting the employee exercise judgment by spending work time and other corporate resources on activities that may lead to discovery, because such resources could have been spent on routine activities. We assume that these costs are a linear function of the time given to the employee. Both parties share the monetary joint surplus in some proportion. We can assume, as is conventional, that they share 50:50. The employee's total benefits are thus the sum of her share of the joint surplus plus her private benefits, while the employer's net benefits are

[14] Aghion and Tirole (1997) make a similar assumption. Anecdotally, the ability to control a certain percentage of one's working hours (a practice associated with firms like 3M) has become an increasing part of many employment packages, particularly in "dynamic" industries (IT, biotech, consulting, etc.). More broadly, much work in motivational psychology points to a close link between intrinsic motivation and conditions that allow individuals to engage in creative pursuits (Gagné and Deci, 2005).

simply his share of the surplus minus his opportunity costs. Given the way these curves have been drawn, the team that maximizes the joint gains from trade (i.e., the net jointly created value) is the one where Jack is employer and Jill is employee.

Given the specification of costs (including opportunity costs) and benefits in Figure 8.1, Figure 8.2 shows the preferred constraints of the parties. Figure 8.2 depicts a curve representing the employer's share of the created value (minus his opportunity costs)[15] and a curve representing the employee's share of the surplus plus her private benefit.[16] Given this, the employer's preferred degree of contractual incompleteness is given by I^*_E and the employee's is given by I^*_e. Thus, the parties disagree about how many constraints should be imposed upon the employee! The parties may strike any contract between I^*_E and I^*_e (this will always be beneficial compared with a situation of no contract). However, given the assumption that a part of the employee's total benefits and the employer's costs are private, bargaining is likely to be costly and dissipate value.

In fact, as the example is constructed, no sharing rule can generate agreement on the preferred degree of contractual incompleteness, and any sharing rule will therefore cause some inefficiency. Moreover, according to Figure 8.2, it is more lucrative to be an employee than to be a principal, which may imply that the party who holds comparative advantages in forming original judgment (i.e., Jack in Figure 8.1) may prefer to be an employee with the party who is comparatively disadvantaged in forming original judgment as an employer (i.e., Jill in Figure 8.1). This is clearly inefficient: As the example has been constructed, the team in which Jack is employer and Jill is employee is more efficient (it creates more value) than the other team.

Absent transaction costs, this inefficiency may be handled through the appropriate choices of sharing rules, side payments, and contractual constraints (Coase, 1960). However, bargaining costs may swamp the benefits from such arrangements (Wernerfelt, 1997). Given bargaining costs, it matters who sets sharing rules and contractual

---

[15] More precisely, the employer receives half the difference between the joint (monetary) benefits of productive proxy-entrepreneurship and the (monetary) cost of destructive proxy-entrepreneurship.

[16] More precisely, the employee receives half the difference between the joint (monetary) benefits of productive proxy-entrepreneurship and the (monetary) cost of destructive proxy-entrepreneurship, plus the (decreasing) benefit of autonomy given by the downward-sloping solid line in Figure 8.1.

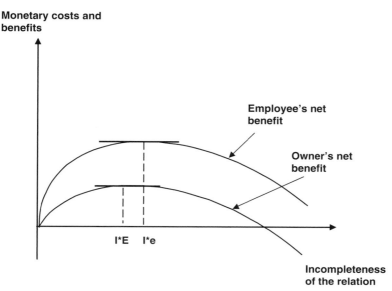

Figure 8.2 The parties' preferred degree of incompleteness

constraints. If, for example, the employee can set the constraints but cannot bribe the principal, not even 100 percent residual claimancy will make it attractive to become the employer, since in this case, the agent will prefer total absence of constraints. In turn, there will be no gains from trade (and the employer still has to suffer the opportunity costs of the employee's entrepreneurial activities). The question then is how these inefficiencies are minimized, that is, choosing the efficient team (i.e., team {Jack is employer, Jill is employee} or {Jill is employer, Jack is employee}), sharing rules and contractual constraints. We argue that ownership to the asset in the relation plays a key role with respect to all three issues.

Implications for economic organization

Who owns what?

Ownership plays a key role in easing entrepreneurship and exchange (i.e., minimizing costs of dissipation). Asset ownership confers a *bundle* of rights, including rights to hitherto unknown attributes of the relevant asset. Ownership reduces information, communication, and contracting costs relative to a situation in which it is necessary to contract over all these rights. Thus, ownership eases the implementation of entrepreneurial judgment in a productive venture by allowing entrepreneurs to acquire, in one transaction, a bundle of rights to attributes (i.e., a distinct asset). This means that the parties do not have to engage in costly bargaining over many rights to single attributes (Barzel, 1997). The dissipation of value is at a minimum. Moreover, ownership also facilitates the use of entrepreneurial judgment in a productive venture by conferring a legally recognized right to define contractual constraints (Coase, 1937; Williamson, 1996).

Recall now the possible inefficiency caused by the wrong assignment of roles, i.e., the individual with comparative advantages in forming original judgment (here, Jack) assuming the role of employee, directed by the comparatively disadvantaged individual (here, Jill), because this would give him higher returns, at the expense of joint value creation. This inefficiency may be avoided if somehow Jack can be made just as well-off as the employer in the efficient team as he would be as the employee in the inefficient team. Simply adjusting the sharing rule with respect to the monetary surplus to compensate Jack will not do: If Jack receives, for example, 100 percent of the surplus, this will not compensate him, if Jill keeps the right to set the constraints. In fact, the greater the employer's share in the surplus, the greater will be the employee's incentive to choose constraints that maximizes his own private benefits at the cost of the joint monetary surplus.

The power to set constraints (limit access) is conferred by asset ownership. Thus, if the employer owns the asset, he can set constraints in such a way that he can influence the size of the surplus that will be shared among the parties, and in this way make sure that he will actually be compensated for assuming the role of principal in the efficient team. In other words, ownership has the function in our example of minimizing the dissipation of value – it means that Jack and Jill do not have to engage in costly bargaining – and of selecting the efficient team, that is, the one that best utilizes the parties' comparative advantages in forming original and derived judgment. To put it in a compact manner, ownership is a means of implementing the principal's preferred degree of incompleteness in a low-cost way. In other words, the party with original or primary judgment – the higher-order judgment described by Lachmann (1956), the judgment about other people's judgment identified by Knight (1921) – establishes the environment in which other agents exercise their own derived or secondary judgment.

Although we have presented our arguments in the context of a static setting, the above functions of ownership are particularly important in a dynamic context, because in such a context an ongoing process of entrepreneurial creation and discovery will require that constraints in a relation are redefined. Thus, in terms of Figure 8.1, the slopes of the D and the P curves are likely to change over time as a result of entrepreneurial activities on the part of both the agent and the principal. The power conferred by ownership allows the principal to adjust the level of contractual constraints to ensure that he has incentives to maintain the role of principal in the efficient team, realizing comparative advantages of entrepreneurship. Indeed, as noted below, the notion that contractual constraints define the scope of entrepreneurship, rather than simply allowing agents to choose the values of particular variables with known distributions, is an inherently dynamic, forward-looking concept of organizational design.

Other applications

Our theory of ownership as a means of implementing a preferred set of constraints in a productive relationship, and therefore a certain combination of productive and destructive entrepreneurship, has application beyond the determination of who should be the owner. It also sheds light on the more general issue of why a certain agent owns a certain asset, independent of his relationships with other agents. The theory of ownership presented in Hart (1995) revolves around the holdup problem: One should own those assets that are complementary to one's (non-contractible) human capital investments, since this increases (*ex post*) bargaining power and therefore the rents that may be expected from investments. This is not a highly general explanation, though; people own many things, the ownership of which cannot be explained by holdup considerations (e.g., standard kitchen utensils in a household).

Another common idea is that those who discover new knowledge have an incentive to use it themselves because of the transaction costs of knowledge transfer. Given this, there is a general tendency for ownership of complementary assets to move to the knowledge source (rather than the other way around), because knowledge is harder to trade than most other resources (Foss, 1993a; Casson, 1997). The problem with this explanation is that it does not allow to distinguish analytically between ownership and rental agreements. Our theory can do this, however.

For example, one could imagine a car rental company that puts very few constraints in the contracts it offers renters, so that the latter could use the company's cars for the purpose of running a taxi business or a truck operation. Thus, the car company does not strongly constrain productive *or* destructive proxy-entrepreneurship. Normally, however, car rental companies circumscribe in a relatively detailed way the possible productive and destructive entrepreneurship that the renter can engage in. For example, usually rental cars cannot be used for commercial purposes, primarily because the company fears that the car will not be driven properly and that this will reduce the demand of other renters for the car's services. Thus, in order to maintain demand and control externalities, the company constrains the use of the car in many ways. However, a renter who wishes to use a rental car for entrepreneurial, commercial purposes is not likely to find the constraints imposed by the car rental company to be optimal. Hence, he may prefer to own the car in order to be able to impose his own, preferred, open-ended way of using the car, particularly under dynamic conditions. In other words, he owns the car in order to carry out his own entrepreneurial plans.[17]

Ownership and the rewarding of employees

The general point that ownership facilitates the use of entrepreneurial judgment in a productive venture by conferring the right to define contractual constraints may also be argued from a property-rights perspective. Specifically, the entrepreneur wants to motivate employees to engage in productive proxy-entrepreneurship. Because their

---

[17] Of course, in this situation car rental companies may increase earnings by offering differentiated products, where rental fees and contractual constraints differ for different segments of the market, or new firms may arise to special-purpose segments of the market. However, even those firms that offer cars with fewer or other contractual constraints may be too constraining for some persons, particularly those who (expect that they) are likely to discover yet unimagined activities (i.e., entrepreneurs). They will still want to become owners.

actions are costly to observe, it will be difficult for the entrepreneur to offer direct compensation for employees' productive actions. In the example so far we have simply assumed that employees will share in the surplus they help to create. To refine the example a bit more, assume employees are rewarded if their exercise of proxy-entrepreneurship, in the form of refining aspects of the entrepreneur's overall plan (finding a new market for the product, improving a production process, etc.), is adopted and implemented. However, not all (potentially sound) business ideas may be adopted, if implementation is costly, and entrepreneurs have different judgments about the likelihood of various outcomes (see Chapter 4). This creates an additional problem: How does an employee form reliable expectations about what projects the entrepreneur will adopt? The basic assumption of property-rights theory (Hart, 1995) is that the *ex ante* investment into an activity – effort into searching for a promising project – is driven by *ex post* bargaining power, that is, the probability of a project being adopted and rewarded.

The *ex post* bargaining position has two components. First, the firm needs to commit credibly to the general practice of rewarding employees for suggesting adopted projects (Kreps, 1990; Baker *et al.*, 1999; Foss, 2003). Second, the firm needs to convey credibly what *kinds* of projects it will adopt. Without clear criteria, employees may be reluctant to exert effort in searching for business opportunities, because they anticipate competition for internal funding among projects, they recognize that the entrepreneur's judgments may differ from their own, and otherwise cannot guarantee that they will reap the expected rewards.[18]

The firm may then be better off adopting a narrow business strategy, as argued by Rotemberg and Saloner (1994, 1995) and Rajan and Zingales (2001). Such a strategy means that the firm commits to consider only business ideas within a narrow, but highly profitable, set of business activities, while disregarding all business opportunities outside that narrow domain. The commitment sends a clearer signal to employees that a project gets funded if it appears profitable and falls within the business domain of a firm. Hence, employees

---

[18] This is analogous to the problem of reliance on subjective, rather than objective, performance criteria – principals cannot commit to particular rewards that might motivate specific actions by agents (Baker, Gibbons, and Murphy, 1994).

will be more motivated to engage in proxy-entrepreneurship within the narrow domain, while disregarding possibilities that lie outside of the narrow business strategy. Obviously, this approach comes at the cost of forgoing attractive opportunities that are incompatible with the firm's current business strategy (and does not, of course, completely eliminate the problem of different judgments under Knightian uncertainty). Viewed from this perspective, "sticking to your knitting" is an effective way to stimulate entrepreneurial activity by employees. The analysis suggests that more innovative firms will have a narrower scope of business activities than less innovative firms.[19]

An alternative approach to motivating proxy-entrepreneurship by strengthening employees' *ex post* bargaining position is to employ a visionary CEO (Rotemberg and Saloner, 2000; Van den Steen, 2005). A visionary CEO articulates and pursues a concrete vision for the business model and evaluates proposed projects according to whether they fit that vision.[20] The CEO is therefore consistently biased toward certain types of projects. In that sense, having a visionary CEO corresponds to employing a narrow business strategy that channels proxy-entrepreneurship within specific parameters. However, the CEO may recognize a sufficiently good project that falls outside the range of her narrow vision and may choose to implement it anyway. For this process to work, the firm needs a layer of semi-autonomous middle managers between the CEO and the employees. In contrast to the CEO, middle managers do not have a bias; they promote projects solely based on their expected profit potential. While the CEO makes the ultimate decision about what projects to implement and reward, middle managers are charged with the responsibility of allocating resources to nascent projects proposed by employees. In this way, the middle managers act as an information filter for the CEO, passing on projects for possible implementation that are either consistent with

---

[19] Note that this approach differs from the standard agency-theoretic conclusion that the greater the uncertainty between an agent's action and his reward, the more the principal must offer in average compensation, to insure the agent against contingencies beyond the agent's control (Holmström, 1979). The adoption of a narrow business strategy also provides a form of insurance by reducing the uncertainty about rewards.

[20] See the discussion of entrepreneurship as "cognitive leadership" in Chapter 2 above.

the CEO's vision or have great profit potential.[21] Employing middle managers as information filters also helps employees to decide how much effort to expend on projects, because decisions by the entrepreneur and middle managers to allocate resources to a project sends a strong signal that it might get implemented and the effort rewarded. This organizational structure mitigates a major weakness of narrow business strategies that eschew all business opportunities outside the narrow domain.

Dispersed knowledge, authority, and firm organization

Hayekian dispersed knowledge as a challenge to authority and hierarchy

Our argument that authority backed up by ownership serves to maximize joint surplus provides additional perspective on the popular argument that dispersed knowledge in the sense of Hayek (1945) and Polanyí (1962) seriously and increasingly challenges existing authority relations and firm boundaries (e.g., Jensen and Meckling, 1992; Minkler, 1993a, 1993b; Cowen and Parker, 1997; Ghoshal, Moran, and Almeida-Costa, 1995; Hodgson, 1998; Rousseau and Shperling, 2003). "Dispersed knowledge" is knowledge that is not possessed by any single mind and which may be private, fleeting, tacit, and subjectively held (O'Driscoll and Rizzo, 1985) – but which is still needed for the effective allocation of resources under complexity as, of course, Hayek (1945) famously argued about the price mechanism. The planning problems posed by Hayekian distributed knowledge have become increasingly pressing for firms (Ghoshal *et al.*, 1995).

Given the increased importance of specialist workers and the increased knowledge-intensity of production, it is argued, coping with the problem posed by Hayekian distributed knowledge is not simply

---

[21] An alternative approach, pursued by Falaschetti and Miller (2011) in the context of public bureaucracy, is to give the middle managers formal authority, to make the CEO's promise to follow the middle managers' guidelines more credible. However, as discussed above, the entrepreneur-owner cannot delegate original judgment to these middle managers, so that the promise not to reject their advice cannot be fully credible. See also Williamson's (1985) discussion of the "impossibility of selective intervention."

a problem for socialist managers and *dirigiste* bureaucrats, but also a problem for managers of large firms in capitalist economies.[22] As hierarchy and planning methods are just as problematic inside firms as they have proved to be outside firms, firms need to harness the ability of markets to utilize, exchange, and build information rapidly in response to changing contingencies. It is not difficult to see how such argument seems to cast doubt on the analytical dichotomy between planned firms and unplanned markets, present not only in Coase (1937) (and most of post-Coasean organizational economics), but also in central Austrian contributions from Mises (1922, 1944, 1949) and Hayek (1973).[23]

The fact that firms exist and thrive would seem to indicate, however, that they can somehow successfully cope with dispersed knowledge. The reason, of course, is delegation. As Mises (1949: 303) emphasized, "entrepreneurs are not omnipresent. They cannot themselves attend to the manifold tasks which are incumbent upon them," so that coping with distributed knowledge leads in the direction of decentralization (see also Hayek, 1945: 83–84), through delegation of decision rights to managers (Mises, 1949: 305). Mises also recognized that delegation leads to agency problems, but argued that the system of double-entry bookkeeping and other control measures may partly cope with such problems. Thus, in the Misesian scheme, an organizational equilibrium obtains where decision rights are delegated in such a way that the benefits of delegation in terms of better utilizing local knowledge (or stimulating productive proxy-entrepreneurship) are balanced against the costs of delegation in terms of agency losses (and destructive proxy-entrepreneurship). This provides a useful

---

[22] Of course, there are longstanding connections between the literatures on organizations and on socialist economic planning, including important discussions in Mises (1922) and Hayek (1933). The early work on mechanism design by Hurwicz (1969, 1973) and associates was motivated by the debates over central planning. See also Mises (1944) and Klein (1996).

[23] A parallel argument asserts that "firms and markets are not exactly the same, but rather they differ in empirical terms. They refer to different means of organizing economic activity, albeit means that *do not differ substantially in kind* ... This ... view does not seek to find a clear-cut distinction between firms and markets. Rather the difference between the firm and the market as a resource allocator involves what might more usefully be viewed as subtle differences relating to contracting" (Cowen and Parker, 1997: 15, emphasis in original).

perspective on many of the loosely structured, emergent organizational forms said to characterize the knowledge economy.

However, while an Austrian perspective is useful for understanding why firms adopt decentralized organizational structures, we still have the puzzle why such teams are organized *inside* firms, being subject to the exercise of authority, rather than organizing them as inter-firm networks, alliances, clusters, and the like, where activities are coordinated by the high-powered incentives of the market. Adding to the puzzle is that authority (at least in the sense of Coase [1937] or Simon [1951]) appears to play at best a very limited role under Hayekian dispersed knowledge. This is because traditional notions of authority in economics assume that a directing principal is at least as knowledgeable about the relevant tasks as the agent being directed.

Authority, ownership, and dispersed knowledge

Although Max Weber had many interesting things to say about authority early in the twentieth century, it was not until Coase (1937) that economists began to conceptualize authority. Coase's understanding, supplemented with a later contribution by Simon (1951), still provides most economists' working definition of authority. Moreover, Coase initiated the tendency to see the employment contract and the authority relation as the defining characteristic of the firm. In Coase (1937), the employment contract is explained as "one whereby the factor, for a certain remuneration (which may be fixed or fluctuating) agrees to obey the directions of an entrepreneur *within certain limits*. The essence of the power is that it should only state the limits to the powers of the entrepreneur. Within these limits, he can therefore direct the other factors of production" (1937: 242, original emphasis). This contractually "agreed upon" right to "direct the other factors of production" is, of course, authority. A later paper by Simon (1951) provided a formalization of Coase's notion of the employment relationship and a clarification of the notion of authority, which is defined as obtaining when a "boss" is permitted by a "worker" to select actions, $A^0 \subset A$, where A is the set of the worker's possible behaviors. More or less authority is then simply defined as making the set A^0 larger or smaller.

How can we reconcile the notions of authority and dispersed knowledge? Note that neither Knight (1921), Mises (1944, 1949), nor

Lachmann (1956) saw a fundamental problem here, as they argued that entrepreneurs exercise judgment about other people's judgment, evaluating employees according to their ability to act as proxy-entrepreneurs, rather than evaluating their specific actions under particular conditions. These writers did not, however, explain exactly how the entrepreneur exercises this judgment of judgment: perhaps he observes indicators of the agents' past and present performance and forms his meta-judgment on this basis. But the Knightian-Austrian literature does not describe specific mechanisms for doing this.

To get some traction on the issue, assume that "hidden knowledge" (Minkler, 1993a, 1993b) obtains in relations between a principal (e.g., the entrepreneur) and an agent (e.g., a hired manager). That is, the problem facing a principal is not just that he is uninformed about what state of nature has been revealed or of the realization of the agent's effort (i.e., hidden information), as in the usual agency model (Holmström, 1979), but that the agent's knowledge is superior to that of the principal with respect to certain entrepreneurial possibilities (i.e., hidden knowledge). The principal may be ignorant about some members of the set of possible actions open to the agent – perhaps because the agent has created or discovered new attributes of the relevant assets – or the agent may be better informed about how certain tasks should (optimally) be carried out. Here are some reasons why, under these conditions, authority may still matter in the sense of promoting efficiency (and the exercise of judgment).

Authority also makes sense when there is a need for urgent coordination. In an argument anticipating later dynamic capabilities arguments (Teece, Pisano, and Shuen, 1997), Langlois (1988) argued that exercising (what we call) entrepreneurial judgment often requires a coordinated and fast deployment of bundles of complementary assets (see also Chapter 5).[24] While Hayek (1945) did much to identify the benefits of the price system in the context of alienable property rights in coping with distributed knowledge and unexpected disturbances, he arguably neglected those situations where efficiency requires that adaptation be "coordinated" rather than "autonomous" (Williamson, 1996). In general, coordinated adaptation or action is likely to be required when actions or activities are complementary (Milgrom and Roberts, 1990; Stieglitz and Heine, 2007) – for example, when it is

[24] Langlois and Robertson (1995) offer several empirical illustrations.

important to make *some* urgent choice (possibly highly inefficient), because doing nothing is worse. In such cases, it may be better to have someone pick a strategy and make everybody play this strategy, if the inefficiencies from picking a bad strategy (e.g., not fully exploiting all distributed knowledge) are smaller than the inefficiencies from delaying a coordinated solution. In the context of a specific model of this kind of trade-off, Bolton and Farrell conclude that "the less important the private information that the planner lacks and the more essential coordination is, the more attractive the central planning solution is" (1990: 805). Moreover, the decentralized solution performs poorly if urgency is important. Centralization is assumed to not involve delay and therefore is a good mechanism for dealing with emergencies, a conclusion Bolton and Farrell argue is consistent with the observed tendencies of firms to rely on centralized authority in cases of emergencies.[25]

Even under distributed knowledge, where the centralized decision-maker lacks at least some local information, he may in many cases still hold the information that is "decisive." Loosely, information is (strongly) decisive if – in a setting involving many cooperating individuals – a decision can reasonably be made on the basis of this information without involving other pieces of information (Casson, 1994). According to Casson (1994), the extent to which a problem involving the knowledge of several individuals is decisive and the cost of transferring knowledge help explain the allocation of decision rights. Organizational economics argues more generally that there are advantages to "co-locating" decision authority and specific knowledge when that knowledge is costly to transfer (Jensen and Meckling, 1992). But that argument treats all kinds of specific knowledge as equal. Here, we are saying that decisive knowledge trumps other kinds of dispersed, specific knowledge. Even if the managers hold particular kinds of specific information, it makes sense to allocate decision rights over the relevant actions to entrepreneurs if the entrepreneurs have decisive knowledge, even if they are uninformed about many other important variables. In other words, the fact that the entrepreneur holds ultimate authority (original judgment) is efficient when the entrepreneur holds decisive knowledge.

[25] See also Boettke (1989).

Minkler (1993b: 23) argues that "if the worker knows more than the entrepreneur, it is pointless for the entrepreneur to monitor the worker," which implies that to the extent that monitoring is a precondition for the exercise of direction, using the authority mechanism also seems to become "pointless." However, even under hidden knowledge, there may still be a role for authority. For example, if the principal has conjectures of the financial results from the agent's activities, he can check whether these conjectures are confirmed using the control systems of the firm. Both Knight (1921) and Mises (1949: 303) clearly allowed for this possibility. Neither assumed that entrepreneurs would have full knowledge of their managers' action set; still, they did assume that the entrepreneur can rationally delegate decisions to managers while retaining appropriate forms of control. Hidden knowledge does not imply that subjective performance measurement is impossible. On the contrary, the more we depart from simple settings in which employees are very easily monitored, and the more complicated the control problem becomes, the more likely the entrepreneur will employ multiple incentive instruments to influence employee behavior (Henderson, 2000). In a dynamic economy, maintaining coherence between such instruments is be a recurrent task (Holmström, 1999) – another facet of the constant combining and recombining of resources that characterizes the entrepreneurial function. Economies of scale in this task suggest centralization. Moreover, centralization is required to the extent that externalities arise when the instruments are controlled by separate firms and transaction costs hinder the internalization of these externalities. Both arguments point towards the centralization of decision rights.

To sum up, authority may be efficient even under dispersed knowledge. Dispersed knowledge challenges narrow notions of authority, such as those of Coase (1937) and Simon (1951) in which authority amounts to a hierarchical superior picking a well-defined action for a subordinate, picking it from an equally well-defined set of actions based on superior knowledge about what actions are efficient responses to contingencies. Both Knight and Mises go significantly beyond this, however. They realized clearly that in many firms decision rights are allocated by the entrepreneur (and the board of directors) to lower levels, presumably to cope with distributed knowledge and to allow for the exercise of the derived judgment by subordinates. Thus, decision rights are delegated in firms, but they are delegated as means to an end (Hayek, 1973); their use is monitored (Jensen and Meckling, 1992) and the top management team reserves ultimate decision rights for itself (Baker *et al.*, 1999). Thus, even in "knowledge-based" firms there is a need for centralized coordination.

Conclusions

In the entrepreneurial judgment approach, the theory of the firm becomes a theory of how the entrepreneur arranges the capital assets he owns or can influence (i.e., human capital), including which combinations of assets he will seek to acquire and which assets he may later divest in an attempt to carry out the commercial experiment that embodies his judgment (Knight, 1921; Casson, 1982; Foss, 1993a; Langlois and Cosgel, 1993; Foss and Klein, 2005). In this chapter we have extended this approach by explaining how entrepreneur-owners delegate decision rights to employees and how the employees' exercise of derived judgment is best circumscribed.

In established economic theories of organizational design, delegation is usually analyzed with a principal-agent model. Such models have been exhaustively treated in the economics literature. A basic implication of this apparatus is that more complete contracts are preferable to less complete contracts. However, under Knightian uncertainty, agents can not only pick an action from a predefined set, but also exercise derived judgment, acting as proxy-entrepreneurs. In this approach, contracts are incomplete not because complete contracts are costly to draft (as in Crocker and Reynolds, 1993), but because complete contracts curb entrepreneurial activities, both productive and destructive. More generally, in the kind of open-ended world envisaged by Knight (1921) as well as Austrian economists (Mises, 1949; Shackle, 1972; O'Driscoll and Rizzo, 1985), limiting employee discretion involves more than simply making formal, written contracts more complete. Discretion is constrained by organizational structure. By the latter we mean not only specialization, departmentalization, formalization, and so on, but also things like informal norms ("corporate culture" and other implicit contracts), and official and unofficial means for resolving disputes (Williamson, 1996), and so on. Ownership conveys the right to define key elements of this organizational structure.[26]

Moreover, in contrast to the new property-rights approach (Hart, 1995), ownership has a variety of implications for firm performance. In the judgment-based perspective, the arrangement of property titles affects not only *ex ante* relationship-specific investments, but also how the firm will perform through time (original judgment rights should be allocated to the party best able to exercise them). Likewise, internal organization affects not only current performance (as in agency theory, mechanism design, etc.), but also dynamics – how derived judgment will be exercised as circumstances change. The judgment approach to organizational design is thus inherently dynamic.

Finally, we note some implications of our perspective for ongoing work in the tradition of Austrian economics. Much of the contemporary Austrian literature focuses on the organic, "spontaneous" nature of market exchange, the distribution of tacit knowledge (Hayek, 1945), and the failure of top-down, central planning (Mises, 1920). However, in our view, the emphasis on "market" over "hierarchy" (to use Williamsonian terms) has resulted in a lack of attention to organizations, the ubiquitous, central features of all modern economies (Simon, 1991).[27] And yet, received Austrian theory can add to our understanding of organizations and their internal organization. This chapter has explored some of this potential.

---

[26] We do not claim that the informal aspects of organizational structure are *completely* controlled, or "designed," by owners. We certainly recognize that, for example, corporate culture can grow and evolve organically, that there is an element of "spontaneous order" within the firm. But we maintain that formal constraints, established and revised by owners, are the ultimate drivers of organizational form.

[27] An obvious exception is Mises (1944). For a critique of the spontaneous-order approach in Austrian economics see Klein (2008a).

9 | *Concluding discussion*

Introduction

The preceding chapters have outlined an entrepreneurial theory of the firm built upon Knightian uncertainty and Austrian capital theory. The theory regards entrepreneurship as an active, owning, controlling agency, the function of assembling, configuring, and reconfiguring bundles of heterogeneous resources under conditions of "true" uncertainty, with strong implications for our understanding of the nature, emergence and boundaries of the firm. It also shows how entrepreneurial judgment about resources is distributed throughout the multi-person firm, as the owner's original judgment is shared with employees who exercise derived judgment on the owner's behalf.

This notion of the entrepreneurial firm is implicit in some of the earliest systematic treatments of economic problems, including Cantillon's (1755) landmark essay, was incorporated by some Classical and Austrian economists, but gradually fell out of favour, losing out to the stylized abstraction of the neoclassical "firm," a production function that is analytically tractable but descriptively vacuous and silent on the key problems of economic organization and entrepreneurship. The transaction cost, agency-theoretic, property-rights, resource-based, and capabilities theories of the firm that emerged in the 1970s, 1980s, and 1990s breathed new life into the theory of the firm, explicating many important problems of firm behavior and performance, but even these did not bring the entrepreneur back into the story. Likewise, entrepreneurship studies became established as a separate field, focusing on start-ups, small-business management, and innovation, but the entrepreneur remained absent from other, mundane topics in economics and management.

A fundamental claim, which we first expressed in Foss and Klein (2005), is that the historic isolation of entrepreneurship studies and the theory of the firm has created substantial unexploited gains from trade. Entrepreneurship should not be treated as a separate domain, focusing on specialized outcomes such as self-employment, business formation, new product introduction, and the like, or as a way of thinking or acting that applies only to a few individuals acting in unique situations. In the most general sense, all human behavior is entrepreneurial, as we live in a world of Knightian uncertainty, not the artificial world of neoclassical economic models.

As economists and management scholars, of course, we are particularly interested in a narrower conception of entrepreneurship, that of the businessperson who invests financial and physical capital in the hopes of earning monetary profits and avoiding monetary losses – not because we think this type of entrepreneur is intrinsically, socially, or morally superior to the everyday entrepreneur, but because business behavior has a larger and more direct effect on the allocation of resources, the basic *explanandum* of economics and its sister disciplines. And therein lies the point: entrepreneurship, in this narrower sense, lies properly at the heart of economics, as well as the applied fields of strategic management, organization theory, innovation, finance, marketing, and so on. This does not mean that "the field of entrepreneurship" is somehow an overarching social science field. Rather, our point is that it makes more sense to think of entrepreneurship as a general category of action rather than as an applied field of economics like labor economics, economic development, or international trade, or a subfield of management research such as the strategic management or organization studies fields.[1]

The implication is that entrepreneurship scholars should focus on implications of their research for organizations and markets, while economists and management scholars should view their work and applied problems through an entrepreneurial lens. As we bring our argument to a close, we provide a summary of our basic narrative, develop and extend some specific implications that we have not dealt with in the previous chapters, offer comments on the development of the fields of entrepreneurship and the theory of the firm, and outline a research agenda for developing a judgment-based entrepreneurial theory of the firm. We follow the same logic of organization as in this

---

[1] At the risk of adding further confusion, this doesn't mean that we see no role for a specialized field focusing on start-ups, venture capital, and the like, provided it is understood that these are subsets of the broader entrepreneurial phenomenon.

book, that is, we begin with entrepreneurship theory, and then move on to the theory of the firm in the context of entrepreneurial judgment and heterogeneous capital.

Implications for entrepreneurship theory

Focusing on the entrepreneur as an uncertainty-bearing, asset-owning, judgmental decision-maker who may delegate his judgment to proxy-entrepreneurs suggests some new directions for emerging entrepreneurship research (Zahra, 2006). The directions are meaningful paths of theoretical development because the entrepreneurship literature so far has been unnecessarily constrained by three important biases that have steered research heuristics in entrepreneurship. The biases we have in mind may be called the start-up bias, the opportunity-discovery bias, and the sole-entrepreneur bias. We have discussed these, in passing (the start-up bias and the sole-entrepreneur bias) or more intensively (the opportunity-discovery bias), already, but a brief summary and explication is in order. We also discuss how entrepreneurship research that proceeds along the lines sketched in this book can overcome these biases.

The start-up bias

While not denying the critical importance of new firms to innovation, economic growth, employment, and other economic outcomes, we think it is a mistake to analyze new firms, small firms, or high-growth firms with a different underlying logic than mature firms, large firms, and less-rapidly changing ones. Hence we part company with entrepreneurship scholars, such as Gartner and Carter (2003: 196) who "consider the processes of organization formation to be the core characteristics of entrepreneurship." Organization formation is an interesting and important topic, to be sure, but we do not see it as uniquely "entrepreneurial," whether from our own judgment-based perspective or from the functional perspectives of Kirznerian alertness, Schumpeterian innovation, Schultzian adaptation, or any similar approach. Judgment, alertness, innovation, and adaptation take place in all kinds of organizations, not only new and nascent ones.[2]

---

[2] Gartner and Carter (2003: 199–201) are careful to point out that studying organization formation is not the same as studying new organizations,

Specifically, we have stressed a notion of entrepreneurship as the exercise of judgment in the specific context of exercising control over heterogeneous resources in the service of satisfying future imagined customer preferences. There is simply no inherent reason why entrepreneurship thus defined cannot be exercised by established firms. And, of course, established firms regularly exercise entrepreneurial judgment. In *Capitalism, Socialism, and Democracy* Schumpeter (1942) famously argued that entrepreneurship should be thought of as a firm-level phenomenon. Indeed, he famously expressed concern regarding the way in which entrepreneurship was somehow becoming subordinate to the R&D routines of the big corporation.[3] Other scholars have also argued that entrepreneurship can be meaningfully conceptualized at the firm level (Baumol, 1990). If entrepreneurship researchers have nevertheless often tied entrepreneurship to new firm formation, one may speculate that this is partly a matter of historical legacy (the "churn" caused by new firm formation became a phenomenon of huge empirical importance in the mid-1970s – as the entrepreneurship field was slowly getting established), as well as an attempt to define and defend an independent subject for entrepreneurship research (entrepreneurship in established firms may be seen as strongly overlapping with, e.g., innovation research).

While we think that the entrepreneurship literature at large still suffers from the start-up bias, we can discern many indications that researchers in other fields are moving beyond this bias, explicitly linking entrepreneurship and established firms. Perhaps most conspicuously the emerging strategic entrepreneurship literature explicitly conceptualizes entrepreneurship at the level of established firms (Hitt *et al.*, 2002; Ireland *et al.*, 2003). Independently of this literature strategic management researchers have emphasized, following Schumpeter (1911), the inherently *temporary* nature of competitive advantages (D'Aveni, 1994; Wiggins and Rueffli, 2002). Empirical work broadly suggests that firm-specific returns that can be linked to specific competitive advantages regress to the industry mean, and

a distinction that much of the applied entrepreneurship literature elides. Still, their approach implies that once an organization is formed, processes of judgment, alertness, innovation, and adaptation cease or operate in fundamentally different ways than before.

[3] For a discussion of this point, and whether it represents a break with Schumpeter's earlier thinking, see Langlois (2007b).

that, moreover, the pace of regression has accelerated over the last few decades (Pacheco-de-Almeida, 2010). In those hypercompetitive environments in which both the rate of innovation and imitation are high, "advantages are rapidly created and eroded" (D'Aveni, 1994: 2). Another literature that links established firms and what we would consider entrepreneurial actions is the "dynamic capabilities view" (Teece *et al.*, 1997; Zahra *et al.*, 2008). This view argues that superior performance comes from a firm's capacity to change its resource base in the face of Schumpeterian competition and environmental change. Dynamic capabilities are defined as the firm's ability to integrate, build, and reconfigure internal and external competences to address rapidly changing environments (Teece *et al.*, 1997: 516). Recent work on dynamic capabilities has increasingly stressed the role of organizational processes for understanding how firms alter its resource base. Teece (2007) opens up the black box of dynamic capabilities by relating the concept to organizational processes of sensing and seizing business opportunities and the constant (re)alignment of resources (see Helfat and Peteraf, 2009). A firm's sensing ability critically depends on the organizational systems and individual capacities to learn and to identify, filter, evaluate, and shape opportunities. Once a business opportunity is identified, the organizational structure, procedures, and incentives influence whether and how a firm seizes the opportunity and creates a new strategic path. What is more, governance and organizational structures shape how firms align their specific resources over time.

We see the judgment approach as, in some important respects, quite close to these recent currents in the strategic management field. What it adds is more explicit concern with much of the micro detail underlying notions like "dynamic capabilities," such as a concern with judgment and its distribution and organization (in terms of original and derived judgment) across the firm. The judgment approach is inherently multi-level. In contrast, much of strategic management theory tends to proceed on only the firm level.

The opportunity-discovery bias

While the main focus of the applied entrepreneurship literature in terms of the *explanandum* phenomenon is start-ups, the main explanatory focus, as noted in Chapter 2, is opportunity discovery, whether in isolation or in combination with the founder's personal characteristics (as in Shane's [2003] "individual–opportunity nexus"). In the judgment-based perspective, however, the unit of analysis is not opportunities, but action – in Knightian terms, the assembly of resources in the present in anticipation of (uncertain) receipts in the future. As we have clarified, "assembly" represents a huge vector of actions, including searching for the right resources, purchasing (including inspecting, measuring, negotiating, etc.) them or otherwise accessing their services, coordinating resource use, monitoring performance, etc. Many of these actions are highly complementary, with direct consequences for their economic organization. The bottom line, however, is that we call for much more emphasis being placed upon the *processes* by which entrepreneurial perceptions are translated into *action* rather than on the psychological aspects of "discovery."

Discovery surely has a long and distinguished history (Foss and Klein, 2010), with roots in Cantillon (1755), Fetter (1905), Wieser (1914), Clark (1918), and Hayek (1946, 1968), and the notion of the entrepreneur as unusually aware, alert, and instinctive has a direct intuitive appeal. Judgment involves anticipation of future conditions, which has some surface similarities to Kirznerian notions of alertness or discovery. Still, the judgment approach goes much further because it calls attention to the many interlocking actions and investments that constitute entrepreneurship. Because Kirzner's conception is extremely stylized, he portrays all of this as one *Gestalt*. As we noted in Chapter 3, he is also insistent that the "pure entrepreneur" does not need a firm to seize opportunities; in fact, he doesn't need to own any assets at all. Adopting Kirzner's views as a foundation for management research on entrepreneurship in our view risks black-boxing too much that should not be black-boxed and strengthens the neglect of the established firm as an entrepreneurial agent.

There are many reasons why the opportunity-discovery lens has become so prominent. One reason is that empirically researching entrepreneurship in ways that go beyond examining, for example, how industry and economy level data are associated with start-ups is very challenging. Survey designs have to cope with the fact that few established measurement scales exist, responses are likely to be highly biased and imprecise, and it is very hard to build in questions that relate to entrepreneurial processes. These are familiar problems in the context of survey design, but they are likely reinforced in the context of entrepreneurship. Given this, it is highly convenient to think of entrepreneurship as located at a clearly identifiable point in time, namely, that of the discovery of the opportunity. The opportunity-discovery view also eases the job of the empiricist, because it implies that a single respondent design may be sufficient, namely the survey may be directed at the entrepreneur-discoverer.

It is, however, quite likely that such an approach misconstrues entrepreneurship, as both our judgment approach and the effectuation approach of Sarasvathy (2008) would indicate. In the judgment approach entrepreneurship is a process that involves the assembly of resources (in the sense defined above) and the coordination, perhaps in an iterative manner, of these resources. This suggests that survey designs that, in the nature of things, face difficulties identifying process aspects, may be problematic research tools. And because judgment can be delegated to lower levels in the organization, single respondent designs may be inadequate. These difficulties can obviously be circumvented by small-N historical research designs, but the development of empirical research tools that are appropriate for researching the judgment view in quantitative terms is a serious methodical challenge.

The sole-individual bias

A third bias in the entrepreneurship literature is the concentration on *individuals*. Thus, entrepreneurs are conceptualized as individuals who believe that they have lower information costs than other people (Casson and Wadeson, 2007), and/or privileged information about, for example, the future preferences of consumers (Knight, 1921; Mises, 1949). Organizations enter the analysis mainly as an instrument of the entrepreneur's vision (Knight, 1921; Mises, 1949) (which also helps explain the strong focus on start-ups in the literature). And yet, a number of contributions to the literature find important roles for groups or teams (Cooper and Daily, 1997; Mosakowski, 1998; Aldrich, 1999; Schoonhoven and Romanelli, 2001; Ruef, Aldrich, and Carter, 2003; Cook and Plunkett, 2006; Felin and Zenger, 2009; West, 2007; Harper, 2008). Burress and Cook (2009) provide a comprehensive review on "collective entrepreneurship," documenting substantial research literatures on intra-organizational employee participation and knowledge management, family- and patron-owned firms such as cooperatives, networks and alliances, clusters and industrial districts, franchise arrangements, and other examples of team or group entrepreneurial behavior.

Some efforts to develop a theory of team entrepreneurship focus on shared mental models, team cognition, and other aspects of the process of identifying opportunities (Harper, 2008; Foss *et al.*, 2008; Foss and Lindenberg, in press). Penrose's (1959) concept of the firm's "subjective opportunity set" is an obvious link to judgment-based theories of entrepreneurship (Kor *et al.*, 2007).[4] Harper (2008) builds on the attempt of Bacharach (2006) to define a role in game theory for team agency, and argues that individuals who perceive that they have common interests, no or only weakly conflicting incentives, and strong complementarities between their entrepreneurial actions are likely to form an entrepreneurial team. In a broader sense, entrepreneurs can also form networks to share expectations of the potential returns to projects (Greve and Salaff, 2003; Parker, 2008).

On the other hand, even if one views the perception of a (subjectively identified) opportunity as an inherently individual act, the *exploitation* of opportunities can be a team or group activity. Venture capital, later-stage private equity, and bank loans are often syndicated. Publicly traded equity is diffusely held. Professional-services firms and closed-membership cooperatives represent jointly owned pools of risk capital. Moreover, the firm's top management team – to whom key decision rights are delegated – can be regarded as a bundle of heterogeneous human resources, the interactions among which are critical to the firm's performance (Foss *et al.*, 2008).

This approach also suggests relationships between the theory of entrepreneurship and the theory of collective action (Olson, 1965; Hansmann, 1996). Once an entrepreneurial opportunity has been perceived, the entrepreneur may need to assemble a team of investors and/or a management team, raising problems of internal governance. Shared objectives must be formulated; different time horizons must be reconciled; free-riding must be mitigated; and so on. Cook and Plunkett (2006), Chambers (2007) and Burress, Cook, and Klein (2008) discuss how these problems are addressed within

[4] Spender (2006: 2) argues that "Penrose's model of managerial learning [is] an accessible instance of the epistemological approach proposed by Austrian economists such as Hayek, Kirzner, and Schumpeter."

closed-membership, or "new-generation" cooperatives. Traditionally organized, open-membership cooperatives suffer from what Cook (1995) calls "vaguely defined property rights." Because their equity shares are not alienable assets that trade in secondary markets, traditional cooperatives suffer from a particular set of free-rider, horizon, portfolio, control, and influence costs problems (see also Alchian, 1965).[5]

In fact, we would tend to think of our conceptualization of the firm as a hierarchy of original and derived judgment as instantiating team entrepreneurship. A classical understanding of teams is that it is a group of individuals who are engaged in "team production," that is, "... production in which (1) several types of resources are used and (2) the product is not a sum of separable outputs of each cooperating resource ... [and] ... (3) not all resources used in team production belong to one person" (Alchian and Demsetz, 1972: 779). Clearly, our approach satisfies condition (1) (firms combine many heterogeneous capital inputs), (2) (difficulties of precisely ascertaining the exercise of delegated judgment means that input and output monitoring are made difficult), and (3) (clearly, proxy-entrepreneurs own their own human capital). Explicating how the established firm may act as a team of entrepreneurs is an important way in which entrepreneurship research may develop.

The entrepreneurial division of labor and organizational design

In a highly influential programmatic statement, Shane and Venkataraman (2000) defined entrepreneurship as the study of the discovery, evaluation, and exploitation of opportunities in terms of, for example, the agents that undertake these actions and the institutional and organization embeddedness of entrepreneurial activities. More than a decade after their ambitious statement, only a fraction of it has been realized in entrepreneurship research. Although we remain sceptical of parts of their program (notably, the emphasis on opportunity discovery), we agree that entrepreneurship can meaningfully be decomposed into entrepreneurial actions that may be carried out by different individuals which need coordination and motivation. In

---

[5] See Cook and Iliopoulos (2000) and Cook and Chaddad (2004) for details.

other words, there is an entrepreneurial division of labor, needing coordination.

The three biases that we discussed above mean, however, that extant entrepreneurship research has not yet explicitly taken this step. For example, Kirzner's classical contribution explicitly treats the many conceptually distinct activities that enter into the exercise of entrepreneurship as essentially taking place simultaneously and undertaken by the same person. Similarly, Lazear's (2005) influential work emphasizes that entrepreneurs are likely to be generalists rather than specialists. However, Lazear, like most writers in the entrepreneurship field, focuses on start-ups. Unlike the individual entrepreneur starting up a new business, established firms may have access to a portfolio of entrepreneurial skill sets through their organizational members. This implies that judgment can be decomposed in terms of such activities as searching for potential opportunities, evaluating those, and undertaking and coordinating the many investments and actions that are necessary to realizing an opportunity. This is what we mean by an "entrepreneurial division of labor."

The need to understand the division of entrepreneurial labor is closely intertwined with the need to examine the impact of organizational designs on entrepreneurial actions. Prior entrepreneurship research has examined what skills or abilities are acquainted with distinct entrepreneurial actions. For example, individuals discover opportunities related to information they already possess (Amabile, 1997; Shane, 2000; Shane and Venkataraman, 2000; Venkataraman, 1997). Hence, acquiring new information about resource uses is fundamental for firms in order to discover new opportunities to leverage (Casson and Wadeson, 2007). However, how firms go about acquiring such information critically depends on their organizational design. For example, we need to separate those effects on entrepreneurship that stem from hiring, promoting, retaining, etc. particularly talented individuals (i.e., selection and matching processes) from the effects of the organizational design itself (i.e., certain reward systems may call forth entrepreneurial initiatives, such as discovery of opportunities, even from employees who do not possess particular entrepreneurial talent to begin with). In a sense, certain organizational designs may compensate (in terms of firm-level entrepreneurial outcomes) for a relative lack of entrepreneurial skills.

However, because the impact of organizational design has not yet been examined in the research literature, we know very little about the relative contributions of individual entrepreneurial actions and organizational design. The relation between these two sets of variables could be one of complementarity, so that entrepreneurial actions (and the skills that underpin them) need to be embedded in the appropriate organizational architectures to become effective. Recent strategic entrepreneurship research has begun to acknowledge the importance of applying both an individual-level perspective and including organizational design when examining how entrepreneurial firms discover and leverage opportunities to create sustained competitive advantage (e.g., Ireland, Covin, and Kuratko, 2009). Adopting a micro focus emphasizing individual (entrepreneurial) actions and examining how firms' organizational designs assist in sourcing, coordinating, and leveraging entrepreneurial skills, will provide much added insight on how firm-level entrepreneurial capacity and outcomes emerge from intra-firm behaviors.

Implications for the theory of the firm

Our focus on the entrepreneur as an uncertainty-bearing, asset-owning, judgmental decision-maker who often delegates judgment to proxy-entrepreneurs also suggests new directions for research in the theory of the firm. As is the case with entrepreneurship research, the judgment approach has the potential of overcoming important biases in the theory of the firm, specifically the free-decision-making bias, the static-incentive-alignment bias, and the finance-as-a-factor-of-production bias.

The free-decision-making bias

Demsetz (1988c) complains that the economic theory of the firm suffers from a fundamental asymmetry: knowledge for the purpose of decision-making is assumed to be scarce (as in agency models with their reliance on asymmetric information), while knowledge for the purpose of production is free. Demsetz argues that taking scarce production knowledge into account implies a different theory of firm boundaries. We agree, and think a third factor needs to be considered as well: decision-making. Standard theories assume that knowledge may be costly, but decision-making is free, meaning that decision-makers can always compute an optimal solution to any decision problem. Even transaction cost economics, which emphasizes bounded rationality (and hence costly decision-making), does not focus on cognitive complexity, as bounded rationality serves mainly to justify the assumption that contracts are incomplete – a role also served by asymmetric information (i.e., non-verifiable information; see Hart, 1995).[6]

The judgment-based approach also implies that decision-making is not free – entrepreneurs cannot simply compute, instantaneously, the solution to complex resource-allocation problems. Modeling them that way is misleading, as it abstracts from the kind of experimentation and learning we have described in earlier chapters. Williamson (1975: 25) likewise emphasizes the need for "adaptive, sequential decision-processes" because these "economize greatly on bounded rationality." One could also say that judgment economizes on bounded rationality. As noted by Simon, "boundedly rational agents experience limits in formulating and solving complex problems and in processing (receiving, storing, retrieving, transmitting) information" (quoted by Williamson, 1981: 553). Bounded rationality makes decision-making localized and path-dependent. This harmonizes with the emphasis in much recent entrepreneurship research on the path-dependent and local character of experience and skills and how these characteristics influence the space of opportunities that an entrepreneur explores (Shane, 2000; Sarasvathy, 2008; see also Chapter 5).

However, there are important differences between the judgment-based and behavioral approaches. Behavioral models tend to model economic actors as hard-wired to choose certain courses of actions: "behavioralists tend to assume that agents are (1) hard-headed rule followers or (2) pre-programmed satisficers *ab ovo*" (Langlois and Csontos, 1993: 118). In contrast, we think that entrepreneurship theory must take the free will of the agent into account at some level

---

[6] Some theorists may take asymmetric information as a condition caused by bounded rationality, but this is never formally explained. Other scholars treat bounded rationality as an umbrella term incorporating all kinds of information costs, but we stick here with the conventional usage in which bounded rationality describes costs of cognition, not simply costs of making suboptimal decisions due to lack of information.

(Knight, 1921; Mises, 1949; for some of the philosophical issues, see Felin and Foss, 2011). Langlois and Csontos (1993: 121) sum up the basic differences between the two models:

An agent who is programmed [i.e., the behavioralist agent] acts in a determinate way even in the most open and unconstrained situations, whereas the agent with free will does not. A strict satisficer stops seeking income when he or she has reached an aspiration level – even if a 50 dollars bill suddenly appears on the sidewalk. The [entrepreneurial actor] might pick up the bill.

The distinction, so basic to behavioralism, between routinized/ programmed and non-routinized/non-programmed behavior, suggests that creativity, new solutions, innovation, and indeed choice "are activities present only in extraordinary, exceptional circumstances" (Bianchi, 1990: 161; see also Grandori, in press). Jensen and Meckling (1994) argue that the view of man in the "rational action" or situational analysis approach (Popper, 1967) is that of a "resourceful, evaluative, maximizing" man (i.e., the REMM model) – a view that they argue is entirely consistent with differences in observed behavior and with learning: "Human beings are not only capable of learning about new opportunities, they also engage in resourceful, creative activities that expand their opportunities in various ways" (1994: 5).[7]

The notion of judgment embodies both the point stressed by behavioralists that decision-making is localized and experiential and the point stressed by Jensen and Meckling that humans "engage in resourceful, creative activities that expand their opportunities in various ways." How can the theory of the firm take this kind of decision-making, really, *natural* decision-making, into account? There are obvious and well-known problems associated with building predictive models of creative decision-making, such as judgment. O'Driscoll

---

[7] It is true that while "economists generally profess fidelity to REMM, their loyalty is neither universal nor constant" (Jensen and Meckling, 1994: 10n). For example, economists may routinely invoke the assumption that individuals are pure maximizers of monetary wealth. However, this is fundamentally an operationalization issue, and the rational action model is not committed to this assumption (Buchanan, 1962; Popper, 1967; Jensen and Meckling, 1992).

and Rizzo (1985: 26) argue that what we should strive for is "intelligibility," so that the

> choice-theoretic explanatory schema must render the given phenomenon [e.g., the way an entrepreneur actually exercised judgment] more likely than if the particular model had not been presented ... Thus, with [the] model a number of alternative decisions can be seen as possible, but, given the model, that which actually did occur is rendered more likely than it would have been given some alternative model.

This calls for "multi-exit" models, that is, models that do constrain the agent's choice to a single, determinate outcome on an *ex ante* basis (although, *ex post*, the choice may be construed thus). Creative search in the sense of explorative efforts in an ambiguous and uncertain context should be central, and be linked to the ability of organizational structures to influence this search process, as we discussed in Chapter 5. While structure does not determine entrepreneurial judgment, it is one of the factors that enable and constrain it.

More effort should be devoted to exploring the consequences of judgments that are costly to formulate and costly (if not impossible) to trade. As we explained in Chapter 4, judgment is not a "resource" with a supply curve in the sense that capital and labor are resources.[8] Judgment is the faculty of decision-making about resources. And yet, one can speak of judgment being "costly," meaning that judgments are not formed instantaneously and that they require complementary (scarce, costly) resources to be made and carried out. Judgment represents a novel conjecture regarding the use of resources for servicing preferences, resides in the head of an entrepreneur (or in the heads of the members of an entrepreneurial team), is difficult to communicate, and so on. This creates trade barriers, and to capture profit from his judgment the entrepreneur must deploy it in the context of his own venture, and hire employees who can work based on their derived judgment. This characterization raises a host of questions, answers to which we have sketched out in this volume. Are all parts of the entrepreneurial conjecture over new resource uses non-contractible? How can judgment be dimensionalized? Is it possible to build a logic

---

[8] Rothbard (1962) sometimes, though not consistently, classifies "decision-making" as a factor of production earning a rent. See Topan (2011) for a critique.

that maps judgment with specific characteristics to be specific organizational forms, as in the "discriminating alignment" principle of transaction cost economics? To what extent does the idiosyncracy of judgment imply authority, because directing someone is a more cost-effective manner of exploiting judgment than communicating it to other agents (see Demsetz, 1988c)? We have dealt with such questions in Chapters 6, 7, and 8, but much work remains along the lines of dimensionalization and working out a full-blown logic of how judgment maps into economic organization.

The static-incentive-alignment bias

As we clarified in Chapter 6, much of the modern economic theory of the firm has a strongly static character. Specifically, efficient economic organization (contracts, ownership, governance structures, reward schedules, etc.) is chosen in an *ex ante*, forward-looking manner. Quite appropriately, Hart (1990: 699, original emphasis) stresses that in the economics of the firm "it is actually very important that agents have a high degree of *computational* ability." In fact, even though parties to a contract cannot write a contract that avoids holdup problems, that is, cannot write down date 0 contingent statements, they have perfect foresight about the consequences of their inability to do this.[9] This may be contrasted with the Knightian view, lucidly expressed by Brian Loasby (1976: 134): "The firm exists because it is impossible to specify all actions, even contingent actions in advance; it embodies a very different policy to emergent events. Incomplete specification is its essential basis: for complete specification can be handled by the market."

Williamson has frequently criticized the emphasis on static *ex ante* alignment, characteristic of the modern economics of organization (e.g., Williamson, 1985, 2000), distinguishing between *ex ante* incentive alignment and *ex post* governance branches of transaction cost economics. Grossman and Hart (1986) and Hart and Moore (1990), Williamson (2000: 605) protests, "vaporize *ex post* maladaptation

---

[9] Indeed, Maskin and Tirole (1999) argue that the transaction costs of describing or foreseeing in advance possible states of nature do not necessarily compromise optimal contracting, provided agents can probabilistically forecast their possible future payoffs (even if other aspects cannot be foreseen); that is, agents can perform dynamic programming.

by their assumptions of common knowledge and costless *ex post* bargaining." Gibbons (2005) goes so far as to attribute to Williamson two theories of the firm, an "adaptation" theory of the firm as well as his better-known, discriminating-alignment, comparative-contracting version (which Gibbons associates with the "rent-seeking" approach of Klein *et al.*, 1978).

Similarly, our view suggests that process perspectives of economic organization should be given more attention. The real problems of economic organization do not involve merely the initial deployment of fully specified, efficient governance structures, but a dynamic process of experimenting with asset combinations to find the right mix. Allocating decision rights, designing incentive and monitoring schemes, adjusting firm boundaries, and the like are part of this process. Given Knightian uncertainty, complete, contingent, Arrow–Debreu-style contracting is impossible, leaving "gaps" that must be filled in the process of experimentation. Like the incomplete-contracting perspective of Hart (1995), we conceive of ownership as a means of filling these gaps, as ownership conveys the rights to make decisions in situations not specified by contract – to exercise original judgment when explicit rules for delegating it have not been designed. The allocation of ownership is not just a matter of "getting the investment incentives right"; it is also a matter of reducing the transaction costs of the experimental process, by allocating authority via the allocation of ownership rights. Moreover, ownership has a speculative dimension (i.e., an entrepreneur may acquire ownership over assets because he thinks they are more valuable in combination with other assets, including his own judgment) that is missing in the established theories of economic organization, but comes into the forefront in an entrepreneurial perspective.

In uncertain settings, the key aspects of organizational design often take the form of relatively fixed rules, rather than discretionary policies (Kreps, 1990). These rules may be informal as well as formal, and relational contracts may be as important as formal contracts within the organization. Hence one way to capture the economic organization of entrepreneurship is by means of the notion of a business model. We are not the first to suggest this possibility. Zott and Amit (2008: 2) explicitly link business opportunity, value creation, and business models: "A business model depicts the design of transaction content, structure, and governance so as to create value through the exploitation of business opportunities." Business models have attracted substantial attention in the practitioner literature, but much less in academic research (see Amit and Zott, 2001; Chesbrough and Rosenbloom, 2003; Zott and Amit, 2008; Teece, 2007 for notable exceptions). A business model may be seen as a set of instructions to address how an entrepreneur creates and appropriates value in combination with other resource owners under uncertainty. In terms of the judgment perspective, entrepreneurs are individuals who decide on, implement, and adapt business models to discover and exploit business opportunities. This entails managing a coalition of resources to create value and to stake out a bargaining position that allows for the appropriation of value (Lippman and Rumelt, 2003b; Ryall and MacDonald, 2004).

The finance-as-a-factor-of-production bias

Conventional approaches to the firm, both the neoclassical "black box" model and modern organizational economics treatments, treat financial capital as just another factor of production. Often firms are modeled as price takers in the capital market, meaning that they can borrow as much as they want at the market interest rate without affecting that rate. Even most of the corporate finance literature, which from Modigliani and Miller (1958) to Jensen (1986) to Williamson (1988) has explained carefully the way firms choose among alternative financial instruments and manage their relationships with creditors, equity holders, and employees to achieve strategic objectives, tends to treat finance as an input the firm purchases along with labor and machines and raw materials. Obviously, this does not square with the approach presented here, in which capital is not a factor or production per se, but an intrinsic aspect of the *function of entrepreneurial ownership and control*. Judgment and finance are inextricably linked.

As we argued in Chapter 4 above, judgment is the act of owning and controlling productive resources under conditions of uncertainty and, therefore, not a resource itself. We quoted Marchal (1951: 551) to the effect that "the entrepreneur, although undeniably providing a factor of production, ... is not himself to be defined in those terms." The entrepreneur stands outside the production process, exercising responsibility toward firm structure and operation. The firm, in an important sense, is an investment, and can usefully be understood in terms of the entrepreneur's financial (and other) investment goals.

A few decades ago, a literature on "firms-as-investments" tried to work out some of these implications (Gabor and Pearce, 1952, 1958; Vickers, 1970, 1987; Moroney, 1972). This literature distinguished between "controlling" and "contracting" factors, with financial capital in the former category, land and labor in the latter. Without adopting their terminology, we share much of these writers' perspective. They argued, for example, that firms should be modeled as maximizing not the level of profit, but the rate of return on invested capital. For this reason, owners will seek to place each dollar where it will generate the highest return, rather than giving each plant manager or division head a fixed amount of capital and directing them to expand output until marginal revenue equals marginal cost (Gabor and Pearce, 1952: 253). Typically, the portfolio-ROI-maximizing level of output for an individual operating unit will be lower than the profit-level-maximizing level of output for that operating unit. Put differently, the standard microeconomic assumptions about profit maximization hold only in the special case where the plant manager is unable to invest financial capital in other activities, such that the opportunity cost of using his allotted capital stock in the current line of production is zero. (Hence the neoclassical, black-box theory of the firm is – at best – not a theory of the firm at all, but a theory of the plant.)

From the judgment-based perspective, the entrepreneur chooses what activities to undertake, and how to undertake them, to maximize the return on his capital, and eventually to increase the size of his capital stock. Potential projects or activities are evaluated according to some concept of ROI or economic value added (EVA). While this perspective is mainstream in the literature on diversification and internal capital markets, it has gone largely unnoticed that all firms are operated essentially this way. The judgmental entrepreneur is an investor, not simply an inventor, manager, or consultant.[10]

---

[10] Continuing a point made in Chapter 4, even pure financial-market speculators, those who take little "active" controlling interest in their investment portfolios, are Knightian entrepreneurs, as their returns are never guaranteed. Corporate raiders, private-equity investors, venture capitalists, hedge-fund owners, and other brokers and market makers are

In some cases treating financiers as entrepreneurs is straightforward, such as the staging of venture finance (Gompers, 1995) and the design of venture-capital agreements (Kaplan and Strömberg, 2003) – venture capitalists maintain tight control of their investments, allocating cash flow rights, control rights, board rights, voting rights, liquidation rights, etc. separately and reserving the right to take them back if particular thresholds aren't met. Another application is the inherent uncertainty of the gains from corporate takeovers. In the absence of uncertainty, one can imagine an equilibrium in which the number of takeovers is suboptimal because shareholders will refuse to tender their shares for anything less than their share of the post-takeover value of the firm (Scharfstein, 1988). In a world of Knightian uncertainty, however, the post-takeover value of the firm is uncertain, and many shareholders, not wanting to bear this uncertainty, will tender their shares to the "raider" at a price above the pre-takeover share value but below the raider's expected post-takeover price. The raider's return to a successful takeover is thus a form of pure entrepreneurial profit (Klein, 1999a: 36–38).[11] We think this perspective applies more

---

speculators, and hence entrepreneurs, exercising judgment about future market movements (Klein, 1999a: 36–38). As Mises (1949: 303) notes, "the changes in the prices of common and preferred stock and of corporate bonds are the means applied by the capitalists for the supreme control of the flow of capital. The price structure as determined by the speculations on the capital and money markets and on the big commodity exchanges not only decides how much capital is available for the conduct of each corporation's business; it creates a state of affairs to which the managers must adjust their operations in detail."

[11] It is easy to conceive of financiers – venture capitalists, angel investors, banks, family members, even corporate shareholders – as entrepreneurs, but harder to see it for "passive" investors like trust-fund babies, absentee owners, small shareholders, the millions of wage-earners and consumers with equities in their retirement funds, but little interest in owning, governing, directing. Here it makes sense to distinguish between an actor's economic function and the quantitative significance of that function. In the judgment-based view, all asset owners are entrepreneurs, but not all of these entrepreneurs play important roles in resource allocation, firm strategy, innovation, and the like. To borrow Jensen's (1989) distinction between "active" and "passive" investors, in our approach the residual control rights which accompany ownership make all resource owners "active," in the sense that they must exercise judgment over the use of their resources, even if only to delegate judgment, explicitly or implicitly, to others. In other words, entrepreneur-owners choose how "Jensen-active" they want to be.

broadly, to any case in which financial capital is being invested under conditions of uncertainty – i.e., in all business ventures.

Implications for public policy

Throughout the volume we have mainly taken the perspectives of the entrepreneur, the manager, the investor, and the employee. Although this is not primarily a policy-oriented book, we think our approach to the entrepreneur and the firm has some important implications for regulation, antitrust, fiscal and monetary policy, and related public policy issues.

Challenges to macroeconomic stimulus policy[12]

The recent financial crisis and subsequent economic downturn are among the most important global economic events since the Great Depression of the 1930s (Elmendorf, 2009). In response to these events, macroeconomists have mustered their traditional theories to understand the causes of the crisis and, equally important, what might be done to help the economy recover more quickly. In the midst of this obsession with macroeconomics, we would like to propose an alternative thesis: Macroeconomics, by itself, is not well-equipped to deal with the current crisis and, in particular, a sole reliance on macroeconomic theory is likely to slow rather than accelerate economic recovery. The reason for this is that mainstream macroeconomic theories, whatever their stripe, all adopt the assumption that factors of production, firms, and industries in the economy are homogenous and fungible. This assumption makes it possible for macroeconomists to conclude that the economy, as a whole, can be managed by adjusting aggregate economy-wide indicators, for example, GDP, money supply, growth rates, and so forth. Everything we have written in this volume denies the assumption that the economy is made up of homogeneous or fungible factors of production.

Mainstream macroeconomic models, given their focus on economy-wide phenomena (e.g., gross domestic or national product, employment, growth rates, etc.) tend to focus on aggregates, that is, industries, sectors, and entire economies. Economic models of

---

[12] The discussion here draws on material in Agarwal *et al.* (2009b).

industries and economies typically start with "representative firms," implying that all firms in an industry are alike (Carlton and Perloff, 2005). This mode of thinking is carried to the extreme particularly in modern mathematical macroeconomic models: all factors of production are assumed to be homogeneous within sectors, what we called "shmoo" in Chapter 5. This type of reasoning originated with David Ricardo (1817), who found it a useful simplification. And it can be. But sometimes economists' assumption of homogeneity can lead to trouble, as in the case of the causes of the current crisis and its proposed solutions, as we explain below.

In contrast, the idea that resources, firms, and industries are different from each other, that capital and labor are specialized for particular projects and activities, that people (human capital), etc. are distinct, is ubiquitous in Austrian economics and, we may add, strategic management. The focus on heterogeneity of resources, including knowledge and managerial ability, in strategy and organization theory stems from heterogeneity being a critical determinant of competitive advantage (Barney, 1991). Superior profitability is seen as emerging from bundles of resources, with different resource bundles associated with different efficiencies. As a consequence, management scholars think of firms as bundles of heterogeneous resources, assets, and/or activities. These assets have different (economic) life expectancies. Such unique and specialized assets can also be intangible, such as worker-specific knowledge or firm-specific capabilities (Barney, 1986; Dierickx and Cool, 1989). These assets can be specific to certain firms, and co-specialized with other assets, such that they generate value only in certain combinations (Lachmann, 1956; Teece, 2009). Further, resource- and knowledge-based scholars often emphasize that heterogeneous assets usually do not give rise independently to competitive advantages. Rather, it is the interactions among these resources, their relations of specificity and co-specialization, that generate such advantages (e.g., Dierickx and Cool, 1989; Barney, 1991; Black and Boal, 1994; Teece, 2009). These interactions, coupled with path-dependent outcomes of past strategic investments in heterogeneous resources (Nelson and Winter, 1982), imply that heterogeneity, rather than homogeneity, is the hallmark characteristic of resources and firm organization of these resources. Models of the economy that are based on the assumption that capital is shmoo inherently cannot capture such heterogeneity and therefore fail to take into account the special problems of organization and allocation raised by the hetero-geneity of capital.

Note that macroeconomics has not always neglected the above resource characteristics. As explained in Chapter 5, the Austrian school has always emphasized capital heterogeneity, closely paral-leling management concepts of heterogeneous resources. The overall picture of the economy painted in this theory – which in important ways is a macro-level mirror of resource-based and other strategic management theories – is one of a web of heterogeneous capital assets that stand in complex relations to each other, and do so for a reason. The resulting structure is one in which capital assets are deployed, combined, etc. in an attempt to direct production towards satisfying consumer preferences, contemporaneous as well as future ones.

To the extent that economic activity is organized within markets, and conducted by for-profit firms, these firms' resource-based strat-egies have important macro-level ramifications; specifically, processes of acquiring or developing, combining, and divesting resources fit into an overall structure of production that ultimately serves the prefer-ences of consumers. The other side of the coin is that our knowledge of these firm-level processes forms an important micro foundation for our reasoning about what happens at the macro level. As a result, the constraints, incentives, opportunities, etc. faced by entrepreneurs must ultimately enter as a crucial element in the understanding of macro phenomena.

The role of heterogeneity

Unfortunately, the bailout and stimulus programs enacted in the US and EU in 2008 and 2009 virtually ignored the heterogeneity of entre-preneurs, assets, firms, and industries. The discussion before, during, and after these programs were enacted took place at a very high level of aggregation. Despite the widely publicized failures of particular financial institutions, such as AIG, Lehman Brothers, Freddie Mac, and Fannie Mae, government officials spoke in terms of "the banking system," "the financial system," and the economy as a whole. The dis-cussion of "frozen credit markets" focused on high-level indicators, with the focus on total lending, not the composition of lending among individuals, firms, and industries.

Few seemed to recognize that a decline in average home prices, reductions in total lending, and volatility in asset price indexes does not reveal much about the prices of particular homes, the cost of capital for specific borrowers, and the prices of individual assets. In analyzing a credit crisis, the critical question are about which loans are not being made, to whom, and why? Indeed, it is impossible to understand the origins of the credit crisis without looking at the lending practices of government-sponsored enterprises like Freddie Mac and Fannie Mae and policies that encouraged lenders to lower underwriting standards, on the assumption that all borrowers were "really" equally credit-worthy (Liebowitz, 2009). The assumption of homogeneity – during a period of rapid central-bank credit expansion – is at the root of the mainstream, Keynesian analysis of the 2008 financial crisis.

In the judgment-based perspective, the critical issues there relate to the composition of lending, not the amount. Total lending, total liquidity, average equity prices, and the like obscure the key questions about how resources are being allocated across sectors, firms, and individuals, whether bad investments are being liquidated, and so on. Such aggregate notions homogenize – and in doing so, suppress critical information about relative prices. The main function of capital markets, after all, is not to moderate the total amount of financial capital, but to allocate capital across activities.

If not all borrowers are the same, it is even more true that not all banks are the same. And yet, bailout programs like the US Treasury's Troubled Assets Relief Program (TARP) were designed explicitly on the premise that the banking system itself, rather than individual banks, was in trouble.[13] By bolstering inefficient banks and creating incentives to keep issuing mortgages that ought not to be issued, in the interests of reviving the macroeconomy, policies such as TARP are repeating the mistakes that caused the problems in the first place.

---

[13] To avoid signaling the financial conditions of specific banks to the market, the Treasury insisted that all large banks take TARP funds, whether they wanted to or not. Ultimately, some 250 banks refused to participate. Of course, such programs create a strong adverse-selection problem; banks that followed more prudent lending policies, did not invest in complex mortgage-backed securities, and the like have little incentive to take government subsidies accompanied by government control of future lending and investment (and even practices such as executive compensation).

More generally, the US stimulus package, and similar proposals around the world, are characterized by Keynesian-style reliance on macroeconomic aggregates. According to the common wisdom, the bank crisis led to a collapse of effective aggregate demand, and only massive increases in government expenditure (and government debt) can kick-start the economy. However, in a world of heterogeneous capital resources, spending on some assets but not others alters the pattern of resource allocation, and, in a path-dependent process, the overall performance of the economy in the future. As Hayek, Keynes' most important intellectual opponent, argued in the 1930s and 1940s, the economy's capital structure is a complex and delicate one that cannot be mashed and pushed like putty (Hayek, 1941). Resources cannot be shifted costlessly from one activity to another, particularly in a modern economy in which much of those resources are embodied in industry-specific, firm-specific, and worker-specific capabilities. Even idle resources can be misallocated – what Hayek and Mises called "malinvestment" – if invested in activities that do not produce the goods and services the economy needs (Hayek, 1933).

Unfortunately, this perspective has mostly been lost in contemporary macroeconomic discussions. As Kenneth Boulding, reviewing Paul Samuelson's *Foundations of Economic Analysis*, wrote in 1948:

[I]t is a question of acute importance for economics as to why the macroeconomics predictions of the mathematical economists have been on the whole less successful than the hunches of the mathematically unwashed. The answer seems to be that when we write, for instance, "let i, Y, and I stand, respectively, for the interest rate, income, and investment," we stand committed to the assumption that the internal structures of these aggregates or averages are not important for the problem in hand. In fact, of course, they may be very important, and no amount of subsequent mathematical analysis of the variables can overcome the fatal defect of their heterogeneity.   (Boulding, 1948: 189)

The nature of entrepreneurial competition

History, rather than macroeconomic perspectives stressing homogeneity, may provide us with valuable lessons regarding the understanding of the micro processes of entrepreneurship and economic recovery. A Kauffman Foundation report (Stangler, 2009) regarding the relationship between what they term "bureaucratic capitalism," financial downturns, and entrepreneurship in the United States over the last 100 years has important implications for potential solutions to the current financial crisis that relate to decentralized entrepreneurial activity. Specifically, the report documents periods when entrepreneurial entry was limited due to the unlevel playing field and concentration of economic power through government regulation that enabled large, sometimes inefficient, firms and powerful labor unions. Further, the report documents evidence that periods of economic downturns exhibit higher than average entrepreneurial activity, where decentralized decision-making ensures that resources flow freely to their highest value uses, given heterogeneity in potential use and ownership of the relevant resources. Cole and Ohanian (2009) also argue that the fruits of the 1930s – the most technologically progressive decade of the twentieth century (Field, 2003) – were delayed or reduced due to the New Deal-related policies that "suppress[ed] competition, and set prices and wages in many sectors well above their normal levels." These lessons indicate that the solutions to the current financial and economic crisis should leverage entrepreneurship and innovation that result from decentralized decision-making, rather than assuming that all resources are homogenous putty that can be allocated centrally, or through government intervention and edict.

One particular example where the standard macroeconomics assumptions of homogeneity and fungibility is likely to create problems is the US government's restructuring plans for the financial and automobile industries, and potentially for other sectors as well, including its proposals for sweeping changes in executive compensation, financial accounting, financial reporting, and more. Consider just one example – the link between Chrysler and Fiat.

Fiat, at the urging of the US government, completed an alliance with Chrysler in June 2009. The justifications for these actions are familiar to anyone who studies corporate strategy – the mythological search for synergy (Larsson and Finkelstein, 1999). Chrysler is supposed to get access to capital and to Fiat's knowledge of how to manufacture small cars profitably, and Fiat gets access to the US market through Chrysler's distribution network. Setting aside the observation that it is not at all clear that the proposed synergies could not be realized through some sort of market contract – what is the market failure that justifies more hierarchical forms of governance in this setting (Williamson, 1996)? Are the proposed synergies likely to be realized in a more integrated Fiat-Chrysler?

The data here are compelling. Most such corporate combinations – even those done voluntarily in non-crisis settings – fail to realize sought-for synergies. For example, Agarwal, Croson, and Mahoney (2009a) provide evidence of significant deviation between potential and realized value creation in alliance settings, even when economic incentives are appropriately aligned. Information asymmetries, communication costs, cultural differences, managerial preferences, conflicts of interests – the reasons for failure are legion. If one had to bet on whether or not any such combination would yield anticipated synergies, the bet would have to be "no." How much less likely, then, will these kinds of "shotgun" marriages, arranged in times of crisis, generate the hoped-for benefits?

In the face of these very consistent results, why the policy of merging Chrysler and Fiat? One explanation – but certainly not the only explanation – is that macroeconomists who have been instrumental in developing this policy fail to recognize the heterogeneity and stickiness of the resources and capabilities of firms like Chrysler and Fiat. It appears the logic is: Chrysler needs small cars, Fiat has small cars, link them. Little problems like culture, language, employment relationships, history, the fact that a similar relationship between Chrysler and Daimler failed – none of these seems to play a large role in this story. But how can they, when economic policy is based on theories that assume away this very heterogeneity?[14]

Policy derived from strategic management and organization theory suggests a different approach. Even casual observation suggests that Chrysler still has some valuable resources and capabilities – the Jeep brand, some reasonably efficient manufacturing operations, some excellent dealerships, and so forth. Strategic management theory asks: How can these valuable resources and capabilities be

---

[14] Of course, private firms can also underestimate the implications of resource heterogeneity and stickiness in realizing cross-firm synergies (Roll, 1986). However, they face resource constraints and incentive schemes that limit aggressive expansion, and operate in a selection environment that punishes poor decisions *ex post*. Public agencies face different, and we would argue, substantially weaker, constraints in reallocating private resources.

reallocated to their most-valued uses? This suggests that many of Chrysler's resources and capabilities might be profitably sold to other firms and that such restructuring could benefit many of Chrysler's stakeholders, including its employees. Of course, this is the trad-itional role of bankruptcy protection – an opportunity for firms to restructure in a way that enables them to realize as much of their value as they can.

If the proposed synergies with Fiat do not materialize soon, stra-tegic management theory suggests that yet another Chrysler bailout looms on the horizon. This theory also suggests that, just maybe, this is what the senior managers at Chrysler and Fiat are counting on.

Public policy for entrepreneurship

What, then, is the proper role of macroeconomic policy, and govern-ment intervention more generally, in a world of heterogeneous cap-ital and human resources? What should governments do to promote entrepreneurship in general, and particularly during an economic downturn? Is there a role for "activist" policy?

First, we think it is critically important to avoid public policies that generate malinvestment in the first place. As noted above, in our view the current crisis is not the result of unfettered markets (or, more colloquially, of "greed," or hubris, or regulators being "asleep at the wheel," or similar op-ed pronouncements), but the result of specific government policies designed to increase bank credit (par-ticularly, but not exclusively, mortgage lending). The roots of the current crisis lie with the credit bubble that preceded it, and the best thing policymakers can do is not to create the next credit bubble. Given that the bubble has burst, however, the fastest way to eco-nomic recovery is to *liquidate the bad investments as quickly as possible*. When resources have been malinvested, the remedy is to redirect those resources to alternative, and higher-valued, uses. Of course, given asset specificity (Williamson, 1985), resources cannot be instantly and costlessly reallocated to alternative uses. However, contracting parties should be allowed to renegotiate resource use without artificial impediments to contract enforcement and resource mobility. Existing mechanisms for liquidating existing investments and organizations, such as bankruptcy, should be used where appropriate.

Obviously, this implies that bailouts – not only banks or industrial firms getting infusions of taxpayer funds to stave off bankruptcy, but delinquent mortgage borrowers being protected by law from foreclosure – do not lead to improvements in long-term economic performance. Rather, they perpetuate the inefficient allocation of resources that characterize the boom and bust.[15] Indeed, the consensus among economic historians is that in the US New Deal policies of massive public works, wage and price controls, forced cartelization, high tariffs, and the like not only did not alleviate the Great Depression, but made what would have otherwise been a sharp, but short-lived, economic contraction into the worst depression in US history (Higgs, 1989; Vedder and Gallaway, 1993; Cole and Ohanian, 2004, 2009; Stangler, 2009). Moreover, the constantly changing mix of economic interventions generated a climate of what Higgs (1997) calls "regime uncertainty" that discouraged the private investment that would have stimulated economic recovery. It is vital that today's policymakers avoid the same mistakes.

Final remarks

Throughout the volume we have tried to be provocative, to challenge and extend received theory in entrepreneurship and organization studies, positioning ourselves not as radical, hostile critics, but as friendly insiders. We were both trained in fairly conventional, "mainstream" economics programs, while also being exposed to "heterodox" ideas from Austrian, evolutionary, and behavioral economics. There is much to admire in contemporary entrepreneurship theory (in management as well as in economics) and in the resource-based, agency-theoretic, transaction-cost, and property-rights approaches to the firm. We consider our work as part of these traditions. But there is much to learn from bringing entrepreneurship and the theory of the firm together in new, or previously underappreciated, ways.

Many of our arguments are tentative, rather than dispositive. There is obviously much work to be done in working through the details,

---

[15] The appropriate role of public policy and private charity in alleviating financial hardships faced by individuals during periods of economic upheaval is, of course, a separate issue that we do not address here.

drawing out specific implications, doing careful empirical work, and so on. Our aim in this book has been to define a research program for research in the intersection of the firm and entrepreneurship, one that revitalizes neglected insights, but does so in the context of modern theory.

References

Abell, Peter, Teppo Felin, and Nicolai Foss. 2008. "Building Micro Foundations for the Routines, Capabilities, and Performance Links." *Managerial and Decision Economics* 29: 489–502.

Abelson, Robert P. and John B. Black. 1986. "Introduction." In James A. Galambos, Robert P. Abelson and John B. Black, eds., *Knowledge Structures*. Hilsdale, NJ: Lawrence Erlbaum Associates.

Acs, Zoltan and David B. Audretsch. 1990. *Innovation and Small Firms*. Cambridge, MA: MIT Press.

Agarwal, Rajshree, Rachel Croson, and Joseph T. Mahoney. 2009a. "Decision Making in Strategic Alliances: An Experimental Investigation." *Strategic Management Journal* 31(4): 413–437.

Agarwal, Rajshree, Jay B. Barney, Nicolai J. Foss, and Peter G. Klein. 2009b. "Heterogeneous Resources and the Financial Crisis: Implications of Strategic Management Theory." *Strategic Organization* 7(4): 467–484.

Aghion, Philippe and Peter Howitt. 1992. "A Model of Growth through Creative Destruction." *Econometrica* 60(2): 323–351.

Aghion, Philippe and Jean Tirole. 1997. "Formal and Real Authority in Organizations." *Journal of Political Economy* 105(1): 1–29.

Ahuja, Gautam and Curba Morris Lampert. 2001. "Entrepreneurship in the Large Corporation: A Longitudinal Study of How Established Firms Create Breakthrough Inventions." *Strategic Management Journal* 22(6–7): 521–543.

Alchian, Armen A. 1950. "Uncertainty, Evolution, and Economic Theory." *Journal of Political Economy* 63: 211–221.

1965. "Some Economics of Property Rights." *Il Politico* 30: 816–829. Reprinted in Alchian, *Economic Forces at Work*. Indianapolis, IN: Liberty Press, 1977.

Alchian, Armen A. and Harold Demsetz. 1972. "Production, Information Costs, and Economic Organization." *American Economic Review* 62(5): 777–795.

Aldrich, Howard E. 1990. "Using an Ecological Perspective to Study Organizational Founding Rates." *Entrepreneurship Theory and Practice* 14(3): 7–24.

1999. *Organizations Evolving*. Thousand Oaks, CA: Sage Publications.

Aldrich, Howard E. and Gabriele Wiedenmayer. 1993. "From Traits to Rates: An Ecological Perspective on Organizational Foundings." In Jerome Katz and Robert Brockhaus, eds., *Advances in Entrepreneurship, Firm Emergence, and Growth*. Greenwich, CT: JAI Press, 145–195.

Alvarez, Sharon A. and Jay B. Barney. 2005. "How do Entrepreneurs Organize Firms under Conditions of Uncertainty." *Journal of Management* 31(5): 776–793.

2007. "Discovery and Creation: Alternative Theories of Entrepreneurial Action." *Strategic Entrepreneurship Journal* 1(1–2): 11–26.

2010. "Entrepreneurship and Epistemology: The Philosophical Underpinnings of the Study of Entrepreneurial Opportunities." *Academy of Management Annals* 4(1): 557–583.

Amabile, Teresa M. 1997. "Motivating Creativity in Organizations: On Doing What You Love and Loving What You Do." *California Management Review* 40(1): 39–58.

Amit, Rafael and Christoph Zott. 2001. "Value Creation in E Business." *Strategic Management Journal* 22(6–7): 493–520.

Anderson, Terry L. and Peter J. Hill. 2004. *The Not So Wild, Wild West: Property Rights on the Frontier*. Stanford, CA: Stanford University Press.

Andrade, Gregor and Erik Stafford. 2004. "Investigating the Economic Role of Mergers." *Journal of Corporate Finance* 10: 1–36.

Andrade, Gregor, Mark Mitchell, and Erik Stafford. 2001. "New Evidence and Perspectives on Mergers." *Journal of Economic Perspectives* 15: 103–120.

Aoki, Masahiko. 1986. "Horizontal vs Vertical Information Structure of the Firm." *American Economic Review* 76: 971–983.

Ardichvili, Alexander, Richard Cardozo, and Sourav Ray. 2003. "A Theory of Entrepreneurial Opportunity Identification and Development." *Journal of Business Venturing* 18(1): 105–123.

Argote, Linda. 1999. *Organizational Learning: Creating, Retaining, and Transferring Knowledge*. Berlin: Springer.

Argyres, Nicholas. 2010. "The Transaction as the Unit of Analysis." In Peter G. Klein and Michael E. Sykuta, eds., *The Elgar Companion to Transaction Cost Economics*. Cheltenham, UK: Edward Elgar, 127–132.

Argyres, Nicholas and Julia Porter Liebeskind. 1999. "Contractual Commitments, Bargaining Power, and Governance Inseparability: Incorporating History into Transaction Cost Theory." *Academy of Management Review* 24(1): 49–63.

Argyres, Nicholas and Kyle J. Mayer. 2007. "Contract Design as a Firm Capability: An Integration of Learning and Transaction Cost Perspectives." *Academy of Management Review* 32: 1060–1077.

Arrow, Kenneth J. 1974. *The Limits of Organization*. New York: W. W. Norton.

Audretsch, David B., Max Keilbach, and Erik Lehmann. 2005. *Entrepreneurship and Economic Growth*. Oxford University Press.

Bacharach, M. 2006. *Beyond Individual Choice*. Princeton University Press.

Baker, George, Robert Gibbons, and Kevin J. Murphy. 1994. "Subjective Performance Measures in Optimal Incentive Contracts." *Quarterly Journal of Economics* 109(4): 1125–1156.

1999. "Informal Authority in Organizations." *Journal of Law, Economics, and Organization* 15(1): 56.

Baker, Ted and Timothy G. Pollock. 2007. "Making the Marriage Work: The Benefits of Strategy's Takeover of Entrepreneurship for Strategic Organization." *Strategic Organization* 5(3): 297–312.

Barney, Jay B. 1986. "Organizational Culture: Can It Be a Source of Sustained Competitive Advantage?" *Academy of Management Review* 11(3): 656–665.

1991. "Firm Resources and Sustained Competitive Advantage." *Journal of Management* 17: 99–120.

Baron, Robert A. 1998. "Cognitive Mechanisms in Entrepreneurship: Why and When Entrepreneurs Think Differently than Other People." *Journal of Business Venturing* 13(4): 275–294.

Barreto, Humberto. 1989. *The Entrepreneur in Microeconomic Theory: Disappearance and Explanation*. London and New York: Routledge and Kegan Paul.

Barzel, Yoram. 1982. "Measurement Cost and the Organization of Markets." *Journal of Law and Economics* 25(1): 27–48.

1987. "The Entrepreneur's Reward for Self-Policing." *Economic Inquiry* 25: 103–116.

1994. "The Capture of Wealth by Monopolists and the Protection of Property Rights." *International Review of Law and Economics* 14: 393–409.

1997. *Economic Analysis of Property Rights*, second edn. Cambridge University Press.

Baumol, William J. 1968. "Entrepreneurship in Economic Theory." *American Economic Review* 58(2): 64–71.

1990. "Entrepreneurship: Productive, Unproductive, and Destructive." *Journal of Political Economy* 98(5): 893–921.

1994. *Entrepreneurship, Management, and the Structure of Payoffs.* Cambridge, MA: MIT Press.

Becarra, Manuel. 2009. *Theory of the Firm for Strategic Management.* Cambridge University Press.

Becker, Gary S. 1962. "Investment in Human Capital: A Theoretical Analysis." *Journal of Political Economy* 70(5): 9–49.

Becker, Marcus C. and Thorbjørn Knudsen. 2003. "The Entrepreneur at a Crucial Juncture in Schumpeter's Work: Schumpeter's 1928 Handbook Entry Entrepreneur." *Advances in Austrian Economics* 6: 199–234.

Begley, Thomas and David Boyd. 1987. "Psychological Characteristics Associated with Performance in Entrepreneurial Firms and Smaller Businesses." *Journal of Business Venturing* 2: 79–93.

Bénabou, Roland and Jean Tirole. 2003. "Intrinsic and Extrinsic Motivation." *Review of Economic Studies* 70(3): 489–520.

Bernardo, Antonio E. and Ivo Welch. 2001. "On the Evolution of Overconfidence and Entrepreneurs." *Journal of Economics and Management Strategy* 10(3): 301–330.

Ben-David, Itzhak, John R. Graham, and Campbell R. Harvey. 2010. "Managerial Miscalibration." NBER Working Paper No. 16215.

Bertrand, Elodie. 2006. "The Coasean Analysis of Lighthouse Financing: Myths and Realities." *Cambridge Journal of Economics* 30(3): 389–402.

Besanko, David, David Dranove, Mark Shanley, and Scott Schaefer. 2010. *Economics of Strategy,* third edn. New York: John Wiley.

Bewley, Truman F. 1986. "Knightian Decision Theory: Part I." Cowles Foundation Discussion Paper No. 807.

1989. "Market Innovation and Entrepreneurship: A Knightian View." Cowles Foundation Discussion Paper No. 905.

Bhardwaj, Gaurab, John C. Camillus, and David Hounshell. 2006. "Continual Corporate Entrepreneurial Search for Long-Term Growth." *Management Science* 52(2): 248–261.

Bhidé, Amar V. 2000. *The Origin and Evolution of New Businesses.* Oxford University Press.

2010. *A Call for Judgment: Sensible Finance for a Dynamic Economy.* New York: Oxford University Press.

Bianchi, Milo. 1990. "The Unsatisfactoriness of Satisficing: From Bounded Rationality to Innovative Rationality." *Review of Political Economy* 2: 149–167.

Bianchi, Milo and Magnus Henrekson. 2005. "Is Neoclassical Economics Still Entrepreneurless?" *Kyklos* 58: 353–377.

Bjørnskov, Christian and Nicolai J. Foss. 2008. "Economic Freedom and Entrepreneurship: Some Cross-Country Evidence." *Public Choice* 134(3): 307–328.

    2010. "Do Economic Freedom and Entrepreneurship Impact Total Factor Productivity?" Working paper, Department of Strategic Management and Globalization, Copenhagen Business School.

Black, Janice A. and Kimberly E. Boal. 1994. "Strategic Resources: Traits, Configurations and Paths to Sustainable Competitive Advantage." *Strategic Management Journal* 15: 131–148.

Blanchflower, David G. 2000. "Self-employment in OECD Countries." *Labor Economics* 7(5): 471–505.

Blau, David M. 1987. "A Time-Series Analysis of Self-Employment in the United States." *Journal of Political Economy* 95(3): 445–467.

Blaug, Mark. 1997. *Economic Theory in Retrospect*. Cambridge University Press.

Boettke, Peter J. 1989. Comment on Joseph Farrell, "Information and the Coase Theorem." *Journal of Economic Perspectives* 3: 195–198.

    2005. "Kirzner." *The Austrian Economists*, September 10. http://austrianeconomists.typepad.com/weblog/2005/09/kirzner.html. Accessed September 16, 2008.

Boettke, Peter J. and David L. Prychitko, eds. 1994. *The Market Process: Essays in Contemporary Austrian Economics*. Aldershot, UK: Edward Elgar.

Böhm-Bawerk, Eugen von. 1884–1912. *Capital and Interest*. South Holland, IL: Libertarian Press, 1959.

    1898. *Karl Marx and the Close of His System: A Critique*. London: T. Fisher Unwin.

Bolton, Patrick and Mathias Dewatripont. 1994. "The Firm as a Communication Network." *The Quarterly Journal of Economics* 109(4): 809–839.

Bolton, Patrick and Joseph Farrell. 1990. "Decentralization, Duplication, and Delay." *Journal of Political Economy* 98(4): 803–826.

Boot, Arnoud W. A., Todd T. Milbourn, and Anjan V. Thakor. 1999. "Megamergers and Expanded Scope: Theories of Bank Size and Activity Diversity." *Journal of Banking and Finance* 23: 195–214.

Boudreaux, Donald J. 1989. "Imperfectly Competitive Firms, Non-Price Competition, and Rent Seeking." *Journal of Institutional and Theoretical Economics* 145: 597–612.

Boudreaux, Donald J. and Randall G. Holcombe. 1989. "The Coasian and Knightian Theories of the Firm." *Managerial and Decision Economics* 10(2): 147–154.

Boulding, Kenneth E. 1948. "Samuelson's *Foundations*: The Role of Mathematics in Economics." *Journal of Political Economy* 56: 187–199.

Bradley, Robert L. 2008. *Capitalism at Work: Business, Government, and Energy*. Salem, MA: M and M Scrivener Press.

Brafman, Ori and Rod A. Beckstrom. 2006. *The Starfish and the Spider: The Unstoppable Power of Leaderless Organizations*. London: Penguin.

Braguinsky, Serguey, Steven Klepper, and Atsushi Ohyama. 2009. "Schumpeterian Entrepreneurship." Working paper, Carnegie Mellon University, Pittsburgh.

Bresnahan, Timothy F., Erik Brynjolfsson, and Lorin M. Hitt. 2002. "Information Technology, Workplace Organization, and the Demand for Skilled Labor: Firm-Level Evidence." *Quarterly Journal of Economics* 117(1): 339–376.

Brickley, James A., Clifford W. Smith, and Jerold L. Zimmerman. 2008. *Managerial Economics and Organizational Architecture*, fifth edn. New York: McGraw-Hill/Irwin.

Brooke, Geoffrey T. F. 2010. "Uncertainty, Profit, and Entrepreneurial Action: Frank Knight's Contribution Reconsidered." *Journal of the History of Economic Thought* 32: 221–235.

Buchanan, James M. 1962. "What Should Economists Do?," in James M. Buchanan, 1979. *What Should Economists Do?* Indianapolis: Liberty Press.

Buchanan, James M. and Viktor J. Vanberg. 1991. "The Market as a Creative Process." *Economics and Philosophy* 7: 167–186.

Buffett, Mary and David Clark. 1997. *Buffettology: The Previously Unexplained Techniques that Have Made Warren Buffett the World's Most Famous Investor*. London: Pocket Books.

Burress, Molly J. and Michael L. Cook. 2009. "A Primer on Collective Entrepreneurship: A Preliminary Taxonomy." University of Missouri, AEWP 2009–4.

Burress, Molly J., Michael L. Cook and Peter G. Klein. 2008. "The Clustering of Organizational Innovation: Developing Governance Models for Vertical Integration." *International Food and Agribusiness Management Review* 11(4): 49–75.

Busenitz, Lowell W. 1996. "Research on Entrepreneurial Alertness." *Journal of Small Business Management* 34: 35–44.

Busenitz, Lowell W. and Jay B. Barney. 1997. "Differences between Entrepreneurs and Managers in Large Organizations: Biases and Heuristics in Strategic Decision-Making." *Journal of Business Venturing* 12(1): 9–30.

Bylund, Per L. 2011. "Division of Labor and the Firm: An Austrian Attempt at Explaining the Firm in the Market." *Quarterly Journal of Austrian Economics* 14(2): 188–215.

Caldwell, Bruce J. 1988. "Hayek's Transformation." *History of Political Economy* 20(4): 513–541.

Caliendo, Marco, Frank M. Fossen, and Alexander S. Kritikos. 2009. "Risk Attitudes of Nascent Entrepreneurs: New Evidence from an Experimentally Validated Survey." *Small Business Economics* 32(2): 153–167.

Camerer, Colin and Marc Knez. 1996. "Coordination: Organizational Boundaries and Fads in Business Practice." *Industrial and Corporate Change* 5: 89–112.

Cantillon, Richard. 1755. *Essai sur la nature du commerce en général.* Henry Higgs, ed. London: Macmillan, 1931.

Carlton, Dennis and Jeffrey Perloff. 2005. *Modern Industrial Organization,* fourth edn. New York: Addison-Wesley.

Carnahan, Seth, Rajshree Agarwal, Benjamin A. Campbell, and April Franco. 2010. "The Effect of Firm Compensation Structures on Employee Mobility and Employee Entrepreneurship of Extreme Performers." Working paper, Department of Business Administration, University of Illinois Urbana-Champaign.

Carson, Kevin A. 2008. *Organization Theory: A Libertarian Perspective.* Charleston, SC: BookSurge.

Casson, Mark C. 1982. *The Entrepreneur: An Economic Theory,* second edn. Aldershot, UK: Edward Elgar, 1999.

  1994. "Why Are Firms Hierarchical?" *International Journal of the Economics of Business* 1(1): 47–76.

  1997. *Information and Organization.* Oxford University Press.

  2000. "An Entrepreneurial Theory of the Firm." In Nicolai J. Foss and Volker Mahn, eds., *Competence, Governance and Entrepreneurship: Advances in Economic Strategy Research.* New York: Oxford University Press.

  2005. "Entrepreneurship and the Theory of the Firm." *Journal of Economic Behavior and Organization* 58: 327–348.

Casson, Mark C. and Nigel Wadeson. 2007. "The Discovery of Opportunities: Extending the Economic Theory of the Entrepreneur." *Small Business Economics* 28(4): 285–300.

Chambers, Molly L. 2007. "Organizational Spawning: Investment in Farmer-Controlled Businesses." Ph.D. dissertation, Department of Agricultural Economics, University of Missouri.

Chandler, Gaylen N. and Erik Jansen. 1992. "The Founder's Self-Assessed Competence and Venture Performance." *Journal of Business Venturing* 7: 223–236.

Chesbrough, Henry and Richard S. Rosenbloom. 2003. "The Dual-Edged Role of the Business Model in Leveraging Corporate Technology Investments." In L. M. Branscomb and P. E. Auerswald, eds., *Taking Technical Risks: How Innovators, Managers, and Investors Manage Risk in High-Tech Innovations.* Cambridge, MA: Harvard University Press, 57–68.

Cheung, Steven N. S. 1970. "The Structure of a Contract and the Theory of a Non-Exclusive Resource." *Journal of Law and Economics* 13(1): 49–70.

  1973. "The Fable of the Bees." *Journal of Law and Economics* 16: 11–34.

  1983. "The Contractual Nature of the Firm." *Journal of Law and Economics* 26(1): 1–21.

Chiles, Todd H. 2003. "Process Theorizing: Too Important to Ignore in a Kaleidic World." *Academy of Management Learning and Education* 2(3): 288–291.

Chiles, Todd H. and T. Y. Choi. 2000. "Theorizing TQM: An Austrian and Evolutionary Economics Interpretation." *Journal of Management Studies* 37(2): 185–212.

Chiles, Todd H., Alan D. Meyer, and Thomas J. Hench. 2004. "Organizational Emergence: The Origin and Transformation of Branson, Missouri's Musical Theaters." *Organization Science* 15(5): 499–519.

Chiles, Todd H., Allen C. Bluedorn, and Vishal K. Gupta. 2007. "Beyond Creative Destruction and Entrepreneurial Discovery: A Radical Austrian Approach to Entrepreneurship." *Organization Studies* 28(4): 467–493.

Choi, Young Back. 1993. *Paradigms and Conventions: Uncertainty, Decision Making, and Entrepreneurship.* Ann Arbor: University of Michigan Press.

Christensen, Clayton M. 1997. *The Innovator's Dilemma: When New Technologies Cause Great Firms to Fail.* Boston, MA: Harvard Business School Press.

Clark, John Bates. 1893. "The Genesis of Capital." *Yale Review* 2: 302–315.

  1918. *Essentials of Economic Theory As Applied to Modern Problems of Industry and Public Policy.* New York: The Macmillan Company.

Coase, Ronald H. 1937. "The Nature of the Firm." *Economica* 4: 386–405.

  1960. "The Problem of Social Cost." *Journal of Law and Economics* 3(1): 1–44.

  1964. "The Regulated Industries: Discussion." *American Economic Review* 54(3): 194–197.

1972. "Industrial Organization: A Proposal for Research." In V. R. Fuchs, ed., *Policy Issues and Research Opportunities in Industrial Organization.* New York: National Bureau of Economic Research, 59–73.

1974. "The Lighthouse in Economics." *Journal of Law and Economics* 17(2): 357–376.

1988. "Notes on the Problem of Social Cost." In R. H. Coase, *The Firm, the Market, and the Law.* University of Chicago Press.

1991. "The Nature of the Firm: Origin, Meaning, Influence." In Oliver E. Williamson and Sidney G. Winter, eds., *The Nature of the Firm.* Oxford University Press.

1992. "The Institutional Structure of Production." *American Economic Review* 82(4): 713–719.

Coddington, Alan. 1983. *Keynesian Economics: The Search for First Principles.* London: George Allen and Unwin.

Cohen, Avi J. and Geoffrey C. Harcourt. 2003. "Whatever Happened to the Cambridge Capital Theory Controversies?" *Journal of Economic Perspectives* 17(1): 199–214.

Cole, Harold L. and Lee E. Ohanian. 2004. "New Deal Policies and the Persistence of the Great Depression: A General Equilibrium Analysis." *Journal of Political Economy* 112(4): 779-816.

Cole, Harold L. and Lee E. Ohanian. 2009. "How Government Prolonged the Depression," *Wall Street Journal*, February 2, http://online.wsj.com/article/SB123353276749137485.html. Accessed July 29, 2011.

Companys, Yosem and Jeffery McMullen. 2007. "Strategic Entrepreneurs at Work: The Nature, Discovery, and Exploitation of Entrepreneurial Opportunities." *Small Business Economics* 28(4): 301–322.

Cone, Judith. 2008. *Teaching Entrepreneurship in Colleges and Universities: How (and Why) a New Academic Field is Being Built.* Kansas City: Ewing Marion Kauffman Foundation.

Connell, Carol Matheson. 2007. "Discerning a Mentor's Role: The Influence of Fritz Machlup on Edith Penrose and the Theory of The Growth of the Firm." *Journal of Management History* 13(3): 228–239.

Conner, Kathleen R. and C. K. Prahalad. 1996. "A Resource-based Theory of the Firm: Knowledge versus Opportunism." *Organization Science* 7: 477–501.

Cook, Michael L. 1995. "The Future of US Agricultural Cooperatives: A Neo-Institutional Approach." *American Journal of Agricultural Economics* 77(5): 1153–1159.

Cook, Michael L. and Fabio R. Chaddad. 2004. "Redesigning Cooperative Boundaries: The Emergence of New Models." *American Journal of Agricultural Economics* 86(5): 1249–1253.

Cook, Michael L. and Constantine Iliopoulos. 2000. "Ill-Defined Property Rights in Collective Action: The Case of US Agricultural Cooperatives." In C. Ménard, ed., *Institutions, Contracts and Organizations*. London: Edward Elgar Publishing, 335–348.

Cook, Michael L. and Brad Plunkett. 2006. "Collective Entrepreneurship: An Emerging Phenomenon in Producer-Owned Organizations." *Journal of Agricultural and Applied Economics* 38(2): 421–428.

Cooper, Arnold C. and Catherine M. Daily. 1997. "Entrepreneurial Teams." In Donald Sexton and Ray Smilor, eds., *Entrepreneurship: 2000*. Boston: PWS–Kent Publishing Company, 127–150.

Cooper, Arnold C., Timothy B. Folta, and Carolyn Y. Woo. 1995. "Entrepreneurial Information Search." *Journal of Business Venturing* 10: 107–120.

Corbett, Andrew C. 2005. "Experiential Learning within the Process of Opportunity Identification and Exploitation." *Entrepreneurship Theory and Practice* 29(4): 473–491.

Covin, Jeffrey G. and Morgan P. Miles. 2007. "Strategic Use of Corporate Venturing." *Entrepreneurship Theory and Practice* 31(2): 183–207.

Cowen, Tyler. 1985. "Public Goods Definitions and Their Institutional Context: A Critique of Public Goods Theory." *Review of Social Economy* 43: 53–63.

1988. *The Theory of Market Failure: A Critical Examination*. Fairfax, VA: George Mason University Press.

Cowen, Tyler and David Parker. 1997. *Markets in the Firm: A Market-Process Approach to Management*. London: Institute of Economic Affairs.

Crocker, Keith J. and Scott E. Masten. 1991. "Pretia Ex Machina? Prices and Process in Long-Term Contracts." *Journal of Law and Economics* 34: 69–99.

Crocker, Keith J. and Kenneth J. Reynolds. 1993. "The Efficiency of Incomplete Contracts: An Empirical Analysis of Air Force Engine Procurement." *Rand Journal of Economics* 36: 126–146.

Csikszentmihalyi, Mihaly. 1996. *Creativity: Flow and the Psychology of Discovery and Invention*. New York: HarperCollins.

Cusumano, Michael A. 1997. "How Microsoft Makes Large Teams Work Like Small Teams." *Sloan Management Review* 39: 9–20.

Cyert, Richard M. and James G. March. 1963. *A Behavioral Theory of the Firm*. Englewood Cliffs, NJ: Prentice-Hall.

D'Aveni, Richard A. 1994. *Hypercompetition*. New York: Free Press.

Davenport, Herbert J. 1914. *Economics of Enterprise*. New York: Macmillan.

Day, David V. and Robert G. Lord. 1992. "Expertise and Problem Categorization. The Role of Expert Processing in Organizational Sense-Making." *Journal of Management Studies* 29: 35–47.

Day, Jonathan D. and James C. Wendler. 1998. "The New Economics of Organization." *McKinsey Quarterly* 1: 4–17.

Debreu, Gerard. 1959. *Theory of Value.* New York: Wiley.

Deci, Edward L. and Richard M. Ryan. 1985. *Intrinsic Motivation and Self-Determination in Human Behavior.* New York: Springer.

De Clercq, Dirk, Xavier Castañer, and Imanol Belausteguigoitia. 2007. "The Secrets of Intrapreneurship." *European Business Forum* 31: 40–45.

Delmar, Frédéric. 1996. *Entrepreneurial Behavior and Business Performance.* Institute of Economic Research at the Stockholm School of Economics.

Demmert, Henry and Daniel B. Klein. 2003. "Experiment on Entrepreneurial Discovery: An Attempt to Demonstrate the Conjecture of Hayek and Kirzner." *Journal of Economic Behavior and Organization* 50(3): 295–310.

Demsetz, Harold. 1964. "The Exchange and Enforcement of Property Rights." *Journal of Law and Economics* 7: 11–26. In Demsetz, *Ownership, Control, and the Firm.* Oxford: Basil Blackwell, 1988.

1967. "Toward a Theory of Property Rights." *American Economic Review* 57(2): 347–359. In Demsetz, *Ownership, Control, and the Firm.* Oxford: Basil Blackwell, 1988.

1969. "Information and Efficiency: A Different Viewpoint." In Demsetz, *Ownership, Control, and the Firm.* Oxford: Basil Blackwell, 1988.

1973. "Industry Structure, Market Rivalry, and Public Policy." *Journal of Law and Economics* 16(1): 1–9.

1983. "The Neglect of the Entrepreneur." In Joshua Ronen, ed., *Entrepreneurship.* Lexington, MA: Lexington Press.

1988a. *The Organization of Economic Activity.* Oxford: Basil Blackwell.

1988b. "Profit as a Functional Return: Reconsidering Knight's Views." In Demsetz, *Ownership, Control, and the Firm.* Oxford: Basil Blackwell, 1988.

1988c. "The Theory of the Firm Revisited." *Journal of Law, Economics, and Organization* 4(1): 141–161.

1991. "The Theory of the Firm Revisited." In Oliver E. Williamson and Sidney G. Winter, eds., *The Nature of the Firm.* Oxford: Basil Blackwell.

Dennen, R. Taylor. 1976. "Cattlemen's Associations and Property Rights in Land in the American West." *Explorations in Economic History* 13(4): 423–436.

Denrell, Jerker, C. Fang, and Sidney G. Winter. 2003. "The Economics of Strategic Opportunity." *Strategic Management Journal* 24(10): 977–990.

Dew, Nicholas, Stuart Read, Saras D. Sarasvathy, and Robert Wiltbank. 2009. "Effectual Versus Predictive Logics in Entrepreneurial Decision-Making: Differences between Experts and Novices." *Journal of Business Venturing* 24(4): 287–309.

Dierickx, Ingemar and Karel Cool. 1989. "Asset Stock Accumulation and Sustainability of Competitive Advantage." *Management Science* 35: 1504–1511.

Dosi, Giovanni. 2000. *Innovation, Organization, and Economic Dynamics: Selected Essays.* Cheltenham, UK: Edward Elgar.

Douglas, Evan J. and Dean A. Shepherd. 1999. "Entrepreneurship as a Utility Maximizing Response." *Journal of Business Venturing* 15(3): 231–251.

Dow, Gregory K. 1987. "The Function of Authority in Transaction Cost Economics." *Journal of Economic Behavior and Organization* 8: 13–38.

Ekelund, Robert B., Jr. and Robert F. Hébert. 1990. *A History of Economic Thought and Method,* third edn. New York: McGraw-Hill.

Ekelund, Robert B.,Jr. and David S. Saurman. 1988. *Advertising and the Market Process: A Modern Economic View.* San Francisco: Pacific Research Institute.

Elfenbein, Daniel W., Barton H. Hamilton, and Todd R. Zenger. 2010. "The Small Firm Effect and the Entrepreneurial Spawning of Scientists and Engineers." *Management Science* 56: 1–23.

Elkjær, Jørgen R. 1991. "The Entrepreneur in Economic Theory: An Example of the Development and Influence of a Concept." *History of European Ideas* 13: 805–815.

Elmendorf, Douglas W. 2009. "The State of the Economy and Issues in Developing an Effective Policy Response." Statement of the Director of the Congressional Budget Office before the Committee of the Budget, US House of Representatives, January 29.

Elster, Jon. 1983. *Explaining Technical Change. A Case Study in the Philosophy of Science.* Cambridge University Press.

Emmett, Ross B. 1999. "The Economist and the Entrepreneur: Modernist Impulses in Frank H. Knight's *Risk, Uncertainty and Profit.*" *History of Political Economy* 31 (Spring): 29–52.

2009. *Frank Knight and the Chicago School in American Economics.* London: Routledge.

2010. "Frank H. Knight on the 'Entrepreneur Function' in Modern Enterprise." Working paper, James Madison College, Michigan State University.

Falaschetti, Dino and Gary J. Miller. 2011. "Constraining Rational Choice: Allocation vs. Efficiency and the Origin of Credible Commitment Problems." Working paper, Department of Political Science, Washington University, St. Louis.

Fama, Eugene and Michael C. Jensen. 1983. "Separation of Ownership and Control." *Journal of Law and Economics* 26(2): 301–325.

Fehr, Ernst, and Simon Gächter. 2000. "Cooperation and Punishment in Public Goods Experiments." *American Economic Review* 90(4): 980–994.

Felin, Teppo, and Nicolai J. Foss. 2005. "Strategic Organization: A Field in Search of Micro-Foundations." *Strategic Organization* 3(4): 441–455.

2011. "The Endogenous Origins of Experience, Routines and Organizational Capabilities: The Poverty of Stimulus." *Journal of Institutional Economics* 7: 257–277.

Felin, Teppo, and Todd R. Zenger. 2009. "Entrepreneurs as Theorists: On the Origins of Collective Beliefs and Novel Strategies." *Strategic Entrepreneurship Journal* 3(2): 127–146.

Fetter, Frank A. 1905. *The Principles of Economics*. New York: The Century Co.

1910. *The Principles of Economics, with Applications to Practical Problems*. New York: Century.

1915. *Economic Principles*. New York: The Century Co.

1977. *Capital, Interest, and Rent: Essays in the Theory of Distribution*. Edited by M. N. Rothbard. Kansas City: Sheed Andrews and McMeel, Inc.

Field, Alexander. 2003. "The Most Technologically Progressive Decade of the Century." *American Economic Review* 93: 1399–1414.

Finkle, Todd A. and David Deeds. 2001. "Trends in the Market for Entrepreneurship Faculty, 1989–1998." *Journal of Business Venturing* 16: 613–630.

Fisher, Franklin M. 1983. *Disequilibrium Foundations of Equilibrium Economics*. Cambridge University Press.

Fisher, Irving. 1930. *The Theory of Interest*. Clifton: Augustus M. Kelley (reissue 1974).

Fleming, Lee. 2001. "Recombinant Uncertainty in Technological Search." *Management Science* 47: 117–132.

Forbes, Daniel P. 2005. "Are Some Entrepreneurs More Overconfident Than Others?" *Journal of Business Venturing* 20(5): 623–640.

Foss, Kirsten. 2001. "Organizing Technological Interdependencies: A Coordination Perspective on the Firm." *Industrial and Corporate Change* 10(1): 151–178.

Foss, Kirsten and Nicolai J. Foss. 2000. "Theoretical Isolation in Contract Economics." *Journal of Economic Methodology* 7: 313–339.

2001. "Assets, Attributes and Ownership." *International Journal of the Economics of Business* 8: 19–37.

2005. "Resources and Transaction Costs: How Property Rights Economics Furthers the Resource-based View." *Strategic Management Journal* 26(6): 541–553.

2008. "Understanding Opportunity Discovery and Sustainable Advantage: The Role of Transaction Costs and Property Rights." *Strategic Management Journal* 2: 191–207.

Foss, Nicolai J. 1993a. "Theories of the Firm: Contractual and Competence Perspectives." *Journal of Evolutionary Economics* 3: 127–144.

1993b. "More on Knight and the Theory of the Firm." *Managerial and Decision Economics* 14: 269–276.

1994. "The Biological Analogy and the Theory of the Firm: Marshall and Monopolistic Competition." *Journal of Economic Issues* 28: 1115–1136.

1996a. "Knowledge-Based Approaches to the Theory of the Firm: Some Critical Comments." *Organization Science* 7: 470–476.

1996b. "The 'Alternative' Theories of Knight and Coase, and the Modern Theory of the Firm." *Journal of the History of Economic Thought* 18: 76–95.

1997. "Austrian Insights and the Theory of the Firm." *Advances in Austrian Economics* 4: 175–198.

1999. "The Use of Knowledge in Firms." *Journal of Institutional and Theoretical Economics* 155: 458–486.

2000. "Equilibrium versus Evolution: The Conflicting Legacies of Demsetz and Penrose." In N. J. Foss and P. Robertson, eds., *Resources, Technology, and Strategy: Explorations in the Resource-based View*. London: Routledge.

2001. "Leadership, Beliefs and Coordination." *Industrial and Corporate Change* 10: 357–388.

2003. "Selective Intervention and Internal Hybrids: Interpreting and Learning from the Rise and Decline of the Oticon Spaghetti Organization." *Organization Science* 14: 331–349.

2005. *Strategy and Economic Organization in the Knowledge Economy: The Coordination of Firms and Resources*. Oxford University Press.

Foss, Nicolai J. and Jens Frøslev Christensen. 2001. "A Market-Process Approach to Corporate Coherence." *Managerial and Decision Economics* 22(4–5): 213–226.

Foss, Nicolai J. and Giampaolo Garzarelli. 2007. "Institutions as Knowledge Capital: Ludwig M. Lachmann's Interpretative Institutionalism." *Cambridge Journal of Economics* 31(5): 789–804.

Foss, Nicolai J. and Peter G. Klein. 2002. *Entrepreneurship and the Theory of the Firm*. Aldershot, UK: Edward Elgar.

2005. "Entrepreneurship and the Economic Theory of the Firm: Any Gains from Trade?" In Rajshree Agarwal, Sharon A. Alvarez, and Olav Sorenson, eds., *Handbook of Entrepreneurship Research: Disciplinary Perspectives*. Dordrecht: Springer.

2010. "Alertness, Action, and the Antecedents of Entrepreneurship." *Journal of Private Enterprise* 25: 145–164.

2011. "Organizational Governance." Working paper, McQuinn Center for Entrepreneurial Leadership, University of Missouri.

Foss, Nicolai J. and K. Laursen. 2005. "Performance Pay, Delegation, and Multitasking Under Uncertainty and Innovativeness: An Empirical Investigation." *Journal of Economic Behavior and Organization* 58: 246–276.

Foss, Nicolai J. and Siegwart Lindenberg. (in press). "Teams, Team Agency, and the Theory of the Firm." *Managerial and Decision Economics*.

Foss, Nicolai J. and Jacob Lyngsie. 2011. "Strategic Entrepreneurship." In Daniel Hjorth, ed., *Handbook of Organisational Entrepreneurship*. Cheltenham, UK: Edward Elgar.

Foss, Nicolai J. and Nils Stieglitz. 2011. "Modern Resource-based Theory." In M. Dietrich and J. Krafft, eds. *Handbook of the Economics of the Firm*. Cheltenham, UK: Edward Elgar.

Foss, Nicolai J., Peter G. Klein, Yasemin Y. Kor, and Joseph T. Mahoney. 2008. "Entrepreneurship, Subjectivism, and the Resource-Based View: Towards a New Synthesis." *Strategic Entrepreneurship Journal* 2(1): 73–94.

Foss, Nicolai J., Keld Laursen, and Torben Pedersen, 2011. "Linking Customer Interaction and Innovation: The Mediating Role of New Organizational Practices." *Organization Science* 22: 980–999.

Foss, Nicolai J., Dana Minbaeva, Mia Reinholt, and Torben Pedersen. 2009. "Stimulating Knowledge Sharing Among Employees: The Contribution of Job Design." *Human Resource Management* 48: 871–893.

Furubotn, Erik G. 2001. "The New Institutional Economics and the Theory of the Firm." *Journal of Economics Behavior and Organization* 45(2): 133–153.

2002. "Entrepreneurship, Transaction-Cost Economics, and the Design of Contracts." In Eric Brousseau and Jean-Michel Glachant, eds., *The Economics of Contracts: Theories and Applications*. Cambridge University Press, 72–97.

2006. "The New Institutional Economics and the Theory of the Multiobjective Firm." In R. Richter, U. Bindseil, J. Haucap, and C. Wey, eds., *Institutions in Perspective: Festschrift in Honor of Rudolf Richter on the Occasion of His 80th Birthday*. Thüringen: Mohr Siebeck, 37.

Futia, Carl A. 1980. "Schumpeterian Competition." *Quarterly Journal of Economics* 94: 675–695.

Gabor, André and Ivor F. Pearce. 1952. "A New Approach to the Theory of the Firm." *Oxford Economic Papers* 4: 252–265.

1958. "The Place of Money Capital in the Theory of Production." *Quarterly Journal of Economics* 72: 537–557.

Gaglio, Connie M. and Jerome A. Katz. 2001. "The Psychological Basis of Opportunity Identification: Entrepreneurial Alertness." *Small Business Economics* 16: 95–111.

Gagné, Marylène and Edward L. Deci. 2005. "Self Determination Theory and Work Motivation." *Journal of Organizational Behavior* 26(4): 331–362.

Galloway, Les. 1996. *Operation Management: The Basics*. London: International Thomson Business Press.

Garrison, Roger W. 2001. *Time and Money: The Macroeconomics of Capital Structure*. London: Routledge.

Gartner, William B. 1988. "Who is An Entrepreneur? Is the Wrong Question." *American Journal of Small Business* 12: 11–32.

2007. "Entrepreneurial Narrative and a Science of the Imagination." *Journal of Business Venturing* 22: 613–627.

Gartner William B. and Nancy M. Carter. 2003. "Entrepreneurial Behavior and Firm Organizing Processes." In Zoltan J. Acs and David B. Audretch, eds., *Handbook of Entrepreneurship Research*. Boston: Kluwer, 195–221.

Gartner, William B. and Karl H. Vesper. 1999. *University Entrepreneurship Programs*. Los Angeles: Lloyd Grief Center for Entrepreneurial Studies, University of Southern California.

Garud, Raghu, and Peter Karnøe. 2003. "Bricolage versus Breakthrough: Distributed and Embedded Agency in Technology Entrepreneurship." *Research Policy* 32: 277–300.

Gatewood, Elizabeth J. and Kelly G. Shaver. 2009. *Handbook of University-Wide Entrepreneurship Education*. Cheltenham, UK: Edward Elgar.

Gavetti, Giovanni. 2005. "Cognition and Hierarchy: Rethinking the Microfoundations of Capabilities' Development." *Organization Science* 16(6): 599–617.

Gavetti, Giovanni and Daniel Levinthal. 2000. "Looking Forward and Looking Backward: Cognitive and Experiential Search." *Administrative Science Quarterly* 45(1): 113–137.

Gavetti, Giovanni and Jan W. Rivkin. 2007. "On the Origin of Strategy: Action and Cognition Over Time." *Organization Science* 18: 420–439.

Ghoshal, Sumantra, Peter Moran, and L. Almeida-Costa. 1995. "The Essence of the Megacorporation: Shared Context, Not Structural Hierarchy." *Journal of Institutional and Theoretical Economics* 151: 748–759.

Gibbons, Robert. 1999. "Taking Coase Seriously." *Administrative Science Quarterly*, 44: 145–157.

2005. "Four Formal(izable) Theories of the Firm." *Journal of Economic Behavior and Organization* 58: 200–245.

Gifford, Sharon. 1999. "Limited Attention and the Optimal Incompleteness of Contracts." *Journal of Law, Economics, and Organization* 15(2): 468–486.

Gompers, Paul A. 1995. "Optimal Investment, Monitoring, and the Staging of Venture Capital." *Journal of Finance* 50(5): 1461–1489.

Gompers, Paul A., Josh Lerner, and David Scharfstein. 2005. "Entrepreneurial Spawning: Public Corporations and the Genesis of New Ventures, 1986 to 1999." *Journal of Finance* 60(2): 577–614.

Grandori, Anna. 2001. "Neither Hierarchy nor Identity: Knowledge-Governance Mechanisms and the Theory of the Firm." *Journal of Management and Governance* 5(3): 381–399.

2010. "A Rational Heuristic Model of Economic Decision Making." *Rationality and Society* 22(4): 477–504.

Grant, Robert M. 1996. "Toward a Knowledge-Based Theory of the Firm." *Strategic Management Journal* 17: 109–122.

Greve, Arent and Janet W. Salaff. 2003. "Social Networks and Entrepreneurship." *Entrepreneurship Theory and Practice* 28(1) 1–22.

Greve, Heinrich R. 2003. *Organizational Learning from Performance Feedback: A Behavioral Perspective on Innovation and Change.* Cambridge University Press.

Grossman, Sanford J. and Oliver D. Hart. 1986. "The Costs and Benefits of Ownership: A Theory of Vertical and Lateral Integration." *Journal of Political Economy* 94: 691–719.

Guzmán, Joaquín and F. Javier Santos-Cumplido. 2001. "The Booster Function and the Entrepreneurial Quality: An Application to the

Province of Seville." *Entrepreneurship and Regional Development* 13: 211–228.

Hansmann, Henry. 1996. *The Ownership of Enterprise*. Cambridge, MA: Belknap Press of Harvard University Press.

Hanusch, Horst and Andreas Pyka. 2005. "Principles of Neo-Schumpeterian Economics." Discussion Paper Series 278, Universitaet Augsburg, Institute for Economics.

Harper, David. 1995. *Entrepreneurship and the Market Process: An Inquiry into the Growth of Knowledge*. London: Routledge.

2008. "Towards a Theory of Entrepreneurial Teams." *Journal of Business Venturing* 23(6): 613–626.

Harsanyi, John. 1967. "Games with Incomplete Information Played by 'Bayesian' Players, I-III. Part I. The Basic Model." *Management Science* 14(3): 159–182.

1968a. "Games with Incomplete Information Played by 'Bayesian' Players, I-III. Part II. Bayesian Equilibrium Points." *Management Science* 14(5): 320–334.

1968b. "Games with Incomplete Information Played by 'Bayesian' Players, I-III. Part III. The Basic Probability Distribution of the Game." *Management Science* 14(7): 486–502.

Hart, Oliver D. 1989. "An Economist's Perspective on the Theory of the Firm." *Columbia Law Review*: 1757–1774.

1990. "Is 'Bounded Rationality' an Important Element of a Theory of Institutions?" *Journal of Institutional and Theoretical Economics* 16: 696–702.

1995. *Firms, Contracts, and Financial Structure*. Oxford: The Clarendon Press.

2011. "Thinking about the Firm: A Review of Daniel Spulber's *The Theory of the Firm*." *Journal of Economic Literature* 49(1): 101–113.

Hart, Oliver D. and John Moore. 1990. "Property Rights and the Nature of the Firm." *Journal of Political Economy* 98(6): 1119–1158.

Hayek, Friedrich A. 1928. "Intertemporal Price Equilibrium and Movements in the Value of Money." In *Money, Capital and Fluctuations: Early Essays*. University of Chicago Press, 1984: 121–137.

1931a. *Prices and Production*. London: Routledge and Sons.

1931b. "Richard Cantillon." In W. W. Bartley III and Stephen Kresge, eds., *The Collected Works of F. A. Hayek*, volume III: *The Trend of Economic Thinking*. University of Chicago Press, 245–294.

1933. *Prices and Production*. London: Routledge and Kegan Paul.

1937. "Economics and Knowledge." In Hayek, *Individualism and Economic Order*. University of Chicago Press, 1948.

1941. *The Pure Theory of Capital*. University of Chicago Press.

1945. "The Use of Knowledge in Society." In Hayek, *Individualism and Economic Order*. Chicago University Press, 1948.

1946. "The Meaning of Competition." In Hayek, *Individualism and Economic Order*. Chicago University Press, 1948: 92–106.

1948. *Individualism and Economic Order*. University of Chicago Press.

1968. "Competition as a Discovery Procedure." Translated by Marcellus S. Snow. *Quarterly Journal of Austrian Economics* 5: 9–23. In Hayek, *New Studies in Politics, Economics, Philosophy, and the History of Ideas*. London: Routledge and Kegan Paul, 1978.

1973. *Law, Legislation and Liberty*, volume I: *Rules and Order*. Chicago University Press.

Hébert, Robert F. and Albert N. Link. 1988. *The Entrepreneur: Mainstream Views and Radical Critiques*. New York: Praeger.

Helfat, Constance E. 1994. "Firm-Specificity in Corporate Applied R & D." *Organization Science* 5(2): 173–184.

1997. "Know-how and Asset Complementarity and Dynamic Capability Accumulation: the Case of R&D." *Strategic Management Journal* 18: 339–360.

Helfat. Constance E. and Margaret A. Peteraf. 2009. "Understanding Dynamic Capabilities: Progress Along a Developmental Path." *Strategic Organization* 7(1): 91–102.

Helfat, Constance E. and Ruth S. Raubitschek. 2000. "Product Sequencing: Co-Evolution of Knowledge, Capabilities and Products." *Strategic Management Journal* 21(10–11): 961–980.

Hellmann, Thomas. 2007. "When Do Employees Become Entrepreneurs?" *Management Science* 53(6): 919–933.

Henderson, Rebecca M. and Kim B. Clark. 1990. "Architectural Innovation: The Reconfiguration of Existing Product Technologies and the Failure of Established Firms." *Administrative Science Quarterly* 35(1): 9–30.

Henderson, Richard I. 2000. *Compensation Management in a Knowledge-Based World*. New York: Prentice-Hall.

Hicks, John R. 1946. *Value and Capital: An Inquiry into Some Fundamental Principles of Economic Theory*. Oxford University Press.

Hicks, John R. and R. G. D. Allen. 1934. "A Reconsideration of the Theory of Value." *Economica* 1(1): 52–76.

Higgs, Robert. 1989. *Crisis and Leviathan: Critical Episodes in the Growth of American Government*. New York: Oxford University Press.

1997. "Regime Uncertainty: Why the Great Depression Lasted So Long and Why Prosperity Resumed after the War." *Independent Review* 1(4): 561–590.

High, Jack C. 1980. *Maximizing, Action, and Market Adjustment: An Inquiry into the Theory of Economic Disequilibrum.* Ph.D. Dissertation, Department of Economics, University of California, Los Angeles.

    1982. "Alertness and Judgment: Comment on Kirzner." In Israel M. Kirzner, ed., *Method, Process, and Austrian Economics: Essays in Honor of Ludwig von Mises.* New York: Lexington Books, 161–168.

Hill, Charles W. L. and David L. Deeds. 1996. "The Importance of Industry Structure for the Determination of Firm Profitability: A Neo-Austrian Perspective." *Journal of Management Studies* 33: 429–451.

Hills, Gerald E., G. Thomas Lumpkin, and Robert P. Singh. 1997. "Opportunity Recognition: Perceptions and Behaviors of Entrepreneurs." In *Frontiers of Entrepreneurship Research* 17: 168–182. Wellesley, MA: Babson College.

Hindle, Kevin. 2004. "Choosing Qualitative Methods for Entrepreneurial Cognition Research: A Canonical Development Approach." *Entrepreneurship Theory and Practice* 28(6): 575–607.

Hitt, Michael A. and R. Duane Ireland. 2000. "The Intersection of Entrepreneurship and Strategic Management Research." In D. L. Sexton and H. Landstrom, eds., *Handbook of Entrepreneurship.* Oxford: Blackwell, 45–63.

Hitt, Michael A., R. Duane Ireland, S. M. Camp, and D. L. Sexton. 2002. *Strategic Entrepreneurship: Creating a New Mindset.* Oxford and Malden, MA: Blackwell.

Hoang, Ha and Bostjan Antoncic. 2003. "Network-Based Research in Entrepreneurship: A Critical Review." *Journal of Business Venturing* 18(2): 165–187.

Hodgkinson, Gerald P. and Gerry Johnson. 1994. "Exploring the Mental Models of Competitive Strategies: The Case of a Processual Approach." *Journal of Management Studies* 31: 525–551.

Hodgson, Geoffrey. 1998. *Economics and Utopia.* London: Routledge.

Holcombe, Randall G. 1992. "Political Entrepreneurship and the Democratic Allocation of Economic Resources." *Review of Austrian Economics* 15: 143–159.

Holmes, Thomas J. and James A. Schmitz. 1990. "A Theory of Entrepreneurship and Its Application to the Study of Business Transfers." *Journal of Political Economy* 98: 265–294.

    2001. "A Gain from Trade: From Unproductive to Productive Entrepreneurship." *Journal of Monetary Economics* 47(2): 417–446.

Holmström, Bengt. 1979. "Moral Hazard and Observability." *The Bell Journal of Economics* 10(1): 74–91.

1982. "Moral Hazard in Teams." *Bell Journal of Economics* 13(2): 324–340.

1989. "Agency Costs and Innovation." *Journal of Economic Behavior and Organization* 12(3): 305–327.

1999. "The Firm as a Subeconomy." *Journal of Law, Economics, and Organization* 15(1): 74–102.

Holmström, Bengt and Paul R. Milgrom. 1990. "Regulating Trade among Agents." *Journal of Institutional and Theoretical Economics (JITE)* 146(1): 85–105.

1991. "Multitask Principal-Agent Analysis: Incentive Contracts, Asset Ownership and Job Design." *Journal of Law, Economics and Organization* 7: 24–54.

1994. "The Firm as an Incentive System." *American Economic Review* 84(4): 972–991.

Holmström, Bengt and Jean Tirole. 1989. "The Theory of the Firm." In R. Schmalensee and R. Willing, eds., *Handbook of Industrial Organization*. Amsterdam: North Holland.

Hood, Jacqueline N. and John E. Young. 1993. "Entrepreneurship's Requisite Areas of Development: A Survey of Top Executives in Successful Entrepreneurial Firms." *Journal of Business Venturing* 8(2): 115–135.

Hoppe, Hans-Hermann. 2007. "The Limits of Numerical Probability: Frank H. Knight and Ludwig von Mises and the Frequency Interpretation." *Quarterly Journal of Austrian Economics* 10(1): 1–20.

Hoskisson, Robert E. and Michael A. Hitt. 1994. *Downscoping: How to Tame the Diversified Firm*. New York: Oxford University Press.

Huerta de Soto, Jesús. 2010. *Socialism, Economic Calculation and Entrepreneurship*. Cheltenham, UK: Edward Elgar.

Hülsmann, Jörg Guido. 2007. *Mises: The Last Knight of Liberalism*, Auburn, AL: Ludwig von Mises Institute.

Hurwicz, Leonid. 1969. "On the Concept and Possibility of Informational Decentralization." *American Economic Review* 59(2): 513–524.

1972. "On Informationally Decentralized Systems." In Charles B. McGuire and Roy Radner, eds., *Decision and Organization*. Amsterdam: North Holland, 297–233.

1973. "The Design of Mechanisms for Resource Allocation." *American Economic Review* 63(2): 1–30.

Hutt, William H. 1939. *The Theory of Idle Resources*, London: J. Cape.

Ibrahim, G. and S. Vyakarnam. 2003. "Defining the Role of the Entrepreneur in Economic Thought: Limitations of Mainstream Economics." Working paper, Nottingham Business School.

Ichniowski, Casey, Kathryn Shaw, and G. Prennushi. 1997. "The Effects of Human Resource Management Practices on Productivity." *American Economic Review* 87(3): 291–313.

Ireland, R. Duan, J. G. Covin, and Donald Kuratko. 2009. "Conceptualizing Corporate Entrepreneurship Strategy." *Entrepreneurship Theory and Practice* 33: 19–46.

Ireland, R. Duane, Michael A. Hitt, and D. G. Sirmon. 2003. "A Model of Strategic Entrepreneurship: The Construct and its Dimensions." *Journal of Management* 29: 963–989.

Jacobides, Michael G. and Sidney G. Winter. 2005. "The Co-evolution of Capability and Transaction Costs: Explaining the Institutional Structure of Production." *Strategic Management Journal* 26(5): 395–413.

Jacobson, Robert. 1992. "The 'Austrian' School of Strategy." *Academy of Management Review* 17: 782–807.

Jarrell, Gregg A., James A. Brickley, and Jeffry M. Netter. 1988. "The Market for Corporate Control: The Empirical Evidence Since 1980." *Journal of Economic Perspectives* 2: 49–68.

Jarvis, Darryl S. L. 2010. "The Political Economy of Risk and Uncertainty: Exploring the Contributions of Frank Knight." Working paper, Lee Kuan Yew School of Public Policy, National University of Singapore.

Jensen, Michael C. 1986. "Agency Costs of Free Cash Flow, Corporate Finance, and Takeovers." *American Economic Review* 76(2): 323–339.

1989. "Eclipse of the Public Corporation." *Harvard Business Review* 67(5): 61–74.

Jensen, Michael C. and William H. Meckling. 1976. "Theory of the Firm: Managerial Behavior, Agency Costs, and Capital Structure." *Journal of Financial Economics* 3(4): 305–360.

1992. "Specific and General Knowledge, and Organizational Structure." In Lars Werin and Hans Wijkander, eds., *Contract Economics.* Oxford: Blackwell.

1994. "The Nature of Man." *Journal of Applied Corporate Finance* 7(2): 4–19.

Jensen, Michael C. and Karen Wruck. 1998. "Science, Specific Knowledge and Total Quality Management." In M. C. Jensen, ed., *Foundations of Organizational Strategy.* Cambridge, MA: Harvard University Press.

Johansson, Dan. 2004. "Economics without Entrepreneurship or Institutions: A Vocabulary Analysis of Graduate Textbooks." *Econ Journal Watch*: 515–538.

Jones, Gareth R. 1983. "Transaction Costs, Property Rights, and Organizational Culture: An Exchange Perspective." *Administrative Science Quarterly* 28: 454–467.

Jones, Gareth R. and John E. Butler. 1992. "Managing Internal Corporate Entrepreneurship: An Agency Theory Perspective." *Journal of Management* 18(4): 733–749.

Kaish, Stanley and Benjamin Gilad. 1991. "Characteristics of Opportunities Search of Entrepreneurs Versus Executives: Sources, Interests, General Alertness." *Journal of Business Venturing* 6: 54–61.

Kaldor, Nicholas. 1934. "The Equilibrium of the Firm." *The Economic Journal* 44(173): 60–76.

Kaplan, Steven and Per Strömberg. 2003. "Financial Contracting Theory Meets the Real World: An Empirical Analysis of Venture Capital Contracts." *Review of Economic Studies* 70: 281–315.

Katz, Jerome A. 2003. "The Chronology and Intellectual Trajectory of American Entrepreneurship Education." *Journal of Business Venturing* 18: 283–300.

——— 2007. "Foreword: The Third Wave of Entrepreneurship Education and the Importance of Fun in Learning." In Alain Fayolle, ed., *Handbook of Research in Entrepreneurship Education*, volume I: *A General Perspective*. Cheltenham, UK: Edward Elgar.

Kauffman, Stuart A. 1993. *The Origins of Order: Self-Organization and Section in Evolution*. New York: Oxford University Press.

Kent, Calvin A. 1989. "Coverage of Entrepreneurship in Principles of Economics Textbooks." *Journal of Economic Education* 20: 153–164.

Kent, Calvin A. and Francis W. Rushing. 1999. "Coverage of Entrepreneurship in Principles of Economics Textbooks: An Update." *Journal of Economics Education* 30(2): 184–188.

Keynes, John Maynard. 1937. "The General Theory of Employment." *Quarterly Journal of Economics* 51: 209–223.

Kihlstrom, Richard E. and Jean-Jacques Laffont. 1979. "A General Equilibrium Entrepreneurial Theory of Firm Formation Based on Risk Aversion." *Journal of Political Economy* 87(4): 719–748.

Kim, Jongwook and Joseph T. Mahoney. 2002. "Resource-Based and Property Rights Perspectives on Value Creation: The Case of Oil Field Unitization." *Managerial and Decision Economics* 23(4): 225–245.

——— 2005. "Property Rights Theory, Transaction Costs Theory, and Agency Theory: An Organizational Economics Approach to Strategic Management." *Managerial and Decision Economics* 26(4): 223–242.

Kirzner, Israel M. 1962. "Rational Action and Economic Theory." *Journal of Political Economy* 70(4): 380–385.

1966. *An Essay on Capital.* New York: Augustus M. Kelley.

1967. *Methodological Individualism, Marked Equilibrium, and Market Process.* New York University.

1973. *Competition and Entrepreneurship.* University of Chicago Press.

1975. "Producer, Entrepreneur, and the Right to Property." In S. L. Blumenfeld, ed., *Property in a Humane Economy.* LaSalle, IL: Open Court.

1976. "Equilibrium versus Market Process." In E. G. Dolan, ed., *The Foundations of Modern Austrian Economics.* Kansas City: Sheed & Ward, 115–125.

1978. "Entrepreneurship, Entitlement, and Economic Justice." *Eastern Economic Journal* 4(1): 9–25.

1979a. *Perception, Opportunity and Profit: Studies in the Theory of Entrepreneurship.* Chicago and London: University of Chicago Press.

1979b. "The Perils of Regulation: A Market Process Approach." Occasional Paper of the Law and Economics Center, University of Miami School of Law.

1982. "Competition, Regulation, and the Market Process: An 'Austrian' Perspective." Cato Policy Analysis No. 18, September 30.

1984. *The Role of the Entrepreneur in the Economic System.* Centre for Independent Studies.

1985. *Discovery and the Capitalist Process.* University of Chicago Press.

1989. *Discovery, Capitalism, and Distributive Justice.* Oxford: Basil Blackwell.

1992. *The Meaning of Market Process.* London: Routledge.

1997. "Entrepreneurial Discovery and the Competitive Market Process: An Austrian Approach." *Journal of Economic Literature* 35: 60–85.

1999. "Mises and His Understanding of the Capitalist System." *Cato Journal* 19(2): 215–232.

2000. "Hedgehog or Fox? Hayek and the Idea of Plan-Coordination." In Kirzner, ed., *The Driving Force of the Market Economy: Essays in Austrian Economics.* London: Routledge, 180–202.

2009. "The Alert and Creative Entrepreneur: A Clarification." *Small Business Economics* 32(2): 145–152.

Kitzmann, Jana and Dirk Schiereck. 2005. "Entrepreneurial Discovery and the Demmert/Klein Experiment: Another Attempt at Creating the Proper Context." *The Review of Austrian Economics* 18(2): 169–178.

Klein, Benjamin, Robert A. Crawford, and Armen A. Alchian. 1978. "Vertical Integration, Appropriable Rents, and the Competitive Contracting Process." *Journal of Law and Economics* 21(2): 297–326.

Klein, Daniel B. and Jason Briggeman. 2009. "Israel Kirzner on Coordination and Discovery." *Journal of Private Enterprise* 25(2): 1–53.

Klein, Peter G. 1996. "Economic Calculation and the Limits of Organization." *Review of Austrian Economics* 9(2): 51–77.

1999a. "Entrepreneurship and Corporate Governance." *Quarterly Journal of Austrian Economics* 2(2): 19–42.

1999b. "F. A. Hayek (1899–1992)." In Randall G. Holcombe, ed., *Fifteen Great Austrian Economists*. Auburn, AL: Ludwig von Mises Institute, 181–194.

2008a. "The Mundane Economics of the Austrian School." *Quarterly Journal of Austrian Economics* 11(3–4): 165–187.

2008b. "Opportunity Discovery, Entrepreneurial Action, and Economic Organization." *Strategic Entrepreneurship Journal* 2(3): 175–190.

Klein, Peter G. and Michael L. Cook. 2006. "T. W. Schultz and the Human-Capital Approach to Entrepreneurship." *Review of Agricultural Economics* 28(3): 344–350.

Klein, Peter G. and Sandra R. Klein. 2001. "Do Entrepreneurs Make Predictable Mistakes? Evidence from Corporate Divestitures." *Quarterly Journal of Austrian Economics* 4: 3–25.

Klein, Peter G., Anita M. McGahan, Joseph T. Mahoney, and Christos N. Pitelis. 2010. "Toward a Theory of Public Entrepreneurship." *European Management Review* 7: 1–15.

Klepper, Steven. 2002. "The Capabilities of New Firms and the Evolution of the US Automobile Industry." *Industrial and Corporate Change* 11(4): 645–666.

Knight, Frank H. 1921. *Risk, Uncertainty and Profit*. New York: August M. Kelley.

1936. "The Quantity of Capital and the Rate of Interest." *Journal of Political Economy* 44: 433–463, 612–642.

1940. "'What Is Truth' in Economics?" *The Journal of Political Economy* 48(1): 1–32.

Koellinger, Philipp D., Maria Minniti, and C. Schade. 2007. "I Think I Can, I Think I Can: Overconfidence and Entrepreneurial Behavior." *Journal of Economic Psychology* 28: 502–527.

Kogut, Bruce, and Udo Zander. 1992. "Knowledge of the Firm, Combinative Capabilities, and the Replication of Technology." *Organization Science* 3: 383–397.

Kor, Yasemin Y., Joseph T. Mahoney, and Stephen C. Michael. 2007. "Resources, Capabilities and Entrepreneurial Perceptions." *Journal of Management Studies* 44(7): 1187–1212.

Kreps, David M. 1996. "Markets and Hierarchies and (Mathematical) Economic Theory." *Industrial and Corporate Change* 5: 561–595.

1990. "Corporate Culture and Economic Theory." In James E. Alt and Kenneth Shepsle, eds., *Perspectives on Positive Political Economy*. Cambridge University Press.

Kuratko, Donald F. 2008. *Entrepreneurship: Theory, Process, and Practice*. Mason, OH: South-Western Pub.

Kyläheiko, Kalevi. 1998. "Making Sense of Technology: Towards a Synthesis between Neoclassical and Evolutionary Approaches." *International Journal of Production Economics* 56: 319–332.

Lachmann, Ludwig M. 1956. *Capital and Its Structure*. Kansas City: Sheed Andrews and McMeel, 1978.

1970. *The Legacy of Max Weber*. Berkeley: The Glendessary Press.

1976. "From Mises to Shackle: An Essay on Austrian Economics and the Kaleidic Society." *Journal of Economic Literature* 14(1): 54–62.

1977. *Capital, Expectations, and the Market Process*. Kansas City: Sheed Andrews and McMeel.

1986. *The Market as a Process*. Oxford: Basil Blackwell.

Laffont, Jean-Jacques and David Martimort. 2002. *The Theory of Incentives: The Principal-Agent Model*. Princeton University Press.

Landa, Janet. 2006. "The Austrian Theory of Entrepreneurship Meets the Social Science and Bioeconomics of the Ethnically Homogeneous Middleman Group." *Advances in Austrian Economics* 9: 177–200.

Landes, David S., Joel Mokyr, and William J. Baumol. 2010. *The Invention of Enterprise: Entrepreneurship from Ancient Mesopotamia to Modern Times*. Princeton University Press.

Langlois, Richard N. 1982. "Systems Theory and the Meaning of Information." *Journal of the American Society for Information Science* 33(6): 395–399.

1985. "Knowledge and Rationality in the Austrian School: An Analytical Survey." *Eastern Economic Journal* 9(4): 309–330.

1986. "The New Institutional Economics." In Langlois, ed., *Economics as a Process: Essays in the New Institutional Economics*. Cambridge University Press.

1988. "Economic Change and the Boundaries of the Firm." *Journal of Institutional and Theoretical Economics* 144: 635–657.

1992. "Transaction Cost Economics in Real Time." *Industrial and Corporate Change* 1(1): 99–127.

1995. "Capabilities and Coherence in Firms and Markets." In Cynthia A. Montgomery, ed., *Resource-based and Evolutionary Theories of the Firm: Towards a Synthesis*. Dordrecht: Kluwer Academic Publishers, 71–100.

1998. "Personal Capitalism as Charismatic Authority: The Organizational Economics of a Weberian Concept." *Industrial and Corporate Change* 7: 195–213.

2001. "Strategy and the Market Process: Introduction to the Special Issue." *Managerial and Decision Economics* 22: 163–168.

2002. "Modularity in Technology and Organization." *Journal of Economic Behavior and Organization* 49(1): 19–37.

2003. "The Vanishing Hand: The Changing Dynamics of Industrial Capitalism." *Industrial and Corporate Changes* 12(2): 351–385.

2007a. "The Austrian Theory of the Firm: Retrospect and Prospect." Mercatus Center at George Mason University, Working Paper No. 80 in Mercatus Center Working Papers.

2007b. *The Dynamics of Industrial Capitalism: Schumpeter, Chandler and the New Economy*. London: Routledge.

2007c. "The Entrepreneurial Theory of the Firm and the Theory of the Entrepreneurial Firm." *Journal of Management Studies* 44(7): 1107–1124.

Langlois, Richard N. and Metin Cosgel. 1993. "Frank Knight on Risk, Uncertainty, and the Firm: A New Interpretation." *Economic Inquiry* 31: 456–465.

Langlois, Richard N. and László Csontos. 1993. "Optimization, Rule-Following, and the Methodology of Situational Analysis." In U. Mäki, B. Gustafsson, and C. Knudsen, eds., *Rationality, Institutions, and Economic Methodology*. London: Routledge.

Langlois, Richard N. and Nicolai J. Foss. 1999. "Capabilities and Governance: The Rebirth of Production in the Theory of Economic Organization." *Kyklos* 52: 201–218.

Langlois, Richard N. and Paul N. Robertson. 1995. *Firm, Markets and Economic Change*. London: Routledge.

Larsson, Rikard and Sydney Finkelstein. 1999. "Integrating Strategic, Organizational, and Human Resource Perspectives on Mergers and Acquisitions: A Case Survey of Synergy Realization." *Organization Science* 10(1): 1–26.

Laursen, K. and Nicolai J. Foss. 2003. "New HRM Practices, Complementarities, and the Impact on Innovation Performance." *Cambridge Journal of Economics* 27: 243–263.

Lavoie, Marc. 2000. "Capital Reversing." *Encyclopedia of Political Economy*. London: Routledge.

Lazear, Edward P. 2004. "Balanced Skills and Entrepreneurship." *American Economic Review* 94(2): 208–211.

2005. "Entrepreneurship." *Journal of Labor Economics* 23(4): 649–680.

Leibenstein, Harvey. 1987. *Inside the Firm: The Inefficiencies of Hierarchy.* Cambridge, MA: Harvard University Press.

Leijonhufvud, Axel. 1968. *On Keynesian Economics and the Economics of Keynes: A Study in Monetary Theory.* Oxford University Press.

LeRoy, Stephen F. and Larry D. Singell Jr. 1987. "Knight on Risk and Uncertainty." *Journal of Political Economy* 95(2): 394–406.

Levinthal, Daniel. 1997. "Adaptation on Rugged Landscapes." *Management Science* 43: 934–950.

Lewin, Peter. 1997. "Hayekian Equilibrium and Change." *Journal of Economic Methodology* 4(2): 245–266.

1999. *Capital in Disequilibrium: The Role of Capital in a Changing World.* New York and London: Routledge.

2005. "The Firm in Disequilibrium: Contributions from the Austrian Tradition." Working paper, University of Texas at Dallas.

Liebowitz, S. J. (2009). "Anatomy of a Train Wreck: Causes of the Mortgage Meltdown." In Randall G. Holcombe and Benjamin Powell, eds., *Housing America: Building Out of a Crisis.* Oakland, CA: Independent Institute.

Lien, Lasse B. and Peter G. Klein. 2009. "Using Competition to Measure Relatedness." *Journal of Management* 35(4): 1078–1107.

2011. "Can the Survivor Principle Survive Diversification?" Working Paper, Department of Strategy and Management, Norwegian School of Economics and Business Administration.

Lippman, Steven A. and Richard P. Rumelt. 1982. "Uncertain Imitability: An Analysis of Interfirm Differences in Efficiency under Competition." *The Bell Journal of Economics* 13(2): 418–438.

2003a. "A Bargaining Perspective on Resource Advantage." *Strategic Management Journal* 24: 1069–1086.

2003b. "The Payments Perspective: Micro-Foundations of Resource Analysis." *Strategic Management Journal* 24: 903–927.

Littlechild, Steven C. 1986. "Three Types of Market Process." In Richard N. Langlois, ed., *Economics as a Process: Essays in the New Institutional Economics.* Cambridge University Press.

Littlechild, Steven C. and G. Owen. 1980. "An Austrian Model of the Entrepreneurial Market Process." *Journal of Economic Theory* 23: 361–379.

Loasby, Brian J. 1976. *Choice, Complexity, and Ignorance.* Cambridge University Press.

1982. "The Entrepreneur in Economic Theory." *Scottish Journal of Political Economy* 29(3): 2–23.

1986. "Competition and Imperfect Knowledge: The Contribution of G. B. Richardson." *Scottish Journal of Political Economy* 33(2): 145–158.

1991. *Equilibrium and Evolution: An Exploration of Connecting Principles in Economics.* Manchester University Press.

Long, Wayne A. and W. Ed McMullan. 1984. "Entrepreneurship Education in the Nineties." *Journal of Business Venturing* 2(3): 261–275.

Lucas, Robert E. 1978. "On the Size Distribution of Business Firms." *Bell Journal of Economics* 9: 508–523.

1986. "Adaptive Behavior and Economic Theory." *Journal of Business* 59: S401–S426.

Lumpkin, G. Thomas and Gregory G. Dess. 1996. "Clarifying the Entrepreneurial Orientation Construct and Linking It to Performance." *Academy of Management Review* 21(1): 135–172.

Lumpkin, G. Thomas and Benyamin Bergmann Lichtenstein. 2005. "The Role of Organizational Learning in the Opportunity-Recognition Process." *Entrepreneurship Theory and Practice* 29(4): 451–472.

Lumpkin, G. Thomas, G. E. Hills, and R. C. Shrader. 2004. "Opportunity Recognition." In Harold L. Welsch, ed., *Entrepreneurship: The Road Ahead.* London: Routledge, 73–90.

Machlup, Fritz. 1963. *Essays on Economic Semantics.* Englewood Cliffs, NJ: Prentice-Hall.

1967. "Theories of the Firm: Marginalist, Behavioral, Managerial." *American Economic Review* 57(1): 1–33.

Machovec, Frank M. 1995. *Perfect Competition and the Transformation of Economics.* New York: Routledge.

MacLeod, W. Bentley. 2002. "Complexity, Bounded Rationality and Heuristic Search." *Contributions to Economic Analysis and Policy* 1(1).

Mahoney, Joseph M. 1995. "The Management of Resources and the Resource of Management." *Journal of Business Research* 33: 91–101.

2005. *Economic Foundations of Strategy.* London: Sage.

Mäki, Uskali. 1992. "On the Method of Isolation in Economics." *Poznan Studies in the Philosophy of the Sciences and the Humanities* 26: 19–54.

1994. "Isolation, Idealization and Truth in Economics." *Poznan Studies in the Philosophy of the Sciences and the Humanities* 38: 147–168.

2004. "Theoretical Isolation and Explanatory Progress: Transaction Cost Economics and the Dynamics of Dispute." *Cambridge Journal of Economics* 28: 319–346.

Makowski, Louis and Joseph M. Ostroy. 2001. "Perfect Competition and the Creativity of the Market." *Journal of Economic Literature* 39(2): 479–535.

Malmgren, Harold B. 1961. "Information, Expectations, and the Theory of the Firm." *Quarterly Journal of Economics* 75: 399–421.

Manne, Henry G. 1966a. "In Defense of Insider Trading." *Harvard Business Review* 44(6): 113–122.

1966b. *Insider Trading and the Stock Market*. New York: Free Press.

2010. "Entrepreneurship, Compensation, and the Corporation." Working paper, George Mason University School of Law.

Marchal, Jean. 1951. "The Construction of a New Theory of Profit." *American Economic Review* 41(4): 549–565.

Marschak, Jacob and Roy Radner. 1972. *The Economic Theory of Teams.* New Haven, CT: Cowles Foundation and Yale University Press.

Marshall, Alfred. 1890. *Principles of Economics*. New York: Macmillan and Co.

Martin, Dolores Tremewan. 1979. "Alternative Views of Mengerian Entrepreneurship." *History of Political Economy* 11(2): 271–285.

Maskin, Eric and Jean Tirole. 1999. "Unforeseen Contingencies and Incomplete Contracts." *Review of Economic Studies* 66: 83–114.

Masten, Scott E. 1988. "A Legal Basis for the Firm." *Journal of Law, Economics, and Organization* 4(1): 181–198.

Matsusaka, John G. 2001. "Corporate Diversification, Value Maximization, and Organizational Capabilities." *Journal of Business* 74: 409–431.

Matthews, John. 2006. *Strategizing, Disequilibrium, and Profit*. Stanford University Press.

Mayer, Kyle J. and Nicholas S. Argyres. 2004. "Learning to Contract: Evidence from the Personal Computer Industry." *Organization Science* 15(4): 394–410.

McCallum, Henry D. and Frances T. McCallum. 1965. *The Wire That Fenced the West*. Norman: University of Oklahoma Press.

McGrath, Rita G. and Ian C. MacMillan. 2000. *The Entrepreneurial Mindset: Strategies for Continuously Creating Opportunity in an Age of Uncertainty*. Boston: Harvard Business School Press.

McMullen, Jeffrey and Dean A. Shepherd. 2006. "Entrepreneurial Action and the Role of Uncertainty in the Theory of the Entrepreneur." *Academy of Management Review* 31(1): 132–152.

McMullen, Jeffrey, Lawrence Plummer, and Zoltan Acs. 2007. "What is an Entrepreneurial Opportunity?" *Small Business Economics* 28(4): 273–283.

McNulty, Paul. 1984. "On the Nature and Theory of Economic Organization: The Role of the Firm Reconsidered." *History of Political Economy* 16: 223–253.

Menger, Carl. 1871. *Principles of Economics*. New York University Press, 1985.

Milgrom, Paul and John Roberts. 1990. "The Economics of Modern Manufacturing." *American Economic Review* 80: 511–528.

1992. *Economics, Organization, and Management.* Englewood Cliffs, NJ: Prentice-Hall.

1995. "Complementarities and Fit: Strategy, Structure, and Organizational Change in Manufacturing." *Journal of Accounting and Economics* 19: 179–208.

Miller, Gary. 1992. *Managerial Dilemmas.* Cambridge University Press.

Minkler, Alanson P. 1993a. "The Problem with Dispersed Knowledge: Firms in Theory and Practice." *Kyklos* 46(4): 569–587.

1993b. "Knowledge and Internal Organization." *Journal of Economic Behavior and Organization* 21(1): 17–30.

Mises, Ludwig von. 1912. *The Theory of Money and Credit.* New Haven, CT: Yale University Press, 1953.

1920. "Economic Calculation in the Socialist Commonwealth." In F. A. Hayek, ed., *Collectivist Economic Planning.* London: Routledge and Sons, 1935.

1922. *Socialism: An Economic and Sociological Analysis.* New Haven, CT: Yale University Press, 1951.

1944. *Bureaucracy,* New Haven, CT: Yale University Press.

1949. *Human Action: A Treatise on Economics.* New Haven, CT: Yale University Press.

1951. *Profit and Loss.* South Holland, IL: Consumers-Producers Economic Services.

Mises, Richard von. 1939. *Probability, Statistics and Truth.* New York: Dover Publications, 1957.

Mitchell, Mark and J. Harold Mulherin. 1996. "The Impact of Industry Shocks on Takeover and Restructuring Activity." *Journal of Financial Economics* 41: 193–229.

Mitchell, Ronald K., Lowell Busenitz, Theresa Lant, P. Patricia McDougall, Eric A. Morse, and J. Brock Smith. 2002. "Toward a Theory of Entrepreneurial Cognition: Rethinking the People Side of Entrepreneurship Research." *Entrepreneurship Theory and Practice* 27(2): 93–104.

Modigliani, Franco and Merton Miller. 1958. "The Cost of Capital, Corporation Finance and the Theory of Investment." *American Economic Review* 48(3): 261–297.

Moroney, John R. 1972. "The Current State of Money and Production Theory." *American Economic Review* 62: 335–343.

Mosakowski, Elaine. 1997. "Strategy Making under Causal Ambiguity: Conceptual Issues and Empirical Evidence." *Organization Science* 8: 414–442.

1998. "Entrepreneurial Resources, Organizational Choices, and Competitive Outcomes." *Organization Science* 9: 625–643.

Nelson, Richard R. 1981. "Research on Productivity Growth and Productivity Differences: Dead Ends and New Departures." *Journal of Economic Literature* 19(3): 1029–1064.

Nelson, Richard R. and Sidney G. Winter. 1982. *An Evolutionary Theory of Economic Change*. Harvard: The Belknap Press.

Nickerson, Jackson and Todd R. Zenger. 2004. "A Knowledge-based Theory of the Firm: The Problem-Solving Perspective." *Organization Science* 15(6): 617–632.

Nisbett, Richard and Lee Ross. 1980. *Human Inferences. Strategies and Shortages of Social Judgment*. Englewood Cliffs, NJ: Prentice-Hall.

Nordhaus, William D. 2004. "Schumpeterian Profits in the American Economy: Theory and Measurement." National Bureau of Economic Research, Working Paper No. 10433.

O'Brien, Dennis. 1984. "The Evolution of the Theory of the Firm." In O'Brien, ed., *Methodology, Money and the Theory of the Firm*, volume I. Aldershot, UK: Edward Elgar, 1994.

O'Driscoll, Gerald P. and Mario Rizzo. 1985. *The Economics of Time and Ignorance*. Oxford: Basil Blackwell.

Olson, Mancur. 1965. *The Logic of Collective Action: Public Goods and the Theory of Groups*. Cambridge, MA: Harvard University Press.

Oppers, Stefan E. 2002. "The Austrian Theory of Business Cycles: Old Lessons for Modern Economic Policy?" IMF Working Paper No. 02/2.

Orr, Julian. 1996. *Talking About Machines: An Ethnography of a Modern Job*. Ithaca, NY: IRL Press.

Osterloh, Margit and Bruno S. Frey. 2000. "Motivation, Knowledge Transfer, and Organizational Forms." *Organization Science* 11(5): 538–550.

Oxfeld, Ellen. 1992. "Individualism, Holism, and the Market Mentality: Notes on the Recollections of a Chinese Entrepreneur." *Cultural Anthropology* 7(3): 267–300.

Pacheco-de-Almeida, G. 2010. "Erosion, Time Compression, and Self-displacement of Leaders in Hypercompetitive Environments." *Strategic Management Journal* 31: 1498–1526.

Parker, Simon C. 1996. "A Time Series Model of Self-Employment under Uncertainty." *Economica* 63: 459–475.

2004. *The Economics of Self-employment and Entrepreneurship*. Cambridge University Press.

2005. *The Economics of Entrepreneurship: What We Know and What We Don't Know.* Boston: Now Publishers.

2008. "The Economics of Formal Business Networks." *Journal of Business Venturing* 23: 627–640.

Pasinetti, Luigi L. and Roberto Scazzieri. 1987. "Capital Theory: Paradoxes." In *The New Palgrave: A Dictionary of Economics.* London and New York: Macmillan, 363–368.

Penrose, Edith T. 1959. *The Theory of the Growth of the Firm.* Oxford: Blackwell.

Peteraf, Margaret A. 1993. "The Cornerstones of Competitive Advantage: A Resource-Based View." *Strategic Management Journal* 14: 179–191.

Peteraf, Margaret A. and Jay B. Barney. 2003. "Unraveling the Resource-Based Tangle." *Managerial and Decision Economics* 24: 309–323.

Phelps, Edmund P. 2006. "Further Steps to a Theory of Innovation and Growth – On the Path Begun by Knight, Hayek, and Polanyí." Paper for the 2006 ASSA meetings.

Pigou, Arthur C. 1928. "An Analysis of Supply." *Economic Journal* 38: 238–257.

Pisano, Gary P. 1990. "The R & D Boundaries of the Firm: An Empirical Analysis." *Administrative Science Quarterly* 35(1): 153–176.

Polanyí, Michael. 1962. *Personal Knowledge.* New York: Harper.

Pongracic, Ivan, Jr. 2009. *Employees and Entrepreneurship: Co-ordination and Spontaneity in Non-Hierarchical Business Organizations.* Aldershot, UK: Edward Elgar.

Popper, Karl R. 1967. "La Rationalité et le Statut du Principe du Rationalité." English translation as "The Rationality Principle" in D. Miller, ed. *A Pocket Popper.* Glasgow: Fontana Press, 1990.

Radner, Roy. 1968. "Competitive Equilibrium under Uncertainty." *Econometrica* 36: 31–58.

Rajan, Raghuram G. and Julie Wulf. 2006. "The Flattening Firm: Evidence from Panel Data on the Changing Nature of Corporate Hierarchies." *Review of Economics and Statistics* 88(4): 759–773.

Rajan, Raghuram G. and Luigi Zingales. 1998. "Power in a Theory of the Firm." *Quarterly Journal of Economics* 113(2): 387–432.

2001. "The Influence of the Financial Revolution on the Nature of Firms." *American Economic Review* 91: 206–211.

Ravenscraft, David, and F. M. Scherer. 1987. *Mergers, Sell-Offs, and Economic Efficiency.* Washington, DC: Brookings Institution.

Read, Stuart and Saras D. Sarasvathy. 2005. "Knowing What to Do and Doing What You Know: Effectuation as a Form of Entrepreneurial Expertise." *Journal of Private Equity* 9(1): 45–62.

Rentsch, Joan R., Tonia S. Heffner and Lorraine T. Duffy. 1994. "What You Know Is What You Get From Experience: Team Experience Related to Teamwork Schemas." *Group & Organization Management* 19: 450–474.

Ricardo, David. 1817. *Principles of Political Economy and Taxation*. London: John Murray.

Richardson, George B. 1972. "The Organisation of Industry." *The Economic Journal*: 883–896.

Ricketts, Martin. 1987. *The New Industrial Economics: An Introduction to Modern Theories of the Firm*. New York: St. Martin's Press.

Rigotti, Luca, Matthew Ryan, and Rhema Vaithianathan. 2011. "Optimism and Firm Formation." *Economic Theory* 46(2): 1–38.

Rivkin, Jan W. 2000. "Imitation of Complex Strategies." *Management Science* 46(6): 824–844.

Robbins, Lionel C. 1932. *An Essay on the Nature and Significance of Economic Science*. London: Macmillan and Co.

Roberts, John. 2004. *The Modern Firm*. Oxford University Press.

Roberts, Peter W. and K. M. Eisenhardt. 2003. "Austrian Insights on Strategic Organization: From Market Insights to Implications for Firms." *Strategic Organization* 1: 345–352.

Robinson, Joan. 1933. *The Economics of Imperfect Competition*. London: Routledge and Kegan Paul.

1934. "What is Perfect Competition?" *The Quarterly Journal of Economics* 49: 104–120.

Roll, Richard. 1986. "The Hubris Hypothesis of Corporate Takeovers." *Journal of Business* 59(2): 197–216.

Rosenberg, Nathan. 1982. *Inside the Black Box*. Cambridge University Press.

1986. "Schumpeter and Marx: How Common a Vision?" in R. M. MacLeod, ed., *Technology and the Human Prospect: Essays in Honour of Christopher Freeman*. London: Pinter, 197–213.

Ross, Stephen A. 1973. "The Economic Theory of Agency: The Principal's Problem." *American Economic Review* 63 (Papers and Proceedings): 134–139.

Rotemberg, Julio J. and Garth Saloner. 1994. "Benefits of Narrow Business Strategies." *American Economic Review* 84: 1330–1349.

1995. "Overt Interfunctional Conflict (and Its Reduction Through Business Strategy)." *RAND Journal of Economics* 26: 630–653.

2000. "Visionaries, Managers, and Strategic Direction." *RAND Journal of Economics* 31: 693–716.

Rothbard, Murray N. 1962. *Man, Economy, and State: A Treatise on Economic Principles*. Princeton, NJ: Van Nostrand.

1974. "Review: Competition and Entrepreneurship." *Journal of Economic Literature* 12(3): 902–904.

1976. "Ludwig von Mises and Economic Calculation Under Socialism." In Laurence S. Moss, ed., *The Economics of Ludwig von Mises: Toward a Critical Reappraisal*. Kansas City: Sheed and Ward, 67–77.

1977. "Introduction." In Frank A. Fetter, *Capital, Interest, and Rent: Essays in the Theory of Distribution*. Kansas City: Sheed Andrews and McMeel, 1–24.

1985. "Professor Hébert on Entrepreneurship." *The Journal of Libertarian Studies* 7(2) (Fall): 281–286. Reprinted as "Professor Kirzner on Entrepreneurship" in *The Logic of Action Two: Applications and Criticism from the Austrian School*. Glos, UK: Edward Elgar, 1987, pp. 245–253.

1991. "The End of Socialism and the Calculation Debate Revisited." *Review of Austrian Economics* 5(2): 51–76.

1995. *An Austrian Perspective on the History of Economic Thought*, volume I: *Economic Thought Before Adam Smith*. Cheltenham, UK: Edward Elgar.

Rousseau, Denise M. and Zipi Shperling. 2003. "Pieces of the Action: Ownership and the Changing Employment Relationship." *Academy of Management Review* 28(4): 553–570.

Ruef, Martin, Howard E. Aldrich, and Nancy M. Carter. 2003. "The Structure of Founding Teams: Homophily, Strong Ties, and Isolation among US Entrepreneurs." *American Sociological Review* 68(2): 195–222.

Rumelt, Richard P. 1984. "Towards a Strategic Theory of the Firm." In R. Lamb, ed., *Competitive Strategic Management*. Englewood Cliffs, NJ: Prentice-Hall, 556–570.

1987. "Theory, Strategy, and Entrepreneurship." In David J. Teece, ed., *The Competitive Challenge*. San Francisco: Ballinger.

Runde, J. 1998. "Clarifying Frank Knight's Discussion of the Meaning of Risk and Uncertainty." *Cambridge Journal of Economics* 22: 539–546.

Ryall, Michael D. and Glenn MacDonald. 2004. "How Do Value Creation and Competition Determine Whether a Firm Appropriates Value?" *Management Science* 50(10): 1319–1333.

Sabbagh, Karl. 1995. *21st Century Jet: The Making of the Boeing 777*. New York: Scribner.

Salanié, Bernard. 1997. *The Economics of Contracts: A Primer*. Cambridge, MA: MIT Press.

Salerno, Joseph T. 1990a. "Ludwig von Mises as Social Rationalist." *The Review of Austrian Economics* 4(1): 26–54.

1990b. "Postscript: Why a Socialist Economy Is Impossible." In L. V. Mises, *Economic Calculation in the Socialist Commonwealth*. Auburn, AL: Ludwig von Mises Institute, 51–71.

1991. "The Concept of Coordination in Austrian Macroeconomics." In R. M. Ebeling, ed., *Austrian Economics: Perspectives on the Past and Prospects for the Future*. Auburn, AL: Ludwig von Mises Institute, 325–343.

1993. "Mises and Hayek Dehomogenized." *Review of Austrian Economics* 6: 113–146.

1999. "The Place of Mises's Human Action in the Development of Modern Economic Thought." *Quarterly Journal of Austrian Economics* 2(1): 35–65.

2002. "Friedrich Von Wieser and Friedrich A. Hayek: The General Equilibrium Tradition in Austrian Economics." *Journal des Economistes et des Etudes Humaines* 12(2).

2008. "The Entrepreneur: Real and Imagined." *Quarterly Journal of Austrian Economics* 11(3): 188–207.

2009a. "Introduction to the Second Edition." In M. N. Rothbard, *Man, Economy, and State with Power and Market*, second edn. Auburn, AL: Ludwig von Mises Institute, xix–l.

2009b. "Lionel Robbins: Neoclassical Maximizer or Proto-Praxeologist?" *Quarterly Journal of Austrian Economics* 12(4): 98–110.

Sarasvathy, Saras D. 2001. "Causation and Effectuation: Toward a Theoretical Shift from Economic Inevitability to Entrepreneurial Contingency." *Academy of Management Review* 26(2): 243–263.

2003. "Entrepreneurship as a Science of the Artificial." *Journal of Economic Psychology* 24(2): 203–220.

2008. *Effectuation: Elements of Entrepreneurial Expertise*. Northampton, UK: Edward Elgar.

Sarasvathy, Saras D. and Stuart Read (in press). "Without Judgment: An Empirically-based Entrepreneurial Theory of the firm. *Review of Austrian Economics*.

Saussier, Stéphane. 2000. "Transaction Costs and Contractual Incompleteness: The Case of Électricité De France." *Journal of Economic Behavior and Organization* 42(2): 189–206.

Sautet, Frederic. 2001. *An Entrepreneurial Theory of the Firm*. London: Routledge.

Savage, Leonard J. 1954. *The Foundations of Statistics*. New York: Dover, 1972.

Say, Jean-Baptiste, 1803. *A Treatise on Political Economy, or the Production, Distribution and Consumption of Wealth.* C. R. Prinsep, trans. and Clement C. Biddle., ed. 1855. Philadelphia: Claxton, Remsen & Haffelfinger.

Scarf, Herbert. 1960. "Some Examples of Global Instability of the Competitive Equilibrium." *International Economic Review* 1: 157–172.

Scharfstein, David. 1988. "The Disciplinary Role of Takeovers." *Review of Economic Studies* 55(2): 185–199.

Schoonhoven, Claudia Bird and Elaine Romanelli. 2001. *The Entrepreneurship Dynamic: Origins of Entrepreneurship and the Evolution of Industries.* Stanford, CA: Stanford Business Books.

Schultz, Theodore W. 1975. "The Value of the Ability to Deal with Disequilibria." *Journal of Economic Literature* 13: 827–846.

1979. "Concepts of Entrepreneurship and Agricultural Research." Kaldor Memorial Lecture, Iowa State University, October.

1980. "Investment in Entrepreneurial Ability." *Scandinavian Journal of Economics* 82(4): 437–448.

Schumpeter, Joseph A. 1911. *The Theory of Economic Development.* Cambridge, MA: Harvard University Press, 1934.

1939. *Business Cycles: A Theoretical, Historical and Statistical Analysis of the Capitalist Process.* New York: McGraw-Hill.

1942. *Capitalism, Socialism, and Democracy.* New York: Harper and Row.

1954. *History of Economic Analysis.* Cambridge, MA: Harvard University Press.

Segal, Gary, Dan Borgia, and Jerry Schoenfeld. 2005. "The Motivation to Become an Entrepreneur." *International Journal of Entrepreneurial Behaviour and Research* 11(1): 42–57.

Selgin, George A. 1988. "Praxeology and Understanding: An Analysis of the Controversy in Austrian Economics." *Review of Austrian Economics* 2: 19–58.

Shackle, George L. S. 1949. *Expectation in Economics.* Cambridge University Press, 1952.

1955. *Uncertainty in Economics, and Other Reflections.* Cambridge University Press.

1972. *Epistemics and Economics.* Cambridge University Press.

1979. *Imagination and the Nature of Choice.* Edinburgh University Press.

Shane, Scott. 2000. "Prior Knowledge and the Discovery of Entrepreneurial Opportunities." *Organization Science* 11: 448–469.

2003. *A General Theory of Entrepreneurship.* Cheltenham, UK: Edward Elgar.

Shane, Scott and S. Venkataraman. 2000. "The Promise of Entrepreneurship as a Field of Research." *Academy of Management Review* 25: 217–226.

Shaver, Kelly G. and Linda R. Scott. 1991. "Person, Process, Choice: The Psychology of New Venture Creation." *Entrepreneurship Theory and Practice* 16: 23–45.

Shepherd, Dean A. and Dawn R. DeTienne. 2005. "Prior Knowledge, Potential Financial Reward, and Opportunity Identification." *Entrepreneurship Theory and Practice* 29(1): 91–112.

Short, Jeremy C., David J. Ketchen, Christopher L. Shook, and R. Duane Ireland. 2010. "The Concept of 'Opportunity' in Entrepreneurship Research: Past Accomplishments and Future Challenges." *Journal of Management* 36(1): 40–65.

Siggelkow, Nicolai and Daniel A. Levinthal. 2003. "Temporarily Divide to Conquer: Centralized, Decentralized, and Reintegrated Organizational Approaches to Exploration and Adaptation." *Organization Science* 14(6): 650–669.

Silverman, Brian. 1999. "Technological Resources and the Direction of Corporate Diversification: Toward an Integration of the Resource-based View and Transaction Cost Economics." *Management Science* 45: 1109–1124.

Simon, Herbert A. 1951. "A Formal Theory of the Employment Relationship." *Econometrica: Journal of the Econometric Society*: 293–305.

1955. "A Behavioral Model of Rational Choice." *Quarterly Journal of Economics* 69: 99–118.

1962. "The Architecture of Complexity." *Proceedings of the American Philosophical Society* 106: 467–482.

1973. "The Structure of Ill Structured Problems 1." *Artificial Intelligence* 4(3–4): 181–201.

1991. "Organizations and Markets." *Journal of Economic Perspectives* 5(2): 25–44.

Solomon, George T., Susan Duffy, and Ayman Tarabishy. 2002. "The State of Entrepreneurship Education in the United States: A Nationwide Survey and Analysis." *International Journal of Entrepreneurship Education* 1: 1–22.

Solow, Robert M. 1957. "Technical Change and the Aggregate Production Function." *Review of Economics and Statistics* 39: 312–320.

Sorenson, Olav and Toby E. Stuart. 2005. "The Evolution of Venture Capital Investment Networks." Federal Reserve Bank of Atlanta, No. 1936 in working paper series.

Spender, J.-C. 2006. "The RBV, Methodological Individualism, and Managerial Cognition: Practicing Entrepreneurship." Paper presented at the Academy of Management conference.

Spulber, Daniel F. 2009. *The Theory of the Firm: Microeconomics with Endogenous Entrepreneurs, Firms, Markets, and Organizations.* Cambridge University Press.

Stangler, Dane. 2009. "The Economic Future Just Happened." *Ewing Marion Kauffman Foundation Report 9.*

Staudenmayer, Nancy and Michael A. Cusumano. 1998. "Alternative Designs for Product Component Integration." Working paper, MIT.

Stenmark, Dick. 2000. "Leveraging Tacit Organizational Knowledge." *Journal of Management Information Systems* 17(3): 9–24.

Stieglitz, Nils and Nicolai J. Foss. 2010. "Opportunities and New Business Models: Transaction Cost and Property Rights Perspectives on Entrepreneurship." Working paper, Center for Strategic Management and Globalization, Copenhagen Business School.

Stieglitz, Nils and Klaus Heine. 2007. "Innovations and the Role of Complementarities in a Strategic Theory of the Firm." *Strategic Management Journal* 28(1): 1–15.

Stigler, George J. 1961. "The Economics of Information." *Journal of Political Economy* 69(3): 213–225.

1962. "Information in the Labor Market." *Journal of Political Economy* 70(5): 94–105.

Strigl, Richard von. 1934. *Capital and Production.* Auburn, AL: Ludwig von Mises Institute, 2000.

Taleb, Nicholas N. 2007. *The Black Swan: The Impact of the Highly Improbable.* New York: Random House.

Tapscott, Don and Anthony D. Williams. 2008. *Wikinomics: How Mass Collaboration Changes Everything.* New York: Portfolio Trade.

Taussig, Frank W. 1911. *Principles of Economics.* London: Macmillan.

Teece, David J. 1986. "Profiting from Technological Innovation." *Research Policy*, 15: 285–305.

2007. "The Role of Managers, Entrepreneurs and the Literati in Enterprise Performance and Economic Growth." *International Journal of Technological Learning, Innovation and Development* 1(1): 43–64.

2009. *Dynamic Capabilities and Strategic Management: Organizing for Innovation and Growth.* Oxford University Press.

Teece, David J., Gary Pisano, and Amy Shuen. 1997. "Dynamic Capabilities and Strategic Management." *Strategic Management Journal* 18(7): 509–533.

Tempelman, Jerry H. 2010. "Austrian Business Cycle Theory and the Global Financial Crisis: Confessions of a Mainstream Economist." *Quarterly Journal of Austrian Economics* 13(1): 3–15.

Thornton, Mark. 1998. "Richard Cantillon and the Origins of Economic Theory." *Journal des Economistes et des Etudes Humaines*: 61–74.

Thornton, Patricia H. 1999. "The Sociology of Entrepreneurship." *Annual Review of Sociology* 25: 19–46.

Tichy, Noel M., and Warren G. Bennis. 2007. *Judgment: How Winning Leaders Make Great Calls*. New York: Portfolio.

Tirole, Jean. 1986. "Hierarchies and Bureaucracies: on the Role of Collusion in Organizations." *Journal of Law, Economics and Organization* 1: 181–214.

Tong, Tony W. and Jeffrey J. Reuer. 2007. "Real Options in Multinational Corporations: Organizational Challenges and Risk Implications." *Journal of International Business Studies* 38(2): 215–230.

Topan, Mihai Vladimir. 2011. "A Note on Rothbardian Decision-Making Rents." Working paper, Department of International Business and Economics, Academy of Economic Studies, Bucharest.

Van den Hauwe, Ludwig. 2007. "John Maynard Keynes and Ludwig von Mises on Probability." MPRA Paper No. 6965.

Van den Steen, Eric. 2005. "Organizational Beliefs and Managerial Vision." *Journal of Law, Economics, and Organization* 21(1): 256–283.

Van Praag, C. Mirjam. 1999. "Some Classic Views on Entrepreneurship." *De Economist* 147(3): 311–335.

Van Zandt, David E. 1993. "The Lessons of the Lighthouse: 'Government' or 'Private' Provision of Goods." *Journal of Legal Studies* 22(1): 47–72.

Vaughn, Karen I. 1992. "The Problem of Order in Austrian Economics: Kirzner vs. Lachmann." *Review of Political Economy* 4(3): 251–274.

1994. *Austrian Economics in America*. Cambridge University Press.

Vedder, Richard K. and Lowell E. Gallaway. 1993. *Out of Work: Unemployment and Government in Twentieth-Century America*. New York: Holmes and Meier.

Venkataraman, Sankaran. 1997. "The Distinctive Domain of Entrepreneurship Research." *Advances in Entrepreneurship, Firm Emergence, and Growth* 3: 119–138.

Vickers, Douglas. 1970. "The Cost of Capital and the Structure of the Firm." *Journal of Finance* 25: 1061–1080.

1987. *Money Capital in the Theory of the Firm: A Preliminary Analysis*. Cambridge University Press.

Viner, Jacob. 1931. "Costs Curves and Supply Curve." *Zeitschrift für Nationalökonomie* 3: 23–46.

Webb, Walter Prescott. 1931. *The Great Plains*. Lincoln, NE: University of Nebraska Press.

Wennekers, Sander and Roy Thurik. 1999. "Linking Entrepreneurship and Economic Growth." *Small Business Economics* 13(1): 27–56.

Wernerfelt, Birger. 1984. "A Resource-Based View of the Firm." *Strategic Management Journal* 5: 272–280.

1994. "An Efficiency Criterion for Marketing Design." *Journal of Marketing Research.* 31(4): 462–470.

1997. "On the Nature and Scope of the Firm: An Adjustment-Cost Theory." *Journal of Business* 70(4): 489–514.

West, G. Page III. 2007. "Collective Cognition: When Entrepreneurial Teams, Not Individuals, Make Decisions." *Entrepreneurship Theory and Practice* 31(1): 77–102.

Wicksteed, Philip H. 1910. *The Common Sense of Political Economy.* London: Macmillan and Co.

Wieser, Friedrich A. von. 1914. *Social Economics.* London: Oxford University Press, 1928.

Wiggins, Robert R. and Timothy W. Rueffli. 2002. "Sustained Competitive Advantage: Temporal Dynamics and the Incidence and Persistence of Superior Economic Performance." *Organization Science* 13: 82–105.

Wiklund, Johan and Dean Shepherd. 2003. "Aspiring for and Achieving Growth: The Moderating Role of Resources and Opportunities." *Journal of Management Studies* 40(8): 1911–1941.

Williamson, Oliver E. 1971. "The Vertical Integration of Production: Market Failure Considerations." *American Economic Review* 61: 112–123.

1975. *Markets and Hierarchies: Analysis and Antitrust Implications.* New York: Free Press.

1979. "Transaction Cost Economics: The Governance of Contractual Relations." *Journal of Law and Economics* 22: 233–261.

1981. "The Economics of Organization: The Transaction Cost Approach." *American Journal of Sociology* 87: 548–577.

1985. *The Economic Institutions of Capitalism.* New York: Free Press.

1988. "The Logic of Economic Organization." *Journal of Law, Economics, and Organization* 4(1): 65–93.

1991a. "Comparative Economic Organization: The Analysis of Discrete Structural Alternatives." *Administrative Science Quarterly* 36: 269–296.

1991b. "Economic Institutions: Spontaneous and Intentional Governance." *Journal of Law, Economics, and Organization* 7: 159–187.

1996. *The Mechanisms of Governance.* Oxford University Press.

2000. "The New Institutional Economics: Taking Stock, Looking Ahead." *Journal of Economic Literature* 38(3): 595–613.

Winter, Sidney G. 1988. "On Coase, Competence, and the Corporation." *Journal of Law, Economics, and Organization* 4(1): 163–180.

Winter, Sidney G. and Gabriel Szulanski. 2001. "Replication as Strategy." *Organization Science* 12(6): 730–743.

Witt, Ulrich. 1998a. "Imagination and Leadership: the Neglected Dimensions of an Evolutionary Theory of the Firm." *Journal of Economic Behavior and Organization* 35: 161–177.

1998b. "Do Entrepreneurs Need Firms?" *Review of Austrian Economics* 11: 99–109.

2007. "Firms as Realizations of Entrepreneurial Visions." *Journal of Management Studies* 44(7): 1125–1140.

Xue, Jian-Hong and Peter G. Klein. 2010. "Regional Determinants of Technology Entrepreneurship." *International Journal of Entrepreneurial Venturing* 1(3): 291–308.

Yates, Andrew J. 2000. "The Knowledge Problem, Entrepreneurial Discovery, and Austrian Market Process Theory." *Journal of Economic Theory* 91(1): 59–85.

Yonekura, Seiichiro and Michael J. Lynskey, eds. 2002. *Entrepreneurship and Organization: The Role of the Entrepreneur in Organizational Innovation.* Oxford University Press.

Yu, Tony Fu-Lai. 1999. "Toward a Praxeological Theory of the Firm." *Review of Austrian Economics* 12(1): 25–41.

2005. *Firms, Strategies, and Economic Change: Explorations in Austrian Economics.* Cheltenham, UK: Edward Elgar.

Zahra, Shaker A. 2006. "Contextualizing Theory Building in Entrepreneurship Research." *Journal of Business Venturing* 22: 443–452.

Zahra, Shaker A., Harry J. Sapienza, and Per Davidsson. 2008. "Entrepreneurship and Dynamic Capabilities: A Review, Model and Research Agenda." *Journal of Management Studies* 43: 917–955.

Zander, Ivo. 2007. "Do You See What I Mean? An Entrepreneurship Perspective on the Nature and Boundaries of the Firm." *Journal of Management Studies* 44(7): 1141–1164.

Zangwill, Willard I. and Paul B. Kantor. 1998. "Toward a Theory of Continuous Improvement and the Learning Curve." *Management Science* 44: 910–920.

Zeckhauser, Richard. 2006. "Investing in the Unknown and Unknowable." *Capitalism and Society* 1: 1–39.

Zingales, Luigi. 2000. "In Search of New Foundations." *Journal of Finance* 55(4): 1623–1654.

Zott, Christoph and Raphael Amit. 2008. "The Fit between Product Market Strategy and Business Model: Implications for Firm Performance." *Strategic Management Journal* 29(1): 1–26.

Zucker, Lynne. 1991. "Markets for Bureaucratic Authority and Control: Information Quality in Professions and Services." *Research in the Sociology of Organizations* 8: 157–190.

Index

To read

Becarra.

Landis

Baker, Gibbons & Turphy, 1994

O'Driscoll & Rizzo, 1985

Gibbons, 2005,